Police Photography

Seventh Edition

D0781476

Police Photography

Seventh Edition

Larry S. Miller

Norman Marin

AMSTERDAM • BOSTON • HEIDELBERG • LONDON
NEW YORK • OXFORD • PARIS • SAN DIEGO
SAN FRANCISCO • SINGAPORE • SYDNEY • TOKYO

Anderson Publishing is an imprint of Elsevier

Acquiring Editor: Sara Scott
Editorial Project Manager: Marisa LaFleur
Project Manager: Punithavathy Govindaradjane
Designer: Greg Harris

Anderson Publishing is an imprint of Elsevier
225 Wyman Street, Waltham, MA 02451, USA

Copyright © 2015, 2011 Elsevier Inc. All rights reserved.

No part of this publication may be reproduced or transmitted in any form or by any means, electronic or mechanical, including photocopying, recording, or any information storage and retrieval system, without permission in writing from the publisher. Details on how to seek permission, further information about the Publisher's permissions policies and our arrangements with organizations such as the Copyright Clearance Center and the Copyright Licensing Agency, can be found at our website: www.elsevier.com/permissions.

This book and the individual contributions contained in it are protected under copyright by the Publisher (other than as may be noted herein).

Notices
Knowledge and best practice in this field are constantly changing. As new research and experience broaden our understanding, changes in research methods or professional practices, may become necessary. Practitioners and researchers must always rely on their own experience and knowledge in evaluating and using any information or methods described herein. In using such information or methods they should be mindful of their own safety and the safety of others, including parties for whom they have a professional responsibility.

To the fullest extent of the law, neither the Publisher nor the authors, contributors, or editors, assume any liability for any injury and/or damage to persons or property as a matter of products liability, negligence or otherwise, or from any use or operation of any methods, products, instructions, or ideas contained in the material herein.

Library of Congress Cataloging-in-Publication Data

Miller, Larry, 1953 August 26-
    Police photography. -- Seventh edition / Larry S. Miller, Norman Marin.
        pages cm
    Includes bibliographical references and index.
ISBN 978-1-4557-7763-1
    1. Legal photography. I. Marin, Norman. II. Title.
    TR822.S26 2015
    363.25–dc23

                                                                    2014014130

British Library Cataloguing in Publication Data
A catalogue record for this book is available from the British Library

ISBN: 978-1-4557-7763-1

For information on all Anderson publications visit our website at
http://store.elsevier.com

Printed and bound in China

Working together
to grow libraries in
developing countries

www.elsevier.com • www.bookaid.org

Dedication

This seventh edition is dedicated to Ruth, Ryan, Casey, Christopher, and Cole.

- Larry S. Miller

I would like to dedicate this book to Michael, Bruni and Maryury Marin.

- Norman Marin

Contents

Acknowledgments

Credit is extended
- To Andrew Davidhazy, Professor, School of Photo Arts & Sciences, Rochester Institute of Technology, 70 Lomb Memorial Drive, Rochester, NY 14623 (email: andpph@rit.edu) for assistance and contributions on high speed photography.
- To Danylo Kozub of Helicon Software, per. Mechanicheski 4, 61068, Ukraine (email: dankozub@helicon.com.ua) for assistance and contributions on Helicon Focus.
- To George Reis of Free Radical Enterprises, 18627 S. Brookhurst, Suite 114, Fountain Valley, CA 92708 for assistance with research and contributions on digital imaging for law enforcement.
- To Ray Smith of Image-Pro Plus, Media Cybernetics, 8484 Georgia Ave. Silver Spring, MD 20910 for assistance with digital software for law enforcement and image contributions.
- To Patrick Nolte of the Anaheim (CA) Police Department for assistance with digital imaging uses for law enforcement.
- To Ward Schwoob of the Florida Department of Law Enforcement, Tallahassee, FL for assistance with crime scene photography.
- To Hayden B. Baldwin of Forensic Enterprises, Inc. for information regarding crime scene and digital photography.
- To Eastman Kodak Company, Rochester, New York for their cooperation in contributing to this book.
- To the United States Department of the Navy for permission granted to use materials employed in their photographic naval training courses.
- To the Johnson City (TN) Police Department for assistance with photographic resources.
- To Arthur Bohanan of the Knoxville (TN) Police Department for assistance with fingerprint comparison and digital imaging techniques.
- To Dr. William Bass and Dr. Murray Marks of The University of Tennessee - Knoxville, Department of Anthropology for information on skeletal identification and forensic anthropology.
- To Linde Christine Rush Burkey, M.A., Ph.D. candidate, University of Arkansas Little Rock, for research assistance and writing the chapter on Identification and Surveillance Photography.

- To Emily J. Will, M.A., CDE, D-BFDE certified forensic document examiner, P.O. Box 58552, Raleigh, NC 27658 for information on ultraviolet and infrared photographic uses in forensic document examination.
- To Heidi H. Harralson, M.A., CDE, D-BFDE, certified forensic document examiner, P.O. Box 65095, Tucson, AZ 85728 for assistance with photographic illustrations in forensic document examinations.
- Edward W. Wallace
- Dr. Peter Pizzola, Ph.D., Pace University
- Jeffrey M. Buszka, Washington D.C. Department of Forensic Sciences
- Dr. Demos Athanasopoulos, Ph.D., Pace University
- Ralph R. Ristenbatt, Penn State University
- To the following companies for their cooperation with photographs or information concerning their products:
    - Free Radical Enterprises, Fountain Valley, CA 92708
    - Media Cybernetics, Image Pro Plus, Silver Spring, MD 20910
    - General Electric, Cleveland, Ohio
    - Luna Pro, Kling Photo Corporation, Woodside, NY 11377
    - Minolta Company, New York
    - Paco Corporation, Minneapolis, MN 55440
    - Polaroid Corporation, Cambridge, MA 02139
    - Saunders Photo/Graphic Inc., Rochester, NY 14611
    - Simmon Bros., Division of Berkey Photo, Inc., Woodside, NY 11377
    - UltraViolet Products Inc., San Gabriel, CA 91778
    - Pete's PhotoWorld, Inc., Cincinnati, OH 45201
    - Tiffen Manufacturing Corp., Hauppauge, NY 11788
    - Sunpak, Division of Tocad America, Inc., Hackensack, NJ 07601
    - Sigma Corporation of America, Hauppauge, NY 11788
    - Electrophysics Corp., Nutley, NJ 07110

Special credits are hereby given to the following individuals for assistance with photographs and information:

Lori Cox, Johnson City Police Arson Unit; William DiGiovanni, Shaker Heights Police Dept., Ohio; Rainer S. Drolshagen, Federal Bureau of Investigation; Edwin Graybeal, Sheriff of Washington County, Tennessee; Stanley Hodges, Tennessee Bureau of Investigation; Todd Hull, 1st Judicial District Attorney General's Office, Tennessee; Martin G. Johnson, Shaker Heights Police Dept., Ohio; John E. Kimmet, Jr., Elyria Police Dept., Ohio; Jeff Kraynik, Palm Bay City Police Dept., Florida; Stan E. Puza, Lorain Police Dept., Ohio; George Rosbrook, Lorain County Community College, Ohio; Leon Smith, Wyoming Police Dept., Michigan; Michael Tomaro, Pepper Pike Police Dept., Ohio; Richard Whitt of the 1st Judicial District Drug Task Force (TN); and, Dr. Jamie Upshaw Downs, forensic pathologist, Georgia Bureau of Investigation.

Digital Assets

Thank you for selecting Anderson's *Police Photography*. To complement the learning experience, we have provided a number of online tools to accompany this edition.

Please consult your local sales representative with any additional questions.

FOR THE INSTRUCTOR

Qualified adopters and instructors need to register at this link for access: http://textbooks.elsevier.com/web/manuals.aspx?isbn=9781455777631

- **Test bank**: Compose, customize, and deliver exams using an online assessment package in a free Windows-based authoring tool that makes it easy to build tests using the unique multiple choice and true or false questions created for *Police Photography*. What is more is that this authoring tool allows you to export customized exams directly to Blackboard, WebCT, eCollege, Angel, and other leading systems. All test bank files are also conveniently offered in Word format.
- **Powerpoint lecture slides**: Reinforce key topics with focused Powerpoints, which provide a perfect visual outline with which to augment your lecture. Each individual book chapter has its own dedicated slideshow.
- **Instructor's guides**: Design your course around customized learning objectives, discussion questions, and other instructor tools.

Preface

The year 1971 was the beginning of a new age for the law enforcement profession. The Law Enforcement Assistance Administration was operating in full resplendence, providing financial assistance to local law enforcement agencies. Criminal Justice programs were emerging in institutions of higher learning across the country. 1971 was also the year Sam J. Sansone's *Modern Photography for Police and Firemen* was first published. As a young Crime Scene Technician, I remember my excitement in obtaining a copy of Mr. Sansone's book. I would never have imagined that, years later, I would be updating his classic work.

This seventh edition of Police Photography is designed, as was the original, to teach the fundamentals of photography and their application to police work. Toward that end, this book is organized into two main themes: (1) the photographic process; and (2) the application of photography to police work. Mr. Sansone's original material has been updated and new material has been added. New material on cameras, digital imaging, equipment and computer application techniques have been included. Of particular mention is the addition of Norman Marin as co-author. Norm has many years of experience as a forensic photographer and has been instrumental in updating several chapters.

We have attempted to maintain Mr. Sansone's proven style of presentation in this edition. We believe we have transformed the book into a current text that Sam would be proud of.

LSM

NM

The Police Photographer

CONTENTS

ABSTRACT

Police have been using photography to document and capture details about crimes for many decades. Generally, the courts have upheld the use of photographic images as evidence at trial. The most widely used system of photography in today's law enforcement community is the digital camera. Digital cameras pose new methods and better technology than traditional film systems to assist police in their duties.

KEY TERMS

Bertillon system
Digital imaging
Digital-single-lens-reflex (DSLR)
Eastman Kodak
Florida v. Victor Reyes
Green v. County of Denver
Luco v. United States
People v. Jennings
Photomacrography

INTRODUCTION

During a routine patrol of a suburban neighborhood, Officer Black receives a call instructing him to investigate a two-car collision a few blocks away. He drives to the scene and, before leaving his patrol car, he notes that, although one of the vehicles has sustained severe damage, no one seems to be injured.

The drivers of the two cars are arguing heatedly (neither driver, Officer Black observes, seems to have been clearly in the wrong), and nearby a passenger is sobbing. Officer Black ensures no one is injured, calms the drivers, soothes the passenger, records each person's description of the accident (there were no witnesses outside the two cars involved), and radios for a tow truck to remove the damaged vehicle. Before the tow truck arrives and the automobiles are moved, he takes a few measurements, sketches the scene, reaches into his pocket and takes out his cell phone, and snaps four photographs of the accident.

In addition to being a calmer of nerves, an investigator, a law enforcer, an impartial witness (although after the fact), an artist, and an agent for the immediate conclusion of a minor catastrophe in the lives of three people, Officer Black is a police photographer. That is not his job description, but neither is his role as a street psychologist. He may never use PhotoShop or hold a digital single-lens reflex camera in his hands. But his function as a police photographer is every bit as important as that of the head of the crime laboratory in his department who takes photographs in his spare time that could vie with the best of those seen in *National Geographic*.

Both Officer Black and the head of his department's crime laboratory are police photographers; this book is for both of them.

POLICE PHOTOGRAPHY: A SHORT HISTORY

Photography is most obviously useful in police work when photographs serve as evidence that may prove invaluable to investigators, attorneys, judges, witnesses, juries, and defendants. Often, a good photograph can be the deciding factor in a conviction or acquittal when no other form of real evidence is available.

Photographs were used in court as early as the mid-1800s. In 1859, a photograph was used in the case of Luco v. United States (64 U.S. (23 HOW.) 515.16

L.Ed. 545 [1859]) to prove that a document of title for a land grant was, in fact, a forgery. The first recorded use of accident photography was in 1875: "Plaintiff, in a horse and buggy, was injured when, in attempting to go around a mud hole in the center of a road he drove off an unguarded embankment" (Blair v. Inhabitants of Pelham, 118 Mass 420 [1875]). The photograph was admitted in evidence to assist the jury in understanding the case. Two years later, photographs were admitted as evidence in a civil suit involving a train wreck (Lock v. The Souix City & P.R.R., 46 Iowa 210 [1879]).

Although neither of these early photographs used in evidence was taken by a police photographer, the use of photography in police work is well established in the early annals of photography. In 1841, 18 years before Luco v. United States, the French police were making daguerreotypes (an early form of photograph) of known criminals for purposes of identification.

One of the first cases to hold that a relevant photograph of an injured person was admissible in evidence was Redden v. Gates in 1879 (52 Iowa 210, 1879). The photograph was a tintype, a photograph made on a thin iron plate by the collodion process. It showed whip marks on the plaintiff's back 3 days after the assault. In 1907, in Denver, Colorado, all intoxicated persons were photographed at the police station.

Speeding motorists were being detected with photographic speed recorders by 1910. The state of Massachusetts approved the use of such devices and gave a full description of their operation. Although radar is a more popular device for this operation today, there has been a resurgence in the use of photo-enforced traffic laws and devices in the past decade.

The use of fingerprint photographs for identification purposes was approved in 1911 in People v. Jennings (96 N.E. 1077, 252 Ill. 534, 1911), although 1882 was the year in which fingerprints were first officially used for identification purposes in the United States. Gilbert Thompson of the US Geological Survey in New Mexico used his own fingerprint on commissary orders to prevent their forgery. In 1902, New York Civil Service began fingerprinting applicants to discourage the criminal element from entering civil service, and also to prevent applicants from having better-qualified persons take the test for them.

The famous Will West case took place at Leavenworth Prison in 1903. When he was received at Leavenworth, Will West denied ever having been imprisoned there before. Clerks at the prison insisted that West had been there and ran the Bertillon instrument (used for identification purposes) over him to verify measurements. When the clerk referred to the formula derived from West's measurements, they were practically identical, and the photograph appeared to be that of Will West. When the clerk turned over the William West record card,

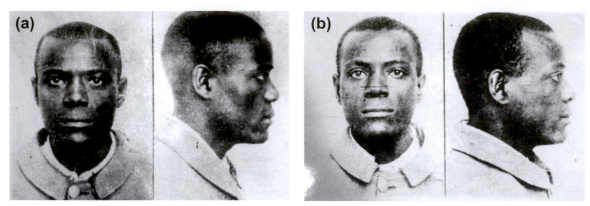

FIGURE 1.1
The Will West–William West case demonstrated that photographs and Bertillon measurements of persons were not accurate methods for identification. Will West (a) and William West (b).

he found that it was that of a man already serving a life sentence for murder. Subsequently, the fingerprints of Will West and William West were compared. The patterns bore no resemblance. The fallibility of three systems of personal identification (photographs, Bertillon measurements, and names) was demonstrated by this one case. The value of fingerprints as a means of identification was established. There was a great similarity in the photographs of Will West and William West (Figure 1.1). An officer must be careful when identifying a person from a photograph. After the Will West–William West case, most police departments began using photographs, Bertillon measurements, and fingerprints on their "mug shot" files. Eventually, the Bertillon system was discarded (Figure 1.2).

One of the early uses of firearms identification is recorded in a 1902 case, Commonwealth v. Best (62 N.E. 748, 180 Mass. 492, 1902). Photographs of bullets taken from the body of a murdered man were put into evidence, along with a photograph of a test bullet pushed through the defendant's rifle. This method of obtaining a test bullet is not proper, according to modern authorities, but the use made of the comparison photographs was to be followed in many later firearms identification cases.

Before the modern electronic flash units of today, photoflash bulbs were used and readily accepted by the public by 1930. Before the photoflash bulbs, people used flash powders—dangerous explosives that produced a great deal of objectionable smoke. The photoflash bulb was a revolutionary development that made possible the taking of many evidence pictures that were otherwise unobtainable. Undoubtedly, their use contributed greatly to the development of police photography.

FIGURE 1.2

Early mug-shot files depicted photographs, fingerprints, and Bertillon measurements. Eventually, Bertillon measurements were discarded as a means for identification. *Courtesy Memphis Police Department.*

Ultraviolet photography was approved in a decision handed down in the 1934 case of State v. Thorp (171 A. 633, 86 N.H. 501, 1934). The picture showed footprints in blood on a linoleum floor, and brought out distinctive marks in the soles of the shoes worn by the defendant that corresponded to the marks shown in the ultraviolet photograph.

In 1938, the Eastman Kodak Company introduced the Super-Six-20, which was a camera featuring fully automatic exposure control by means of a photoelectric cell coupled to the diaphragm of the lens. After 1945, Kodak again introduced cameras that were automatic and in a price range that everyone could afford. Today, such features are used in most cameras and are within a price range that is affordable to most people. You can get an automatic camera that meets almost all of a person's photographic needs, and most cell phones are equipped with sophisticated camera systems. There are even lens attachments, such as Sony's QX Cyber-Shot, that can be mounted to digital tablets and smart-phones to create a high-end camera system.

The first appellate court case passing on the admissibility of color photographs was Green v. County of Denver (142 P.2d 277, 111 Colo. 390, 1943). The court upheld the use of color photographs as evidence.

The Eastman Kodak Company introduced a color transparency using sheet film in 1935, called Kodachrome. It quickly became extremely popular, resulting in the widespread use of color photographs in police photography. Then, in 1941, a color process known as Kodacolor made it possible to make color slides, color prints, or black-and-white prints from a color negative.

In 1963, the Polaroid Company introduced Polacolor film, which made it possible to take finished pictures in black-and-white or color in less than 1 min. This was one of the most significant developments in the history of photography and led to the extensive use of color photographs as evidence. Many Polaroid camera devices were incorporated into traditionally police photographic uses, such as mug shots, fingerprint photography, microscope photography, and forensic photography. Digital photography has replaced Polaroid as the primary police camera system.

In 1965, another important invention was placed on the market. It was the introduction of a fully automatic electronic flash unit, which made it possible to take exposed strobe flash photographs at distances from 2 to 20 feet without changing the lens opening or shutter speed. Automation was thus achieved by means of the lighting equipment rather than the camera.

In 1967, we saw the beginning of the use of videotapes as legal evidence. Sony introduced the Betamax videotape cameras and recorders/players in the mid-1970s, making them affordable for the average household. At the same time, the Matsushita Company introduced the VHS series of cameras and recorders/players in direct competition of the Betamax system. Consumers chose the VHS over the Betamax. Today, many law enforcement agencies use videography for surveillance, recording crime scenes and interrogations, and training purposes.

In the 1980s, we saw the introduction of quality 35-mm "point-and-shoot" cameras, fully automatic 35-mm SLRs with automatic lens focusing, and a host of new and better films. During the late 1980s, we saw faster personal computers with high memory capabilities, allowing for the introduction of the CD Photo system and digital imaging.

The 1990s produced more advances in the field of photography than in previous decades. Primarily because of the progress of electronics and computer systems, new photographic media were developed. During the late 1990s, a new photographic medium emerged, digital imaging. When the digital video disc (DVD) was introduced in the late 1990s, it set the stage for the eventual replacement of the videocassette, the laser disc, the CD-ROM, and even the audio CD with one system for digital media storage. The DVD is now being replaced with portable chip devices in "flash drives" and digital smart-cards.

Today's twenty-first century cameras are fully automatic, to an extent. The police photographer can now concentrate more on the subject of the picture than on the intricacies of the camera. Professionals and amateurs now use cameras equipped with semiautomatic or fully automatic controls. Digital imaging allows photographers to take images and manipulate and enhance them using a computer rather than a darkroom. With the wide variety of good cameras today, there is no excuse for a police photographer not to be able to obtain suitable pictures for evidence.

THE MANY USES OF PHOTOGRAPHY IN POLICE WORK

The modern police department considers photography more than just a way to record evidence or identify a known criminal. Note the role of photography in the following aspects of law enforcement:

Identification files: Criminals, Missing Persons, Lost Property, Licenses, Anonymous Letters, Bad Checks, Laundry Marks, and Civilian or Personnel Fingerprint Identification Files. In the case of a catastrophe, such as an airplane crash, the fingerprints from a civilian file are proving helpful in making positive identifications.

Communications: Investigative Report Files, Accident Files, Transmission of Photos (Wire Photo, FAX, and e-mail), and photographic supplements to reports. With modern-day computers, accident reports can be made in seconds and sold to insurance adjusters for nominal fees. An excellent source of revenue for a department is the sale of photographs of traffic accidents to insurance companies and lawyers.

Evidence: Crime Scenes, Traffic Accidents, Homicides, Suicides, Fires, Objects of Evidence, Latent Fingerprints, Evidential Traces. Evidence can frequently be improved by contrast control (lighting, filters, and software), by magnification (photomicrography and photomacrography), and by invisible radiation (infrared, ultraviolet, soft X-rays, and hard X-rays).

Offender detection: Surveillance, Burglar Traps, Confessions, Re-enactment of Crimes, Intoxicated-Driver Tests. One of the newest applications of police photography is to record on videotape arrests in which the suspect offers resistance.

The practice has been instituted by many law enforcement agencies to counter charges of police brutality.

Court exhibits: Demonstration Enlargements, Individual Photos, Projection Slides, Videography and Computer Presentations (i.e., Power-Point presentations).

Reproduction and copying: Questionable Checks and Documents, Evidential Papers, Photographs, Official Records and Notices.

Personnel training: Photographs, Computer Presentations, and Videos relating to police tactics, investigation techniques, mob control, and catastrophe situations.

Crime and fire prevention: Hazard Lectures, Security Clearance, Detector Devices, Photos of Hazardous Fire Conditions made when fire prevention inspections are made.

Public relations: Slides, Computer Presentations, and Videos that pertain to safety programs, juvenile delinquency, traffic education, public cooperation, and homeland security.

In general, then, there are four primary ways of using photography in police work: (1) as a means of identification; (2) as a method of discovering, recording, and preserving evidence; (3) as a way to present, in the courtroom, an impression of the pertinent elements of a crime; and (4) as a training and public relations medium for police programs.

Public Relations

Aside from the obvious uses of photography in police work, the photographer must be aware of the importance of police photography in public relations. For instance, burglary has a low clearance rate: approximately 12% (US Department of Justice, 2011). The inability of police departments to catch these particular criminals is, of course, founded in the elusiveness of the criminal and his or her ability to vanish into the dark. The public, however, regards this poor percentage as ineptitude on the part of the police. Careful and thorough photography of a burglary scene can go a long way toward solving the crime, thus dispelling this and other misconceptions of the public.

POLICE PHOTOGRAPHY AND FIRE INVESTIGATION

Arson is probably the least investigated index crime for two reasons. First, it is difficult to show that a fire was, in fact, intentionally set. Second, a controversy exists as to who should investigate arson. Should it be the police, who have extensive knowledge and experience in investigations? Or should it be the fire department, which has much more knowledge about the causes of fires? In large cities and some states, this problem is solved because they have their own arson investigation units. But, in smaller towns and states without a state arson investigation unit, this may not be the case; neither department wants to get involved in this problem, so it may go unsolved.

Regardless of who is responsible for photographing the scene during an arson investigation, his or her chief role is to document the fire from its origin to its completion. Another aspect of this job is to document aspects of the operation for the training of new fire fighters, to show both correct and incorrect procedures for future study.

The primary principle to remember in police photography is that a finished photograph must be accurate. As a means of evidence, a photograph can be factual and, in many cases, revealing. In other words, the essence of photography lies in its ability to both record and clarify. To use the camera to its fullest advantage, then, it becomes necessary to learn the fundamentals of the photographic process: to learn and understand the techniques of, and wide range of possibilities for, photography in law enforcement.

EVIDENTIAL PHOTOGRAPHS

Court photographs serve two purposes: (1) the photograph itself is documentary evidence; and (2) the photograph is a record of evidential objects that may or may not be present in the courtroom. When the photograph itself is evidence, it implicates a defendant in a criminal act. This is apparent in surveillance and "sting" operations, in which photographs or videotapes depict identifiable persons engaging in illegal activity. When the photograph serves as a record of items or situations of evidential value, the photograph is used to illustrate details of the evidence or scene, or to represent evidence that is not present or unseen in court. Crime scene photographs, microphotographs, macrophotographs, medicolegal photographs (autopsies), and photographs of objects that cannot be conveniently brought into the courtroom are examples.

When photographs are introduced as evidence in court, the photograph will not stand alone. A person, present when the photograph was taken, must be able to testify that the photograph accurately and fairly depicts the scene as it was and that the photograph is not misleading or sensational. For this reason, no photograph of evidential value may be altered or retouched in any manner that would distort the actual subject. Objections may even be raised over placing identification markings on photographs, such as in the case of fingerprint comparisons. When in doubt as to whether such markings may be objectionable to the court, it is advisable to prepare two sets of photographs, one with and one without such markings. A removable transparent overlay may also be used for such markings on one photograph. As early as 1899, a court observed the following:

> It is common knowledge that as to such matters, either through want of skill on the part of the artist, or inadequate instruments or materials, or through intentional and skillful manipulation, a photograph may not only be inaccurate but dangerously misleading.
>
> Cunningham v. Fair Haven & Westville R. Co., 72 Conn. 244 at 250, 43 A. 1047 at 1049, 1899

Videos, color photographs, and digital images are generally admissible on the same grounds as black-and-white photographs if: (1) they depict relevant issues in the case; (2) they are true and accurate representations (which may require the testimony of the photographer); and (3) their probative value is not outweighed by their prejudicial effect (i.e., gruesomeness or inflammatory character). Digital images may be enhanced to bring out more detail. However, the original, unenhanced, image must be kept to maintain integrity (Washington v. Hayden, 90 Wash. App. 100, 950 P.2d 1024, Wash. App. Div. 1, Feburary 17, 1998).

In Wright v. State (250 So. 2d 333, Fla. App. 1971), the court held that three of eight color photographs introduced were grossly inflammatory and unnecessary to explain or elucidate any portion of the state's case. However, in Albritton v. State (221 So. 2d 192, Fla. App. 1969), the same court held that color and black-and-white photographs depicting injuries to a 16-month-old baby demonstrated visual evidence of the extent and severity of the child's injuries.

Color photographs in and of themselves do not determine their admissibility or inadmissibility as evidence. The legal requirement lies in the effect of the photographs, whether in color or in black-and-white. Generally, if the inflammatory character of "gruesome" photographs is overemphasized and their probative value is minimized, the courts may find error in their admissibility. Criminal cases reflect broad discretion in the trial court for admission of photographs when the probative value is found to outweigh prejudicial impact (People v. Cruz, 26 Cal. 3d 233, Cal. Rptr. 1 1980). The best advice is to show only those photographs that explain and demonstrate, and nothing more.

Although digital images are much easier to manipulate than traditional film photographs, they have stood the same legal tests. In 1997, the International Association for Identification adopted a resolution endorsing the use of digital imaging, stating that it was a natural progression in the history of photography and, therefore, fell under the same criteria as photographic evidence. Despite defense attorneys' objections to the use of digital imaging because of

FIGURE 1.3
The World Trade Center 9/11 hoax photograph.

the ease at which they can be manipulated, the courts have allowed digital photographic images on the same basis as traditional film photographs (Berg, 2000). However, defense attorneys will continue to aggressively point out how easily digital prints can be manipulated. In a 2002 murder trial in Florida, police used software known as More Hits to enhance a smudged palm print on duct tape. Although the court allowed the evidence to be presented, the defense argued that it was "junk science" and introduced testimony from an art professor to demonstrate how easy it was to manipulate images using Adobe Photoshop. The defendant was acquitted (Florida v. Victor Reyes, 17th Jud. Cir. Ct., Case 99-11535CF10A, Opinion and Order on Defendant's Motion in Limine, 21 October 2002). Photographic hoaxes, such as the World Trade Center 911 photograph that appeared widely on the internet, are common, which may encourage defense attorneys in attempting to disqualify digital photographs in court (Figure 1.3).

LEGAL CONSIDERATIONS

The terms *manipulate* and *enhance* are often used interchangeably with digital imaging. However, depending on the definition used, there may be a legal distinction between the two terms. Certainly, brightness/contrast, color balance, and cropping of digital images can all be manipulated with a computer using Adobe Photoshop. But, in a legal sense, the term manipulation may be construed to mean changing an image to reflect something different than the true portrayal of the scene, or subject. It would be better said that the common photographic changes (density, contrast, color balance, burning, and dodging) are, in fact, enhancements. But, as many celebrities have testified, tabloid papers have been accused of using digitally manipulated photographs in their publications. It is easy to put one person's head onto another person's body by manipulating the images on the computer. In the same vein, it might be easy to digitally remove, or to add, a piece of evidence at a crime scene and, therefore, to make the defendant look guilty. If data from the original image are either removed from or added to, that changes the intent of the original photograph. That is considered manipulation. For example, it is easy to use the brightness/contrast controls to make bruises and lacerations appear more serious than they really are with digital imaging. And so, the term *digital manipulation* has a deceitful context. However, the term *enhance* indicates that nothing was removed, changed, or added, to the image that would change the intent of the photograph. Therefore, for purposes of testifying in court, regarding what was done to a digital image, the photographer should use the term *enhancement* rather than *manipulation*. This will tend to avoid being attacked on the subject during cross-examination. There is a false assumption that film is more secure from manipulation than digital images. Although it may be a little harder and more time-consuming to do so, film photographs can, also, be manipulated by anyone who can do darkroom work. In fact, if a standard operating procedure (SOP) for digital images is in place with a police agency, digital images may be more secure than film images.

As with film photographs, the photographer usually must testify in court that any images produced digitally are a reasonably true and accurate reproduction of the scene or subject. If a digital image has been altered, or enhanced, in any way, the photographer must testify as to the protocols followed with enhancement. To ensure that a digital image is accepted as photographic evidence in court, the police department should establish rigid SOPs and follow them. At a minimum, SOPs should include the following:

1. *Camera original images must be archived in an unalterable form soon after the photographs are made.* This can be done by using digital disks with a serial number. The serial number of the disk should be recorded in the case file. This archival copy is made before any image editing work.
2. *A photographic log should be maintained to record information about the images.* This can be a written log, similar to film photographic logs. In most digital cameras of today, a file is generated by the camera, itself. This file is called a metadata file, or more commonly, an Exif header file. These often record the camera make, model, serial number, camera settings, and date/time of the image. When the image is saved, the data file goes with it as a normally hidden file. However, the date and time of the camera must be set correctly. It is advisable to check this before any imaging task.
3. *Chain of custody must be maintained.* As with any form of physical evidence, image files must be controlled and secured. Documentation should be kept on who had possession of materials, what was done to them, and where they were/are located at all times.

4. *Enhancements and alterations to digital images must be documented.* Any alteration or enhancement to images is done using a copy of the archival disk images. Detailed records of what types of enhancements were performed must be recorded. There is a history function in Adobe Photoshop that will record everything that was done to the image. Another way to create documentation is to use the macro feature on the computer. The macro records all the keystrokes made in a session, and these keystrokes can be played back.

THE FUTURE OF PHOTOGRAPHY

Astounding developments are being made in photography that are going to lead to even greater use of police photography. Years ago, people laughed when someone suggested that any size photograph could be produced almost immediately without the use of a darkroom. Photographic prints can be produced today on an inexpensive ink jet printer that rivals that of traditionally produced prints. The traditional darkroom as we know it is going to disappear. Photographic evidence will be produced not only more quickly but more economically, and at the same time will be of excellent quality.

Because revolutionary changes are in progress and are happening so quickly, it will be difficult to keep up with them. Contemporary police photographers have more technologically advanced materials available to them than did their earlier counterparts. Even though photography continues to develop as a digital medium with pictures recorded and stored electronically, the basic principles of photography will not change. We will still have the basic laws of perspective and correct tone reproduction. Photographic processes are but a means to an end, and police are primarily concerned with whether the final photographic exhibit is a fair and accurate representation of a subject, rather than how it was reproduced.

The future of photography continues to be in electronic digitization. Great strides in electronics have been made in the past decade and have invaded the photographic finishing and development areas more fully. Already, videos and digital recordings of depositions, interrogations, and crime scene investigations are becoming common, and digital imaging is becoming common, with crime scene investigations, latent fingerprint examinations, and other areas of forensic science. Color photographs have virtually supplanted black-and-white photographs in all but certain scientific branches of police photography in which color would have no advantage (i.e., infrared and ultraviolet photography). Sophisticated, yet easy-to-operate, digital cameras are being developed on an almost-daily basis. No book can possibly keep up with all the changes taking place in the field of photography. The serious police photographer should subscribe to one of the many photographic magazines (e.g., *Popular Photography*) to keep abreast of new developments.

Photographic evidence is an important specialty—a powerful tool recognized as indispensable in the proof of facts in court. The opportunities for use of photographic evidence in the future will be limited only by our ability to understand and appreciate the power of the photographic picture and to comprehend its limitless value.

REFERENCES

Berg, E. C. (October, 2000). Legal ramifications of digital imaging in law enforcement. *Forensic Science Communications, 2*(4), 1–12.

U.S. Department of Justice. (2011). *Crime in the United States 2010*. Washington, DC: Federal Bureau of Investigation.

Cameras

ABSTRACT

There have been many cameras available for police use since the advent of photography in the nineteenth century. During the past decade, the use of digital cameras has proved to be as good as traditional film cameras for police use. In addition to still cameras, the use of camcorders has seen an increasing use with police in recording crime scenes, crimes in progress, and surveillance. The ideal police camera is a professional-grade, digital, single-lens reflex with interchangeable lenses and attachments.

KEY TERMS

Camcorder
CCD
CMOS
Digital single lens reflex (DSLR)
ISO
Video cameras
White balance

INTRODUCTION

More than almost any other art form, photography requires equipment. The primary piece of equipment for taking photographs is, of course, the camera. Yet, a camera itself does not produce a photograph. The camera requires a photographer to manipulate it. And, the photographer must be able to reproduce the photographic image through the use of computer software and printing. These three items—camera, photographer, and reproduction—working together, constitute a system of photography.

The system, and therefore the capabilities of the system, may be enlarged with the addition of various pieces of equipment (each of which must be compatible with the system). For instance, a simple digital camera manipulated by a photographer is a very limited system that may be enlarged and adapted to indoor use by adding a compatible flash attachment.

As demands on photographers are increased, they must refine the capabilities of the system by adding pieces of equipment, replacing pieces of equipment, simplifying the operation of equipment, using new computer software applications, and by augmenting their knowledge of photography. The photographer chooses a particular camera and organizes all photographic work and equipment around that camera. The camera should serve all the needs of the photographer, so that one camera can be used for most, if not all, facets of the work. Then, the photographer must set up computer software needs and printing capabilities for the finished photograph.

The camera must be compatible with the photographer's needs, abilities, and budget. With the current proliferation of cameras, the photographer is given a wide choice of cameras that vary in performance, complexity, and price. Careful consideration and research should be undertaken when choosing a camera system. One should keep in mind that many camera accessories, especially lenses, are only compatible with their own maker. For instance, Nikon makes lenses, but their lenses are, in general, compatible with Nikon cameras only. A Nikon lens would not fit on a Canon camera and vice versa. The selection of a particular camera must also include the accessories that may be needed for that camera (e.g., lenses, external flash units, underwater housings, and so on).

When Sony first announced the Mavica (magnetic video camera) in 1982, many thought it would replace traditional still photography much in the same way that camcorders have replaced home movie film cameras. As of this date, digital cameras have largely displaced film cameras among amateur consumers. Professional photographers, too, are leaving film cameras behind. Perhaps the company hurt most by the introduction of digital cameras has been Polaroid. Polaroid enjoyed great success with consumers with their instant photographs, rather than traditionally developed film. Consumers like the idea of being able to see immediately what their pictures look like, and Polaroid delivered in this respect. Digital cameras do the same thing: instant gratification. Photographers can see what the picture looks like and can retake a shot if it does not look right. Kodak also has been hurt by the introduction of digital cameras. The point-and-shoot line of cameras for which Kodak has long been known has been replaced with digital cameras. Although Polaroid and Kodak began producing their own lines of digital cameras and equipment in an effort to keep in business with the general public, they were unsuccessful.

Digital cameras are a cross between conventional film-based cameras and a digital scanner. The front of the camera uses a lens, aperture, and shutter to focus an image; however, the image is not focused onto light-sensitive film, but onto a semiconductor chip called a charge-coupled device (CCD) or a complementary metal oxide semiconductor (CMOS). Data are passed to an analog-to-digital converter chip, compressed, and then recorded on either built-in memory chips or a removable memory card. With some digital cameras, there may be as much as a half-second delay between when the shutter is pressed and when the camera actually takes the picture. This delay is the time necessary for the light sensor to read the scene, adjust the diaphragm opening (f-stop) or change the shutter speed, check the autofocus, and trigger the flash. Because of this delay, there may be a problem with the shot when subjects move. Also, there may be as much as a 4–9-second delay when the camera is converting the image into digital form, compressing and saving the image and recycling the flash. With some digital cameras, this additional delay prevents exposures from being made until after the camera recycles. With other camera models, one or more exposures may be taken while the camera is "busy" (processing) the first image. This is done by the camera having a "buffer" memory. Depending on the memory device and the camera quality settings, more than 1000 pictures may be stored in one memory chip before the chip is full and needs to be downloaded to a computer or other large storage device, such as an external hard drive. Like videos, these digital media devices can be reused by deleting unwanted pictures on the camera and/or formatting the media. Most are equipped with a liquid crystal display (LCD) viewfinder screen, which allows photographers to see what the picture looks like almost immediately. As mentioned, if photographers are not pleased with the result, they can retake the picture.

The quality of the pictures is based on the image sensor (CCD or CMOS) in the camera and the method of storing the image. Image sensors are often described by pixel count. *Pixel* is an abbreviation of picture elements. These elements are individual places (usually square) that, together, make up the sensor. One can imagine the sensor as looking much like a very small checkerboard, with each pixel being a square on the board. The more pixels the sensor has, the more detail it can detect. The size of the image sensor is also important, and it is measured diagonally (usually one-half inch or one-third inch). A small image sensor might yield poorer low-light sensitivity than a large one with the same, or lower, pixel count. Digital cameras often range from the lowest pixel resolution of 640 × 480 (0.3 megapixels) to as much as 32 megapixels. Thirty-two-megapixel cameras are relatively expensive, but a 12–14-megapixel camera can be found at a very reasonable price. In general, if enlargement prints of 8 × 10 inches or more are needed, a digital camera should have a 10-megapixel capability or better. When a digital image is enlarged beyond its resolution capability, the prints may become "pixelated" (broken up into blocky squares). This is a particular problem with the low-end point-and-shoot digital cameras with resolutions of 5 megapixels or less. Most digital cameras can record 256 shades of tone (light or dark) and color (Figures 2.1 and 2.2).

FIGURE 2.1
Charge-coupled device (left) and complementary metal oxide semiconductor chip (right).

FIGURE 2.2
Example of a pixelated image.

INTERNATIONAL STANDARDS ORGANIZATION/ AMERICAN STANDARDS ASSOCIATION

International Standards Organization (ISO)/American Standards Association (ASA) refers to the film speed of the camera. In 35-mm film photography, silver halide film of a fine grain meant the film required some time to gather light to form an image. As the size of the film grain was increased, the light-gathering ability of the film increased as well. The speed by which film could gather light was gauged as an ISO/ASA number. As the ISO of film used increased from 100–800 ASA, the film became more sensitive to light, quickening exposures in low-light conditions. However, as the grain size of photographic film increased, there was also a reduction in resolution, such that photographs could appear "grainy" and slightly blurred.

The sensitivity of a digital camera sensor to light is also measured in ISO, where ISO is the effective film speed of the camera. As the ISO of the digital camera increases, the sensor's light-gathering ability also increases. Most digital cameras will have an ISO range of 100–6400; however, high-end cameras can boost their light-gathering ability to the 51,000-ISO range, making these cameras very useful in low-light conditions. As with film, there are limitations to usable ISO. As the sensitivity of the camera sensor increases, the sensor may produce ISO noise, which may appear as "off-color" pixels in an image. This phenomenon may be referred to as *chroma noise*. High ISO noise—like grainy, high-ISO film—can affect the resolution of a photograph. In general, low ISO settings correspond to higher quality better resolved images, but they require longer shutter speeds. High ISO settings can be used to achieve faster exposure times, but they are associated with grainy, poorly resolved images.

A persistent problem with digital imaging is color balance. The white balance setting for a camera adjusts the color of an exposure for a given type of illumination. If the white balance settings and illumination source are matched incorrectly, color shifts occur that result in off-color photographs. The camera must be balanced for the type of illumination used. For example, sunlight and electronic flashes are balanced for "daylight" settings whereas floodlights and tungsten filament lamps are balanced for tungsten lighting. It is important that the correct setting be used with the available lighting so the color of the photographic subject is represented properly (Figure 2.3).

The image sensors used currently in digital cameras have very little color–temperature latitude. Most CCD or CMOS chips are balanced automatically for direct sunlight and electronic flash, and do not do well with other light sources. Therefore, any digital photograph taken with illumination other than sunlight or electronic flash may appear with less detail, low contrast, and incorrect color balance. However, most cameras can be set to the various types of lighting that might be encountered. With this in mind, one can say there are many digital

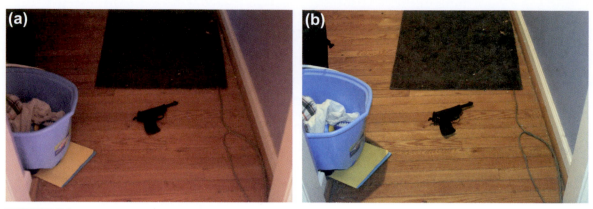

FIGURE 2.3
Example of white balance. (a) Photo taken without white balance correction. (b) Photo taken with white balance correction.

cameras available that are of use to law enforcement, given the many lighting situations that may be encountered.

Digital cameras are designed for applications in which viewing a picture on a television monitor or transmitting images via the Internet is convenient or desirable. This fits with the needs of law enforcement. However, one must keep in mind that picture quality varies in models and price category. Digital photographs also have the advantage of being printed easily in seconds. This, too, is an advantage for law enforcement. And, because the filing and storage of records is of concern to police departments, the ability to store photographs in a computer, or on digital media, adds another important advantage. In most police departments, mug shots, accident photographs, photographs of fingerprints, crime scene photographs, and other images are currently stored on computer media. Regular film negatives (or prints) in older, archived records may now be scanned using a film scanner, and they are digitized for storage or Internet transmission.

DIGITAL SINGLE-LENS REFLEX

The single-lens reflex (SLR) camera allows photographers to view a subject through the main lens of the camera. The image seen through the viewfinder window is a replica image; when using a standard lens, the image is similar in size and appearance to the scene in front of the unaided eye. The optical system for viewing the image is comprised of (1) the main lens, (2) a mirror for diverting light away from the film (or sensor), (3) a prism for reversing and inverting the image as reflected (upside down and reversed) from the mirror, (4) a focusing screen, and (5) a viewfinder. Thus, a change in lenses causes an automatic change in the optical system; no compensation by the photographer

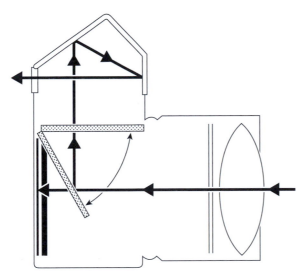

FIGURE 2.4
Cross-section of single-lens reflex optical system.

is necessary. Also, parallax (the difference between the image in the camera viewer and the image recorded by the camera sensor) is eliminated because there is only one point from which to view.

The mirror is mounted on a hinge and flips up and down automatically before and after the shutter opens and closes, blocking out the viewfinder only at the instant of the exposure. The majority of standard, wide-angle, and moderately long-focus lenses are fitted with an automatic iris control so the lens is always wide open for focusing and viewing, but the lens closes down to the pre-selected shooting aperture when the shutter is released.

The digital single-lens reflex (DSLR) camera operates in the same way. Instead of film, a digital sensor sits in place behind the mirror. The photographer has the option of looking through the eyepiece to compose the shot or through a light-emitting diode screen (Figure 2.4).

With the introduction of digital photography during the mid 1980s, many believed it would eventually replace photography as we know it. Although it is true that digital cameras have replaced film and traditional cameras, the basic function of photography has not changed. As mentioned earlier, after Sony introduced its Mavica digital camera in 1982, a number of leading camera and electronic companies began producing digital cameras and computer software designed especially for computer imaging. Most digital cameras produced during the 1990s were designed for amateur consumer use and resembled the 35-mm point-and-shoot cameras. Casio, Canon, Nikon, Kodak, Epson, Minolta, and others produced a large line of point-and-shoot-type digital cameras that stored images on magnetic or electronic storage media. Camera images could be downloaded into various computer software programs for printing, storing, and/or manipulation. Currently, manufacturers are producing more professional-grade digital cameras that allow for interchangeable lenses and accessories. Most cell phones and digital tablets now have camera capabilities that rival top-end digital SLR cameras.

There are numerous advantages for using digital cameras. The most obvious is the ability to store large numbers of photographic images on digital media. Other advantages include the following:

1. The ability to produce color photographs quickly and without the need of a darkroom or film developing.
2. The ability to manipulate or enhance images on a computer for contrast, color, and size.
3. The ability to produce "slide" presentations for training or educational purposes via a computer and television monitor.
4. The ability to transmit photographs over phone lines via e-mail and the Internet.
5. The ability to view images immediately after they have been taken and to make necessary adjustments to exposure if needed.

Some disadvantages include the need for high-speed computer equipment, printers capable of producing high-quality prints, and the inability to send large data-size images via e-mail. Also, digital cameras are notorious for consuming battery power. Police photographers may find themselves at a disadvantage at a crime scene when the camera battery fails and they have no extra batteries.

VIDEO CAMERAS

Technological advances in electronics have made video cameras and camcorders relatively inexpensive, portable, and highly sophisticated. After the initial investment is made in the camera, video media are very inexpensive and may even be the same type of memory card used with the department's DSLR. Video has several advantages over still photographs: (1) video gives immediate results without the need for processing; (2) depending on the media, video can be used more than once simply by recording over previous videos; (3) visual movement allows the viewer to perceive the scene accurately, as it is shown; and (4) sound may be included.

The terms *video camera* and *video camcorder* are used somewhat interchangeably. The primary difference between a video camera and a video camcorder is that a camcorder has a built-in recorder/playback unit whereas a video camera must be attached to a separate recorder/playback unit.

The uses of video in police work are numerous. Videos are excellent means for documenting traffic stops (with the camera mounted inside the police vehicle), interviews, interrogations, and lineups. Videos are useful to show a judge how "drunk" a drunk driver was at the scene of an accident or at the police station during booking. Videos are also used to demonstrate probable cause for stopping suspicious vehicles in suspected drug-trafficking operations. And, videos can help demonstrate that a charge of police brutality during a traffic stop or arrest is founded or unfounded. Camcorders can be used at crime scenes and autopsies, to detail a fire in progress, and for surveillance and "sting" operations. The portability and low cost of camcorders make them suitable for a wide range of police work.

Camcorder Formats

Nearly all the commercially available camcorders are digital and use a CCD or CMOS image sensor. Depending on the size of the image sensor, resolutions range from about 340,000 pixels to well more than 1 megapixel on many consumer and professional-grade cameras. And, almost all digital camcorders have high lines of resolution. Normal analog broadcast television has about 250 lines of resolution whereas digital camcorders have more than 500 lines. Most digital camcorders store images on memory chips or "sticks," and the images are then downloaded via a computer hookup (Figure 2.5).

Camcorder Features
Image Sensors

Many video cameras use a CCD image sensor. This sensor dictates the expense of the camcorder. The larger the sensor, the more expensive the camera. For instance, lower priced camcorders with excellent features may have a one-sixth-inch CCD sensor capable of producing about 340,000 pixels of resolution. A camera equipped with a one-fifth-inch CCD sensor is capable of producing an

(a)   **(b)**   **(c)**

FIGURE 2.5
Various models of consumer and professional-grade video cameras (a–c).

actual pixel resolution of about 690,000. Some higher end camcorders use three CCD image sensors to produce much greater pixel resolution. Nearly all digital camcorders are infrared sensitive—that is, they can be used with an infrared filter—which makes digital camcorders very useful for police work when infrared images may need to be photographed. Sony takes advantage of this feature by marketing some of their cameras with a "Night Vision" ability. Sony cameras with Night Vision capability have a built-in infrared light so images may be seen (much like using a night vision scope) and captured in total darkness. It is the same feature used frequently on TV ghost-hunting shows.

Lenses

Almost all camcorders have motorized zoom lenses controlled with a three-position rocker switch on the handgrip. Zoom ratios are usually from 6:1 to 10:1, and many have macro capabilities. Lenses are usually fixed-mounted, so there are few interchangeable lens models available. On camcorders that do allow interchangeable lenses, the standard mount is the "C" mount, as found on most dash-mounted police vehicle cameras. There are accessory wide-angle and telephoto lenses available that attach directly to fixed-mounted camcorder lenses. Most camcorders are also equipped with an autofocus mode. The autofocus can be switched to manual focus if desired.

The amount of light entering the lens is controlled by an iris diaphragm. Most video cameras are equipped with an automatic iris that opens and closes automatically to adjust for exposure. Many camcorders allow the automatic iris to be adjusted manually, as well, to compensate for bright backgrounds and shadows. The iris control may also be used for fading in and out of scenes, rather than an abrupt on/off at the beginning or end of a scene. Some camcorders have an automatic backlight switch that lightens the main scene to compensate for unusually bright backgrounds.

A camcorder's sensitivity to light is determined by lens speed (f-number) and the characteristics of the image sensor. Video camera light sensitivity is specified using a lux unit. A lux unit is the minimum amount of light necessary to produce a video image. Lux ratings may be as high as 20 lux or as low as 1 lux for camcorders (0 lux for Sony's Night Vision system). The lux brightness scale is the metric version of the foot-candle scale. Seven lux equals three-fourths of 1 foot-candle. One lux is about the amount of light 10 birthday candles produce. The recommended light level for a good-quality video image is at least 500 lux. Less than 500 lux, image quality and contrast become poor.

Many camcorders are equipped with electronic shutters that allow the camera operator to select a shutter speed. Many camcorders allow 1/60-second, 1/500-second, and 1/1000-second shutter speeds. Fast-action scenes may be recorded at higher speeds to reduce blurring of moving objects.

Viewfinders

Most camcorders have an electronic viewfinder containing a miniature LCD television screen. Because camcorders are single-lens recorders, the viewfinder shows exactly what the lens sees. The viewfinder can also be used as a monitor to play back recorded images. Various messages are also indicated in the viewfinder, such as the amount of time remaining on the tape, light levels, battery charge, and mode of operation.

Some camcorders are equipped with a character generator and a date/time indicator. A character generator allows titles to be superimposed over the scene being recorded. On some camcorders, the character generator looks like a tiny typewriter keyboard, and some models have an optional separate keyboard. An automatic calendar/clock imprints the date and time on the tape during recording. This feature is particularly useful for police work. The imprinted date/time provides evidence the tape was not tampered with or edited.

The viewfinder also indicates the white balance level. The white balance control allows a scene to be recorded with correct color balance. Most camcorders have an automatic white balance that can be overridden manually. Before shooting a scene, the camera may be color balanced for the scene's available light by pointing the lens at a white background and pushing the white balance control button. The camera then adjusts the color continually for the best balance.

Use of Camcorders

Although there are many advantages for video camcorders in police work, there are a few disadvantages. First and foremost is the quality of the video image. Because the final image must be viewed on a television screen, the screen's quality is most important. High-resolution digital monitors do improve the quality of the image. Large-screen television monitors or digital projectors are a must if the video is to be shown to a group (such as a jury).

The fact that video camcorders also record sound can prove to be a source of frustration. Although audio capabilities are an advantage when videotaping interviews and interrogations, they may be a disadvantage when recording surveillance operations or crime scene investigations. It may be disconcerting for a jury to view and hear a videotape with excessive background noise or police officers behaving inappropriately at the crime scene. Video camera operators should disable or disconnect the microphone from the camera if they do not wish to record what is being said.

The selection of a camcorder for police work is basically a matter of use and budget. For dash-mounted police vehicle cameras, the choice is a small camera with high resolution. For crime scene, interview, and interrogation recordings, a small, consumer camcorder is sufficient. For serious surveillance work, a professional-grade camcorder with telephoto capabilities should be considered.

THE POLICE CAMERA

All cameras are basically alike. Each is a box with a sensor (film) at one end and a hole at the other. The hole is there so light can enter the box, strike the surface of the sensor, and make a picture. Every camera, from the most primitive to the most modern, is based on the slogan created by Eastman Kodak: "You press the button; we do the rest." Automatic and computerized modern cameras try to make picture taking as easy as possible by choosing the shutter speed or aperture for you or by presetting the focus.

Most of today's DSLR cameras do practically everything for you. They focus, select the aperture, and select the shutter speed for you; there is no reason why a police photographer cannot take a good picture. The photographer may still make choices, even though the cameras are fully automatic, and there are a multitude of things that can be done with today's cameras. Photographers may freeze the motion of a speeding car or let it race by in a blur, or bring an entire accident scene into sharp focus or zoom in to isolate a single vehicle. The photographer can exaggerate the distances of the vehicles in an accident or show the actual distances between the vehicles.

For most on-the-job crime scenes, auto accidents, and other police functions, photographers do very well with DSLR cameras, especially because today's better cameras have many more functions than the cameras of the past. Police photographers have a wide range of cameras from which to choose. Our recommendation is to select a camera that performs all the functions required for general police and evidence photography, including the following:

1. The camera should be a DSLR.
2. The camera should be capable of being adjusted manually for specialized photographic situations and films.
3. The camera should be able to use a wide variety of interchangeable lenses that are readily available and relatively inexpensive.
4. The camera should be rugged, lightweight, compact, and easy to operate, transport, and store.
5. The camera should be able to adapt to all phases of police photography, including traffic accident and crime scene photography, close-up evidence photography, microscope photography, ultraviolet and infrared photography, surveillance photography, aerial photography, underwater photography, and identification photography (Figure 2.6).

FIGURE 2.6
Various models of professional-grade digital single-lens reflex cameras (a–c).

Given these considerations, the recommended police camera is a DSLR with at least 10 megapixels. Another camera that gives police photographers additional versatility is a video camcorder. Digital cameras are electronic and do not fare well when exposed to moisture. It is problematic when police photographers arrive at a secluded outdoor crime scene in rainy weather only to have their camera short-out after becoming wet. Having a backup camera saves considerable time and trouble. Batteries are also cause for consideration. Police photographers should always carry extra batteries for the camera or be able to recharge batteries at the scene.

Optics and Accessory Equipment

CONTENTS

ABSTRACT

One of the advantages of using a digital single-lens reflex (SLR) camera for police work is the availability of lenses and equipment. Different lens focal lengths enable the photographer to capture images over a wide range of situations, from wide-angle to telephoto. In addition, the use of macro lenses will enable the photographer to take detailed close-up pictures of single items of evidentiary importance. Filters help ensure that images are captured with as much detail and contrast as needed. The uses of tripods are a necessity in police photography to help stabilize cameras, as well as for long exposures. In some cases, underwater photography will be required and there are specially designed camera housings for underwater photography.

KEY TERMS

Normal lens
Wide-angle lens
Telephoto lens
Autofocus
Macro lens
Filters
Polarizing
Tripod

LENSES

The police photographer frequently needs a change of lens in order to accomplish a given task. The need for special lenses that can be readily purchased and easily interchanged is often a primary factor in the photographer's choice of a camera.

Lenses for special purposes add great flexibility to a system of photography and allow photographs to be taken that would have been incomplete, misleading, or even prejudicial had the photographer been restricted to using only the "normal" lens on the camera.

A lens is an optical device that gathers light from a subject and focuses onto a screen, film, or digital sensor. Lenses used for photography are plastic or glass, bounded either by two curved surfaces, or one curved surface and one plane. The lens is usually the most expensive component of any camera system.

A simple lens (a single piece of glass or plastic) is known as a lens element. Two or more elements, cemented together, comprise a lens component. Freestanding single elements may also be considered components; thus, an optical system that includes two freestanding lenses and two lenses cemented together is said to have three components.

One of the main advantages of using a digital single-lens reflex (SLR) camera is the wide selection of lenses available. Each camera maker produces a variety of lenses for their cameras, and a number of independent lens manufacturers widen the selection and cost range.

There are three basic categories of lenses for use in photography: normal lenses, wide-angle lenses, and telephoto lenses (Figure 3.1).

Normal Lenses

Lenses are generally referred to by the measure of their focal length. A lens with a focal length of 4 in is a 4-in lens, although it may only be a half-inch in diameter. In photography, a normal lens is one with a focal length equal to the diagonal measure of the image area. The image area of a 35 mm camera is 24 × 36 mm; thus, a normal lens for any 35 mm camera is 50 mm. By international standards, the acceptable measured focal length of a lens may be within 4% of its marked nominal value; a 50 mm lens may then have an actual focal length of 48–52 mm. The lens maker generally does not mark such deviations.

The normal lens is usually standard equipment on a camera, and is the intermediate between wide-angle and telephoto lenses. The picture angle of a

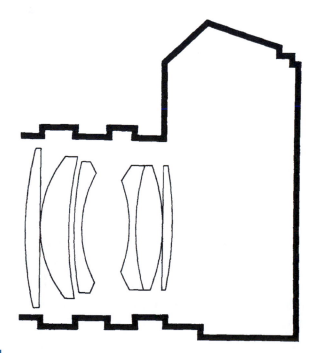

FIGURE 3.1
Lens elements.

normal lens is 45°, which corresponds to the viewing angle of the human eye. Therefore, a "normal" lens allows you to view your subject nearly the same as your unaided eye, neither reducing nor enlarging the image.

For the average police photographer who will be photographing accidents, crime scenes, and other general scenes, the normal lens is adequate. However, it is not an all-purpose lens. There is no all-purpose lens; the advanced or professional police photographer must look to specialized lenses for particular purposes.

Most digital camera lenses provide focal lengths based on 35 mm camera equivalents. Because focal length is based on the size of the film, focal length will be different for digital camera lenses. The "film size" for digital cameras is based on the size of the charge coupled device or complementary metal oxide semiconductor chip, which varies with different camera makes and models. The camera manual should provide information on the digital camera lens 35 mm equivalent. Johnson (2005) has devised a formula that can be used to approximate 35 mm equivalents for digital camera lenses. For example, if a digital camera has a 9.3 mm lens (the actual focal length) then it would be considered a "normal" lens based on 35 mm equivalency using Johnson's formula:

$$\text{Actual Focal Length}/.19 \text{ or}, \ 9.3/.19 = 49$$

WIDE-ANGLE LENSES

Selection of a lens is governed by the distance from a subject at which the photographer must work and by the field that must be encompassed within the picture area. The wide-angle lens has a shorter focal length than the normal lens and, as a result, it covers a picture angle wider than 60°. It enables photography of a widely extended scene from a close proximity or within a confined area. In police work, wide-angle lenses should be used under restricted conditions when the police officer is unable to cover the desired picture area with a lens of longer focal length.

Typical uses for the wide-angle lens are for photographing buildings, street scenes, and interiors of homes where a crime has been committed. Crimes committed in bathrooms, for instance, are not easily photographed without a wide-angle lens.

The wide-angle lens is also convenient for the photographer who is doing candid work where exact focusing is not always possible. The large depth of field resulting from the short focal length of a wide-angle lens compensates, to a degree, for inexact focusing.

A remarkable effect that can be achieved by the wide-angle lens is exaggeration of perspective. A close subject will appear larger than usual in the ultimate picture. Such exaggeration may sometimes result in a distorted impression, depending on the subject and viewing angle, and it gives a peculiar, interesting effect that cannot be attained otherwise.

The range of wide-angle lenses for 35 mm cameras includes 8, 20, 21, 24, 28, and 35 mm. The 28 and 35 mm are the most important for general wide-angle police work. Nikon produces a 35 mm PC lens that can correct for parallax. The 20 mm lens has the shortest focal length usable with viewfinder focusing; a certain amount of edge distortion will be noted. This is a problem with all wide-angle lenses, regardless of the manufacturer. The peripheral light rays are recorded with some degree of elongation, which is due to the angle at which they are received. Apparent perspective distortions are magnified by wide-angle lenses. When shooting with a wide-angle lens, the photographer should use a tripod and a small level to maintain normal perspective effects.

Wide-angle lenses for reflex cameras are also subject to design limitations caused by the need for an adequate back focus to clear the reflex mirror. This calls for inverted type construction.

Hasselblad has a very good super wide-angle camera that can be held in the palm of the hand. Used by many professionals for close-up candid work, it will only accept a 40 mm lens.

TELEPHOTO LENSES

A telephoto, or long-focus, lens has a longer focal length and provides a close-up image of a distant subject. In contrast to the wide-angle lens, the telephoto covers a smaller field of view and a shallower depth of field. Because of this shallowness, the ultimate picture assumes a relief-like quality, resulting from the lack of sharpness of the out-of-focus areas. Another characteristic of the telephoto lens is production of a flat composition; far objects appear enlarged while near objects do not appear proportionately large (Figure 3.2).

Normally, lenses beyond 58 mm come within the telephoto group. A technical distinction should be made between telephoto and long-focus lenses: a true telephoto has a shorter physical length while achieving the same angle of view as the long-focus lens. The shortening and physical convenience of the true telephoto lens is accomplished through use of negative rear elements for image dispersion. The front elements converge; the rear elements diverge. Optical aberrations are more easily corrected in regular long-focus lenses (whose physical size approximates focal length) than in telephoto lenses. Optical designers have overcome telephoto lens aberrations, but the effort in doing so is reflected in the cost of an advanced lens. In actual practice, all long lenses are usually called telephotos or telelenses.

FIGURE 3.2
Various lenses. (a) Nikkor 24–120 mm, (b) Sigma 170–500 mm, (c) Sigma 28–135 macro, and (d) Sigma 800 mm telephoto.

Telephoto lenses are used to bring inaccessible objects into the image area in greater size than would be the case with a normal lens. Image magnification is proportional to focal length. A lens of about 100 mm shows twice as much detail as a 50 mm lens would. The area covered is much less; the 100 mm lens covers the image area of a 50 mm lens. When using a telephoto lens, always shoot with the shortest telephoto lens that adequately encompasses the desired picture area.

Two other operational uses of telephoto lenses are: (1) to achieve better perspective control by being able to work at a distance and (2) to maintain the relative size of objects placed at varying distances from the camera. These purposes are served mostly by lenses up to about 200 mm.

For identification shots in police work, lenses of 85–135 mm focal length are frequently used. Many departments photograph their arrested persons with medium telephotos which effectively avoid lending undue prominence to the nose, lips, and chin of a subject. Also, they crop out extraneous matter while best utilizing the image area with reproducible matter of importance.

Long telelenses are those beyond 200 mm. Their angle of view and areas of image coverage are progressively narrowed as focal length becomes greater, but they show details in greater size and clarity than would be possible with an enlarged section of a picture made with a shorter focal length lens. The particular hazard of the long telephoto lenses is camera movement. Lenses up through 200 mm represent a safe limit for hand-held camera use, but the slightest movement during exposure of a camera with a long lens will show up as image displacement and blurring on the image. This becomes increasingly apparent as lenses with narrow angles of view are used.

The longest hand-held exposure should be the reciprocal of the focal length to the nearest shutter setting. For a 50 mm lens, this would be 1.60 s; for a 135 mm lens, 1.125 s. To minimize camera movement, the photographer should use a tripod, cable release, the highest feasible shutter speeds, and self-timer for shutter triggering. Sometimes, supports can be improvised from the back of a chair, a fence top, a table top, top of a car, a tree, or any other fixed object. The photographer may use bean bags on top of his tripod to stop the vibration of his camera. The bean bag technique is a good one and can be used for many shots in police work.

ZOOM LENSES

The convenience of zoom lenses has made them increasingly popular with photographers. Zoom optics offer the advantages of rapid changing of focal lengths without changing lenses and having one lens serves the purpose of several, being both economical and space saving.

There are many focal length ranges covered by zoom lenses. Among the most popular are those covering the short to medium telephoto ranges, such as 80–200 mm and 70–210 mm lenses. Wide-angle to short telephoto zoom lenses, such as 28–85 mm and 35–70 mm, are very popular because one lens covers all three lens areas: normal, wide-angle, and telephoto. Longer zoom lenses, such as 75–250 mm and 120–600 mm, are available but are heavier, larger, and often slower in speed.

LENS SPEED

The "speed" of a lens refers to the minimum amount of light that is passed through the shutter plane or "iris" of the lens. The speed is measured as an f-number, a system denoting the lens aperture, therefore, the smaller the f-number, the faster the lens. For example, an f-1.2 lens is faster than an f-2.8 lens. Telephoto and zoom lenses typically have slower speeds than wide-angle and normal lenses. Also, slower lenses are usually less expensive than faster lenses because of the number of lens elements required. For police surveillance in low-light conditions, this may be a disadvantage. For instance, a 200 mm telephoto lens may have a speed of f-4.5 while a 500 mm lens may have a speed of only f-8. It would take more light for exposure with the 500 mm lens than with a 200 mm lens. Some zoom lenses are described as having one maximum aperture, such as 75–205 mm f-3.8. The f-number remains constant throughout the zoom range. On other zoom lenses, there may be two maximum apertures included in their descriptions, such as 28–80 mm f-2.8-4.0. This means that the f-number gradually changes as you zoom from one end of the zoom range to the other. The shorter end of the zoom range is "faster" than the other end.

AUTOFOCUS LENSES

Most camera and lens manufacturers produce autofocus (AF) lenses. Autofocusing cameras use an infrared sensing module to determine distance of the subject and high-speed motor-driven focusing. AF lenses allow the photographer freedom from manual focusing so that he or she can concentrate on exposure and framing. They are particularly advantageous when photographing quick scenes or when the subject is moving. Many cameras even have a predictive focus control to track moving subjects.

AF lenses are generally more expensive than their manual counterparts. When purchasing an AF lens or camera, be sure it has a manual override capability for special focusing situations. Also, AF lenses will not operate on non-AF cameras, but manual focusing lenses will generally operate on AF cameras.

LENS MOUNTS

Lens mounts come in two basic choices: bayonet and screw thread. Although the mounts on most of the different brands of bayonet mount lenses appear the same, there are enough differences so that a lens designed for one brand of camera will not fit another. For example, a Minolta lens will not fit a Nikon, Pentax, Canon, or any brand of camera other than Minolta. One exception is the Pentax "K" bayonet mount, which may be used on Ricoh, Cosina, and Chinon cameras. Some private label cameras use Pentax K mounts as well.

Lens companies, such as Sigma and Vivitar, make their lenses available for most all camera brands. When purchasing a lens, be sure to specify the mount system for your camera. Generally, adapters are not available to adapt a lens with one mounting style to a different mount. Such an adapter would add some distance between the lens and the camera, thereby preventing the lens from focusing out to infinity. High-end SLR digital cameras, such as Canon and Nikon, accept the same lenses used by film cameras. If the photographer has two cameras manufactured by two different companies, such as Canon and Nikon, the lenses for the Canon will not work on the Nikon. If, on the other hand, the photographer had two Nikon digital cameras, lenses and other equipment would be compatible.

MACRO LENSES

Macro lenses are designed primarily for close-up work, but can be used for conventional photography as well, because they focus to infinity. Most macro lenses are in the normal (50–55 mm) or moderate telephoto (90–105 mm) focal length ranges with speeds ranging from f-2.8 to f-4.5. Macro lenses are also available on some zoom lenses. The advantage of macro lenses for police work is that they can focus on small articles of evidence (such as fingerprints) at the scene or in the crime laboratory without the use of a microscope or lens attachments. Many macro lenses will focus close enough for a 1:2 reproduction ratio (about 91.2 in). A reproduction ratio is a comparison of the actual size to the reproduction size on film. For example, a 1:2 reproduction ratio is 1.2 life size, and a 3:1 ratio is 3 times life size, or 3× magnification. A matched extension tube that permits 1:1 reproduction ratio is usually included with macro lenses or available as an option.

CARE OF LENSES

A dirty lens cannot yield sharp pictures; the lens must be kept clean. Cleaning must be done carefully or scratches in the lens will result. All outside optical surfaces should be protected as much as possible from dust, dirt, and finger marks. Carrying cases should be closed over lenses when not in use, and lens covers should be placed over the lens. Many professionals keep an ultraviolet (UV) or haze filter on their lens at all times for protection and also to improve the quality of their pictures.

To clean a lens safely:

1. Blow on it gently, either with your breath or with a rubber bulb syringe.
2. If the lens is still dirty, dust it with a soft camel's-hair brush, and blow again. Do not use this brush for any other purpose. Keep the brush covered and protected from dust and grit.

3. A smear or fingerprint can be removed by breathing on the surface (which leaves a film of moisture) then wiping the surface with a clean piece of lens tissue. Use a circular motion. Do not wipe with a rag or handkerchief. If the lens is still dirty, a drop of cleaning fluid may substitute for breath vapor.
4. Brush and blow again to remove any lint left by the tissue.

Lenses should be protected from jars and jolts and from extreme and sudden temperature changes. They should not be stored in hot or moist places.

Do not attempt to take a lens apart. If the lens or mounting requires adjustment, bring it to the attention of an experienced camera repair person.

FILTERS

As the photographer becomes more proficient in the use of basic pieces of equipment, he or she may wish to improve the quality of work by modifying the light that reaches the sensor. This can be done by using filters.

Filters are used to change the composition of available light before allowing it to strike the sensor. These changes may be desired for artistic effect, to increase or decrease contrast, or for photographing certain colors at the exclusion of other colors. The intelligent use of filters improves a large percentage of photographs. Photographic filters selectively transmit wavelengths of light while blocking others. They can be long-pass (passing only long wavelengths), short-pass (passing only short wavelengths), or band-pass (blocking some long and some short wavelengths).

When the term "filter" is used in a photographic discussion, it usually refers to a transparent colored medium used to regulate either the color or the intensity of the light used to expose the image. The color of the filter determines the color of the light that reaches the sensor, but in cases of a neutral density or colorless filter, only the intensity of the light is regulated. Filters for these purposes vary considerably because they are composed of transparent materials that may be colored to a greater or lesser degree. Some are so nearly colorless that they escape casual notice, whereas others are so deeply colored that they appear almost opaque. In all cases, however, the filter is used to modify the light that passes through the camera lens to the sensor.

A good photographer can make a good picture without a filter but a professional photographer can make a better picture with the use of the proper filter. A number of photo optical companies produce filters for commercial and professional photographic use. The labeling system for filters is generally the Wratten system. Frederick Wratten was a British inventor at the turn of the twentieth century who developed a series of colored photographic filters. He sold his company to Eastman Kodak in 1912 and they continued using the Wratten labeling system. The system is still in use today and used by several filter manufacturers. The Wratten system is usually a number sometimes followed by a letter. For instance, a Wratten 2A filter is a pale yellow color and a Wratten 25 is a red colored filter. See Table 3.1 for a list of the more common filters and their use.

Table 3.1 Common Wratten Filter Designations

Wratten Number	Visible Color	F-Stops Correction	Uses and Characteristics
1A			Called a skylight filter, this absorbs UV radiation, which reduces haze in outdoor landscape photography.
2A	Pale yellow		Absorbs UV radiation. Long-pass filter blocking wavelengths below 405 nm.
2B	Pale yellow		Absorbs UV radiation, slightly less than #2A. Long-pass filter blocking wavelengths below 395 nm.
2C			Absorbs UV radiation. Long-pass filter blocking wavelengths below 390 nm.
2E	Pale yellow		Absorbs UV radiation, slightly more than #2A. Long-pass filter blocking wavelengths below 415 nm.
3	Light yellow		Absorbs excessive sky blue, making sky look slightly darker in black-and-white images. Long-pass filter blocking wavelengths below 440 nm.
4	Yellow		Long-pass filter blocking visible wavelengths below 455 nm.
6	Light yellow		Not a long-pass filter.
8	Yellow		Absorbs more blue than #3. Long-pass filter blocking visible wavelengths below 465 nm.
9	Deep yellow		Absorbs more blue than #8. Long-pass filter blocking visible wavelengths below 470 nm.
11	Yellowish-green		Color correction. Not a long-pass filter.
12	Deep yellow		Minus blue filter; complements #32 minus-green and #44A minus-red. Used with infrared films to obtain false-color results. Long-pass filter blocking visible wavelengths below 500 nm.
15	Deep yellow		Darkens the sky in black-and-white outdoor photography. Long-pass filer blocking visible wavelengths below 510 nm.
16	Yellow-orange		Performs like #15, but more so; long-pass filter blocking visible wavelengths below about 520 nm.
18A	Visually opaque		Transmits small bands of UV radiation and infrared radiation.
18B	Very deep violet		Similar to #18A but with wider bands of transmittance in both UV and infrared, a less "pure" filter.
21	Orange		Contrast filter for blue and blue-green absorption. Long-pass filer blocking visible wavelengths below 530 nm.
22	Deep orange		Contrast filter, greater effect than #21. Long-pass filter blocking visible wavelengths below 550 nm.
23A	Light red		Long-pass filter blocking visible wavelengths below 550 nm.

Continued...

Table 3.1 Common Wratten Filter Designations *Continued*

Wratten Number	Visible Color	F-Stops Correction	Uses and Characteristics
24	Red		Used for color separation of transparency films, complements #47B and #61. Long-pass filter blocking visible wavelengths below 575 nm. Red for "two color photography" (daylight or tungsten). White flame arc tri-color projection.
25	Red tricolor		Used for color separation and infrared photography long-pass filter blocking below 580 nm.
26	Red		Long-pass filter blocking below 585 nm.
29	Deep red		Used for color separation, complements #47 and #61. In black-and-white outdoor photography, makes blue skies look very dark, almost black. In infrared photography, blocks much visible light, increasing the effect of the infrared frequencies on the picture. Long-pass filter blocking below 600 nm.
32	Magenta		Minus-green. Complements #12 minus-blue and #44A minus-red.
34A	Violet		Used for minus-green and plus-blue separation.
38A	Blue		Absorbs red, some UV and some green light.
40	Light green		Green for "two color photography" (tungsten).
44	Light blue-green		Minus-red filter with much UV absorption.
44A	Light blue-green		Minus-red, complements #12 minus-blue and #32 minus-green.
47	Blue tricolor		Used for color separation. Complements #29 and #61.
47A	Light blue		By removing lots of light that is not blue, blue and purple objects show a broader range of colors. Used for medical applications that involve making dyes fluoresce.
47B	Deep blue tricolor		Used for color separation. It is also commonly used to calibrate video monitors while using SMPTE color bars.
50	Deep blue		
56	Light green		
57	Green		Green for "two color photography" (daylight).
58	Green tricolor		Color separation.
60	Green		Green for "two color photography" (tungsten).
61	Deep green tricolor		Color separation, complements #29 and #47.
70	Red		Used for color separation and infrared photography long-pass filter blocking below 650 nm.
80A	Blue	2	Color conversion. Raises the color temperature, causing a 3200 K tungsten-lit scene to appear to be daylight lit, approximately 5500 K. This allows use of a daylight balanced film with tungsten lighting.
80B	Blue	1 + 2/3	Similar to #80A; 3400–5500 K.
80C	Blue	1	Similar to #80A; 3800–5500 K. Typically used so that old-style flashbulbs can be used on a daylight film.

Table 3.1 Common Wratten Filter Designations *Continued*

Wratten Number	Visible Color	F-Stops Correction	Uses and Characteristics
80D	Blue	1/3	Similar to #80A; 4200–5500 K.
81A	Pale orange	1/3	Warming filter to decrease the color temperature slightly; this can also be used when shooting tungsten type B film (3200 K) with 3400 K photoflood lights. The opposite of #82A.
81B	Pale orange	1/3	Warming filter, slightly stronger than #81A. The opposite of #82B.
81C	Pale orange	1/3	Warming filter, slightly stronger than #81B, opposite of #82C.
81D	Pale orange		Warming filter, slightly stronger than #81C.
81EF	Pale orange	1/3	Warming filter, stronger than #81D.
82A	Pale blue	1/3	Cooling filter to increase the color temperature slightly. The opposite of #81A.
82B	Pale blue	2/3	Cooling filter, slightly stronger than #82A and opposite of #81B. Can also be used when shooting tungsten type B film (3200 K) with household 100 W electric bulbs (2900 K).
82C	Pale blue	2/3	Cooling filter, slightly stronger than #82B and opposite of #81C.
85	Amber	2/3	Color conversion, the opposite of the #80A; this is a warming filter that takes an outdoor scene lit by sunlight (which has a color temperature around 5500 K) and makes it appear to be lit by tungsten incandescent bulbs around 3400 K. This allows an indoor balanced film to be used to photograph outdoors. These filters were used in super 8 movie cameras that were designed to use tungsten film.
85B	Amber	2/3	Similar to #85; converts 5500–3200 K.
85C	Amber		Similar to #85; converts 5500–3800 K.
85N3	Amber		Neutral density of 1 stop + color conversion, the opposite of #80A; this is a warming filter that takes an outdoor scene lit by sunlight (which has a color temperature around 5500 K) and makes it appear to be lit by tungsten incandescent bulbs around 3400 K. This allows an indoor balanced film to be used to photograph outdoors.
85N6	Amber		Neutral density of 2 stops + color conversion, the opposite of the #80A; this is a warming filter that takes an outdoor scene lit by sunlight (which has a color temperature around 5500 K) and makes it appear to be lit by tungsten incandescent bulbs around 3400 K. This allows an indoor balanced film to be used to photograph outdoors.
85N9	Amber		Neutral density of 3 stops + color conversion, the opposite of the #80A; this is a warming filter that takes an outdoor scene lit by sunlight (which has a color temperature around 5500 K) and makes it appear to be lit by tungsten incandescent bulbs around 3400 K. This allows an indoor balanced film to be used to photograph outdoors.
87	Opaque		Passes infrared but not visible frequencies. Blocks wavelengths below 740 nm.

Continued...

Table 3.1 Common Wratten Filter Designations *Continued*

Wratten Number	Visible Color	F-Stops Correction	Uses and Characteristics
87A	Opaque		Passes infrared but not visible frequencies. Blocks wavelengths below 880 nm.
87B	Opaque		Passes infrared, blocks visible frequencies. Blocks wavelengths below 820 nm.
87C	Opaque		Passes infrared, blocks visible frequencies. Blocks wavelengths below 790 nm.
88	Opaque		Passes infrared, blocks visible wavelengths below 700 nm.
88A	Opaque		Passes infrared, blocks visible frequencies below 720 nm.
89B	Near-opaque red		Passes infrared, long-pass filter blocking visible wavelengths below 690 nm (very deep red). Aerial photography is one use.
90	Dark grayish amber		Used for viewing scenes without color before photographing them, in order to assess the brightness values. Not used for actual photography.
92	Red		Color densitometry. Long-pass filter blocking visible wavelengths below 625 nm.
93	Green		Color densitometry.
94	Blue		Color densitometry.
96	Gray		Neutral density filter. Blocks all frequencies of visible light approximately evenly, making scene darker overall. Available in many different values, distinguished by optical density or by filter factor.
98	Blue		Like #47B plus #2B filter.
99	Green		Like #61 plus #16 filter.
102	Yellow-green		Color conversion; makes a barrier-level type photocell respond as a human eye would.
106	Amber		Color conversions; makes an S-4 type photocell respond as a human eye would.

SMPTE, Society of Motion Picture and Television Engineers; UV, ultraviolet.

A filter of poor construction may cause distortion in a photograph; thus, filters should be carefully chosen if used. Never use a filter that is merely held over the lens. This type of filter is extremely unpredictable. Also, care should be taken when using filters with and without lens shades on wide-angle lenses. A condition known as vignetting, which allows the image to pick up the edges of the filter on the lens, may occur. The finished photograph may result with a circular border that may be difficult to crop out later.

An adequate filter is constructed of filter material sandwiched between pieces of glass. When buying a filter for a threaded lens, it is necessary to know the correct size of the lens. Do not mistake the focal length engraved on the front of the lens as the filter size. The focal length of a lens is its optical length that has no bearing on the filter size, which is the diameter of the filter threads on the front of the lens. One should check the instruction manual or carefully measure the diameter of the filter threads with a metric ruler. Most normal (50 mm) lenses accept 49, 52, or 55 mm filters. Wide-angle, zoom, and tele-photo lenses may accept one of these sizes also, or 58, 62, 67, 72, or 77 mm.

The photographer with more than one lens may purchase filters to fit the larger of his or her lenses and an adapter-reducer for fitting the filter to the smaller cam-era or lens. These adapters are known as step-reducing rings or step-increasing rings and are much less expensive than purchasing filters for each lens.

Some filters are used for black-and-white photography, some for color, and a few for both color and black-and-white. Among the filters used for both color and black-and-white photography are: skylight, haze, neutral density, and polarizing filters.

Skylight and haze filters reduce excessive blue caused by haze and UV rays. They are useful for outdoor photographs and may be kept in place on the lens at all times for lens protection.

Neutral density filters are used to reduce light transmission. They do not oth-erwise affect color or tonal quality of the scene. They are very handy when photographing under bright light conditions, or where the use of a slow shutter-speed or wide aperture is desired for a creative effect. Neutral density filters are available in strengths designed to reduce specific amounts of light by f/stop units.

Polarizing filters, like neutral density filters, are a neutral gray and do not affect the transmitted color in a way that will change its color temperature. When light is reflected by a nonmetallic surface, such as water, it is polarized. With a polarizing filter (in a rotating mount) the photographer can intercept this polarizing light and dramatically reduce reflections in the photograph. These filters also increase the saturation of a blue sky in a color photograph (or darken the tone of the sky in black-and-white photography) as long as the lens/filter combination is not pointing directly at the sun. This is the only filter that can increase the blue saturation in the sky in a color photograph without altering the remaining colors in the scene. The polarizing filter is very handy for photographing vehicles in automobile accidents.

There are a number of different polarizing filters produced by manufacturers. Basically, there are two main types: (1) the type used over the camera lens, and (2) the type designed to be used over studio lights. Polarizing screens and filters may be used for both black-and-white and color photography. Polarizing devices used over the lenses have small posts known as indicator handles projecting from the rims of the metal cells for aligning the axis of the polarizing grid.

The polarizing filter may be thought of as a screen with an optical grid or slots, which stops all light that is not vibrating in a plane parallel to the axis of the grid. This film or sheet of plastic may be used by itself, or may be cemented between thin sheets of glass and mounted in metal cells. The mounted filters are attached to a lens by means of screw threads, a filter holder, or lens shade (Figure 3.3).

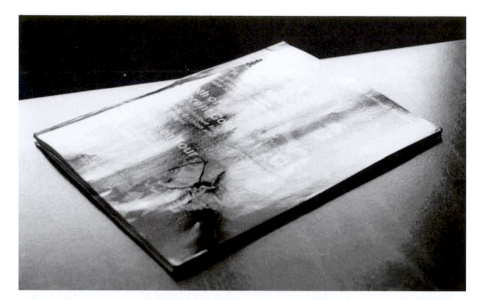

FIGURE 3.3

Example of how polarizing filter reduces glare. The photograph above was taken without a polarizing filter and the one below with a polarizing filter.

Colored filters for black-and-white photography stop one or another color of light from passing through and striking the sensor. They are useful to highlight a subject that would not normally contrast readily with its surroundings. Using a deep red filter (e.g., Wratten no. 25) to photograph a red automobile will cause the automobile to print as white or light gray in black-and-white mode. This relationship between filter and subject color is a reciprocal one. In addition to a color that is lightened, there is also at least one color darkened. The greatest darkening occurs when the color is complementary or opposite of the filter color. Most digital cameras have a black-and-white or monochrome mode setting that can be used. Color images may also be effectively filtered using computer software programs, such as Adobe PhotoShop.

Complementary colors are often depicted as a color wheel or circle. Normally, both additive colors (red, green, and blue) and subtractive colors (magenta, cyan, and yellow) are included (see Figure 3.4). Colors that receive the greatest print darkening are located directly opposite on the color wheel. Because cyan is directly opposite red on the color wheel, it will be darkened more than any other color with a red filter. Colors adjacent to cyan (blue and green) will be darkened to a lesser degree.

Blue Filters
A blue filter can be used effectively when photographing blood in black-and-white. When used outdoors, a blue filter will make the sky, or any blue object, appear white in the photograph.

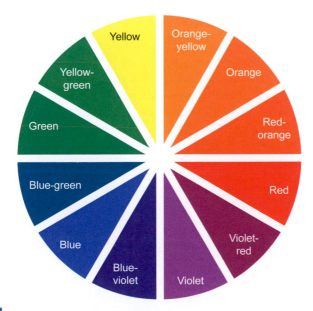

FIGURE 3.4
Color wheel.

Green Filters

Green filters are often used in place of blue filters for photographing blood in black-and-white. Often, they work better than blue filters. Green filters will also bring out the contrast of red stop signs.

Yellow Filters

Yellow filters can be used to photograph white cars; the detail of the car will stand out with black-and-white. Yellow filters also cut through haze to a certain extent, and can be used with good results to photograph an accident scene on a hazy day. A dark yellow filter will emphasize tire marks in photographs of accident scenes.

Filters are often used extensively in questioned document examination photographs, particularly UV and infrared. Additional discussion of these uses can be found in later chapters.

Color photograph filters are basically color balancing filters that allow daylight film to be exposed with artificial light and film balanced for artificial light to be used with daylight. For instance, an 80A filter allows daylight film to be exposed under 3200 K artificial illumination with natural looking results. This is particularly important when photographing documents with daylight balanced color film under artificial tungsten illumination. With digital cameras, one would use the white balance feature on the camera to balance artificial illumination.

Care of Filters

Colored glass filters and filters cemented between two pieces of glass should be treated as carefully as lenses. If dirty or injured, they detract from the quality of the final picture. Filters of this type should be cleaned by polishing them with lens cleaning tissue. Any lint or dust on them, however, should first be removed with a camel's-hair brush. A lens tissue slightly moistened in lens cleaner or pure alcohol may be used, if necessary, but care must be taken to keep the liquid away from any exposed edges of cemented filters.

When not in use, filters should be stored in their cases. All filters must be protected from moisture, excessive heat, and unnecessary exposure to strong light.

MISCELLANEOUS EQUIPMENT

Lens Attachments

There are several camera/lens attachments available for close-up (macro) photography. Close-up lens sets are lens elements that screw into normal or telephoto lenses like filters. These single-element lenses are usually sold in sets of three, each with a different "strength" of magnification expressed as a diopter rating. The larger the diopter rating, the closer the lens will focus. Most close-up lens sets contain +1, +2, and +4 diopter lenses that are double threaded so that any combination of the three lenses can be mounted together (Figure 3.5).

Extension tubes are hollow metal tubes that fit between the camera body and the lens and allow the lens to focus closer than normal. Extension tubes are also usually sold in sets of three, each being a different length. The longer the tube, the closer it will enable the lens to focus. Extension tubes reduce the exposure in proportion to their length, the larger the tube, the greater the light loss.

Bellows attachments are essentially the same as a flexible extension tube but are usually used for ultra-close-up photography (greater than life size).

Reversal rings screw into the front of the lens filter threads and permits the lens to be mounted backwards onto the camera body. By doing so, a normal 50 mm lens that focuses to only about 18 in can be focused close enough for a 1:1 reproduction ratio.

Extension tubes, bellows attachments, and reversal rings are available with or without camera metering coupling mechanisms. If a metering coupling mechanism exists for the attachment, the camera's internal meter system can be used

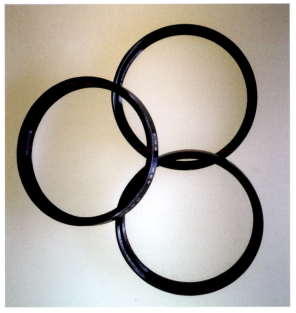

FIGURE 3.5
Screw-on type close-up filters.

for exposure determination. If there is no meter coupling, the photographer may have to "bracket" exposures, assuring at least one properly exposed photograph. Bracketing of exposures is accomplished by taking a normal exposure reading, then making exposures at two f-stops below, one f-stop below, and one exposure at the normal reading.

Another form of lens attachment is the teleconverter. Teleconverters are normally used with telephoto lenses to increase magnification from 1.5X to 2.0X. They tend to be expensive and hard to use. Most do not allow the use of AF capability and many do not allow the use of internal metering systems of cameras. The police photographer would be wise to avoid purchasing a teleconverter and opt to purchase a longer lens.

Tripods

For exposures of long duration and for added accuracy with an exposure of any length, a tripod is a necessity. This is particularly true in the case of cameras that have a long, heavy telephoto lens. Tripods provide a degree of stability that is not possible when a camera is hand held.

Many tripods are available from camera supply shops; the photographer must be careful when choosing a tripod to be sure to purchase one that is stable and does not prove to be a hindrance.

The legs should be given special attention. Most tripods are built with telescoping legs. The legs lock at full extension; or, in the case of some tripods, they can be tightened at any length desired by the photographer. The more sections a leg uses to extend, the less stable the tripod will be; the most stable tripod will be the one with the fewest sections.

The locking mechanisms of tripods' legs are usually of two types: those that snap, and those that must be screwed. The latter is preferable because the tightening of the lock tends to strengthen the leg, but the photographer must be sure that the locks are in good working order and must not allow the leg sections to "creep."

Most tripods include a cranking rack-and-pinion type elevator on the center column that allows the photographer to further adjust the height of the camera once the legs are adjusted and locked. The elevator must be of sturdy construction and must not have "play" that may transmit vibrations to the camera even though the legs are stable. The center column should also be removable and allowed to be inverted. This is handy when making photographs of footprints, tire prints, or small items where the camera must be level with the subject (see Figure 3.6).

The head of the tripod on which the camera is mounted should be large, and balanced enough to support the weight of the camera without vibration. It

FIGURE 3.6
Tripod with center column inverted.

should allow the camera, when mounted, to move freely both vertically and horizontally until locked.

Any time a camera is mounted on a tripod, the danger of accidental damage to the camera is increased. For this reason, it is strongly recommended that a camera never be left unattended while on a tripod. To lessen the danger of breakage, set the tripod on firm footing with its legs spread well apart. On a hard surface, where a tripod leg may slip and allow the camera to fall, use a tripod brace or a triangle to prevent the legs from spreading. A triangle is an adjustable, folding device made of lightweight metal especially for use with tripods. If this device is not available, a triangular-shaped frame can be constructed of wood to serve the same purpose. Hanging a weight, such as a camera bag, between the legs of the tripod will also increase its stability. If possible, the tripod should always be set up with one leg pointing forward. This places the legs in such a position that more freedom of movement about the camera is allowed, with less danger of tripping over one of the legs and upsetting the camera (Figure 3.7).

Tripod Substitutes

Where storage space is limited, or when the photographer needs more versatility in camera placement, there are substitutes that, although not wholly replacing a tripod, can help to steady a camera. The monopod is simply one leg, usually collapsible, of a tripod. The monopod steadies the camera to a degree but will not, of course, permit the photographer to stand free of the camera.

There are also numerous mounts to which a camera may be attached and steadied. Some rest on the shoulder of the photographer. Some merely have a large handgrip that transmits less vibration from the hand to the camera. Some are even constructed like a gun butt. These mounts can be more of a hindrance than a help, but are available should the photographer want or need them.

Cable Release

As with a tripod, a cable release is essential for lessening vibration during long exposures. A good rule is this: always use a tripod and a cable release together. They can eliminate all but the slightest vibration. Cable releases come

FIGURE 3.7
Tripods. These tripods may be used for still and video cameras.

in various lengths and are flexible with a cloth, plastic, or wound metal cover that permits the photographer to stand close to or away from the camera, as he or she pleases. Some cable releases have locks for time exposures. Wireless remote control releases are available on many camera models. Most SLR digital cameras have a timer system that allows for the photographer to get into the picture him or herself. This self-timing function can be used in lieu of a cable release to avoid vibration for long exposures.

Underwater Housings

The police photographer may be faced with photographing evidence or a "crime scene" underwater. Many police departments are located near coastal areas or bodies of water where body recovery or locating evidence may be performed underwater. The police photographer in these areas may also need to be a diver. Several companies manufacture water-tight housings for a number of common digital cameras. Water-tight housings tend to be expensive and, unless underwater photography is frequently needed in a particular jurisdiction, the police photographer might opt to purchase an inexpensive underwater camera, such as the Sealife Reefmaster or Jazz cameras (see Figure 3.8 for examples).

Lens Brush

Lens brushes are usually made of camel's hair, and some are attached to a rubber bulb that, when squeezed, creates a stream of air to blow dust off of a lens. Brushes should be covered (there are retractable brushes that, when capped, resemble a tube of lipstick) when not in use to prevent them from collecting loose dust.

(a)   **(b)**   **(c)**

FIGURE 3.8
(a) The Nexus underwater housing for the Nikon digital camera, (b) The Sealife Reefmaster underwater camera, and (c) Jazz underwater camera.

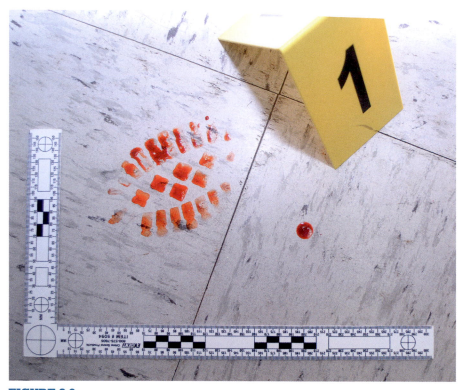

FIGURE 3.9
Numerical evidence marker photograph placards and measurement scale.

NOTE TAKING AND MEASUREMENT SCALES

Although a picture can tell a thousand words, two pictures may become hopelessly confused in the photographer's mind and may need a word or two to distinguish them. He or she should always carry note writing materials in order to annotate photographic shots or the work may become as worthless as it would be had he or she left the lens cap on. Also, the police photographer should carry placard evidence markers and measurement scales to include in photographs (Figure 3.9).

REFERENCE

Johnson, D. (2005). *How to do everything with your digital camera* (4th ed.). New York: McGraw-Hill.

Light Theory and Digital Imaging

CONTENTS

ABSTRACT

Light is the photographer's most important tool. Whether using traditional film or digital imaging cameras, the proper use of light will ensure proper exposure. Digital cameras are capable of recording light images over a wide range of the electromagnetic spectrum, from ultraviolet through infrared. Light is manipulated through the camera lens and recorded on film or a digital imaging sensor by the time and amount of light striking the light-sensitive material.

KEY TERMS

Concave
Convex
Focal length

Focus
Infinity
Infrared light
Inverse square law
Lens
Luminous light
Reflection
Refraction
Shutter
Ultraviolet light
Visible light

INTRODUCTION

A photograph is the result of a manipulation, a recording—and in some cases, creation—of light. The entire science of photography is concerned with light manipulation and recording. The camera and its parts (shutter, diaphragm, focus) filter light, exposure meters record light, and flash units and lamps create light.

Light is radiation. When an atom in a light source is changed physically (the cause of the physical change is irrelevant for our purposes), it emits a photon (electromagnetic radiation) that behaves like a wave and, at the same time, like a particle. For the purposes of photography, light may be discussed as photons that behave like waves.

Light can be compared to a ripple over a pond. If a stone is thrown into a still pond, a series of concentric ripples can be seen that radiate from the source. The concentric ripples are formed because the energy from the disturbance is radiating in straight lines and in all directions over the surface of the pond. A cross-section of the ripples in the pond would show that the energy moving across the pond has formed waves that are characterized by their peaks and troughs.

The distance from a peak crest to an adjacent peak crest in a wave is called the wavelength of the wave. The number of waves per unit of time is called the frequency of the wave (Figure 4.1).

Light, heat rays, X-rays, and radio waves are all forms of radiant energy, each differing from the others in wavelength. Radiant energy can be identified by its wavelength and listed on a number line called the electromagnetic spectrum (Figure 4.2).

The portion of the electromagnetic spectrum that affects the sense of sight in humans is called the visible spectrum and is limited to radiations of extremely short wavelength. These radiations are seen as colors, the longest of which is seen as "red," and the shortest of which is seen as "violet" (Figure 4.3). Photography is not only concerned with these radiations and with those lying

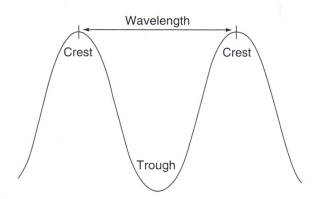

FIGURE 4.1
Wavelength.

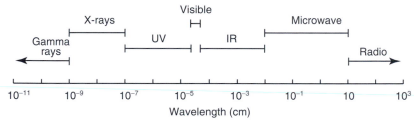

FIGURE 4.2
The electromagnetic spectrum.

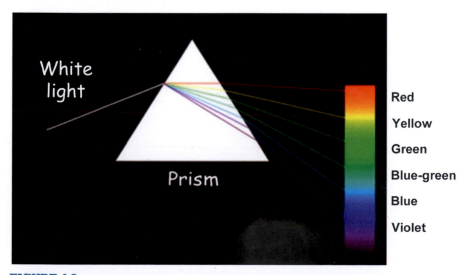

FIGURE 4.3
The visible spectrum.

adjacent to red and violet, but also to those outside the visible spectrum: infrared and ultraviolet.

When all wavelengths of the visible spectrum are radiated by a light source in equal amounts, the mixture is seen as "white" light. In places where no radiations from any light source can be seen, the absence of light is called "black." Whenever any wavelength of light is present in greater abundance than others, the resulting light is colored.

Light travels through a vacuum and through the air at a speed of 186,000 miles/s but can be slowed by dense mediums such as glass or water. Mediums that merely slow the speed of light but allow it to pass freely in other respects are called transparent objects.

Objects that divert or absorb light, but allow no light to pass through, are called opaque. Thick metal, stone, and wood are opaque.

There are some objects that allow light to pass through them in such a way that the outline of the light source is not clearly visible. These objects are spoken of as translucent; a few examples are opal glass, ground glass, and waxed paper.

Light sources such as the sun, flames, white-hot metals, and stars emit radiations within the visible spectrum and are called luminous objects. All other objects, called nonluminous objects, are visible because they reflect light from luminous objects. Reflection occurs whenever an object changes the direction of a light wave but does not allow the wave to pass through it. Reflected light can be either specular or diffuse. Practically all surfaces reflect both specular and diffuse light. Smooth surfaces reflect more specular light and rough surfaces reflect more diffuse light. Diffuse light is more common than specular light; most objects are seen and photographed by diffuse light reflected from their surfaces (Figure 4.4).

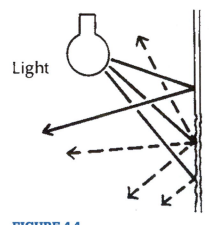

Light

Diffuse reflected light

Specular reflected light

FIGURE 4.4
Light reflected from a sheet of pitted glass.

All surfaces vary in their ability to reflect light. A black cloth will reflect scarcely any light, whereas a white handkerchief reflects a great deal of light.

REFRACTION

When light passes through a piece of glass, the light is slowed from its normal speed of 186,000 miles/s. If the light passes through a sheet of flat glass, such as a modern window pane, it will resume its normal speed when it has passed through, but it will have changed direction. Flat glass, because of its physical properties, corrects the change in direction of the light and no change is readily noticeable (Figure 4.5).

If a piece of glass is made with sides that are not parallel, the glass will not self-correct the bending of the light. In fact, the glass may intensify the change of direction. A prism is a good example of this (Figure 4.6).

A lens is simply a piece of glass that has been constructed so that all the light rays that pass through it are bent toward or away from one point that is determined by the maker of the lens.

Light rays that meet at one point after they pass through a lens converge; those that bend away from a given point diverge. Lenses that cause light rays to converge are usually thick in the center and thinner at their edges; these are called convex lenses. Lenses that are thin at the middle and thick around the edges are concave; these usually make light rays diverge (Figure 4.7).

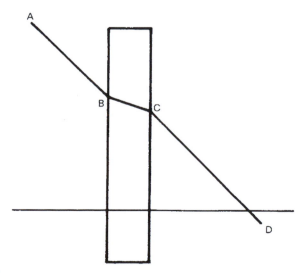

FIGURE 4.5
Refraction of light through flat glass.

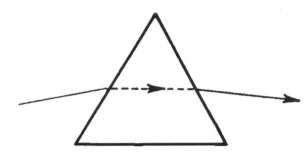

FIGURE 4.6
A prism bends a ray twice.

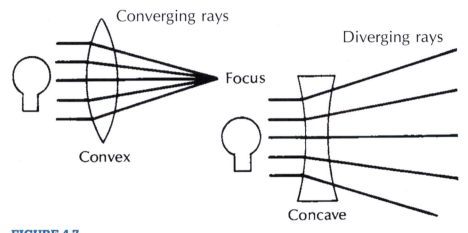

FIGURE 4.7
Convex and concave lenses.

The point at which light rays converge is called the focus. For any lens, this point is not the same for a subject 10 feet away as it is for a subject 20 feet away. The farther a subject is from the lens, the closer the focus will be to the lens. Subjects more than 600 feet away from a lens, however, will focus at very nearly the same distance from the lens. The difference between the focus of a subject 600 feet from the lens and another subject 1000 feet from the lens is nearly negligible.

Distances of 600 feet or more are called infinity. In order that the lens maker can describe the properties of a lens that he has made, he can say that the lens will focus subjects at infinity at a certain distance from the lens. This distance is called the focal length of the lens (Figure 4.8).

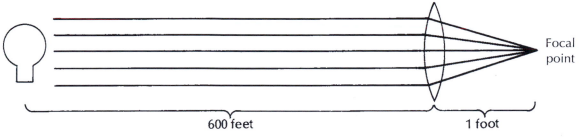

FIGURE 4.8
The focal length of this lens is 1 foot.

LIGHT

For the police photographer, photographs are statements of what he or she saw. The eye sees a photograph and translates the image to the mind; the mind then reacts and within itself it equates, evaluates, and responds to the photograph.

We become capable of describing photographs with words, but more important, the police photographer must develop the ability to describe words with photographs. This is what it is all about: communicating with photographs.

Objectively, photography is a combination of the following tools:

1. Light
2. Camera
3. Lens
4. Digital sensor (film)
5. Computer software
6. Composition

Light—Our Most Important Tool

There is little doubt that light is our most important tool. Light brushes on the lines; sculpts our subject; provides shadows, highlights, and middle-light values; and emphasizes, subdues, lifts out, hides, and dramatizes our subject. Light can flatter or be terribly brutal to our subject.

All cameras are essentially boxes that support the lens and contain the "film" or a digital imaging chip. All lenses are optics. They vary in characteristics and optical quality. Digital imaging chips, the electronic "film," vary with degree of resolution, known as megapixels.

And, there are limitations in hardware and software. The photographer must learn the limitations of equipment and software to prevent mistakes.

A potentially valuable evidential photograph might be lost if the photographer fails to learn these limitations early on.

Another tool—composition—is a Pandora's box. One group in photography bases its approach on the rules of classic composition, while another boldly claims that photography must stand on its own. Composition is a principle of artistic photography. In art photography, the composition of a photograph through light and shadow is as important as the subject matter. Art photography attempts, through composition, to enhance an image, beautify, or express a meaning that may or may not be present in the subject being photographed. In police photography we are not striving for the beautiful or artistic picture. Artistic composition has no place in evidential photography. We are interested in obtaining all the facts of the case, so that we can present them to the jury. In this sense, the police photographer is concerned with using light and shadow to the extent that the photograph taken portrays a true and factual image.

While we find that we have a limited number of cameras, lenses, software, and digital technology to work with, light alone remains as the tool of greatest selection. Here the possibilities are enormous and the selection is ours.

Intensity of Light

One important aspect of light is its intensity as it reaches the subject, and how it is reflected by the subject. This is very important for the police officer to understand, because the intensity of light on a subject varies considerably when the distance between the light source and the subject of the film is changed. The relationship of intensities is governed by the inverse square law that is shown graphically in Figure 4.9.

If an object, such as a card, is placed 1 foot from a light source, the light striking the card will be of particular intensity. If it is then moved 2 feet away from the light, the intensity of the light falling on the card will be one-fourth as great. As the card is moved farther away, the intensity of the light reaching the card decreases further as the square of the distance from the source increases. This property of light is very important to the police photographer, especially when shooting vehicle accidents outdoors at night with flash or floodlight. The officer's failure to correct the exposure as the subject moves farther from the light source will result in badly underexposed photographs due to the inverse square law.

DIGITAL IMAGE FORMATION

Prior to the introduction of digital photography, police photographers had to rely on film cameras. The primary function of film is to record the image that is focused upon it by the lens of the camera. The film, being composed of

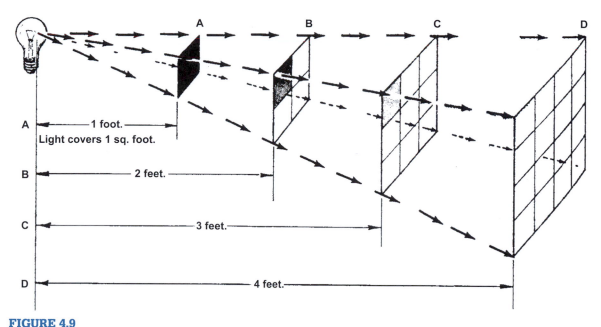

A — 1 foot. —
Light covers 1 sq. foot.

B — 2 feet. —

C — 3 feet. —

D — 4 feet. —

FIGURE 4.9
Graphic representation of the inverse square law.

acetate, is coated with a light-sensitive emulsion that chemically changes when exposed to light. The exposed film must then be developed through chemical means (darkroom) to display the negative image. Digital cameras operate the same way as film cameras with the exception of the film. Instead of film, digital cameras use a digital electronic chip, called a charged-coupled device (CCD) or complementary metal-oxide semiconductor (CMOS). Most newer digital cameras use the CMOS due to it being less expensive than CCD chips. These chips record light much like traditional film does.

There has been much debate over the quality of film images compared to digital images. Generally speaking, film is usually superior to digital images. However, because of the vast array of film types, digital images may be superior in many instances. For example, a photograph taken with a 110 pocket film camera could not stand up to a digital image made on a 6 megapixel digital camera. By the same token, a photograph made on a 120 medium format film camera would be much superior to a digital image made on a 14 megapixel or higher digital camera. For purposes of comparison, this discussion will compare 35 mm film with digital images.

Sharpness of a film is usually measured by its ability to resolve the difference between light and dark contrasts (diffusion). The less diffusion or the smaller the contrasting lines and spaces that can be resolved, the greater the resolution. Lines of resolution (measured as lines/mm) are used as the primary measure of a film's sharpness. A film's measured resolution, or resolving power, is also dependent on lighting conditions, exposure, focus, and so on.

Fuji's Fujicolor Superia (CS) 100 in 35 mm has a resolving power of about 60 lines/mm in low contrast according to the film's data sheet. Fuji's Fujichrome Velvia 100F professional slide film in 35 mm has a resolving power of about 160 lines/mm in high contrast. Using these two extreme values, a range between 60 and 160 lines/mm can be used to represent typical 35 mm ISO 100 film resolutions. Highton (2003) provides a formula for converting film resolution to a digital equivalent. A 35 mm frame is approximately 24 × 36 mm. To get an approximate pixel equivalent, multiply 24 mm × lines/mm × 36mm × lines/mm. The result can be multiplied by 3 for 8-bit RGB color to obtain an approximate uncompressed file size for the digital image.

For Fujicolor Superia CS 100 the formula would be:

$$24 \text{ mm} \times 60 \times 36 \text{ mm} \times 60 = 3{,}110{,}400. \text{ Or, about 3 megapixels}$$
$$(8.9 \text{ megabyte file size for the image}).$$

For Fujichrome Velvia 100:

$$24 \text{ mm} \times 160 \times 36 \text{ mm} \times 160 = 22{,}118{,}400. \text{ Or, about 22 megapixels}$$
$$(63.3 \text{ megabyte file size for the image}).$$

This can be compared to the performance of professional grade digital cameras:

Canon EOS 1D	18 megapixels
Nikon D300	12 megapixels
Nikon D3200	24 megapixels
Canon EOS 6D	20 megapixels
Nikon D800	36 megapixels

Obviously, the choice of film will have a bearing on the results. Kodak Technical Pan with an ISO of 25 will have much more resolving power (about 18 megapixels) and Konica Centuria Super 1600 with an ISO of 1600 will have much less resolving power (about 2 megapixels). The major concern with most photographers is the ability to enlarge photographs. If a photographer wished to enlarge only to no more than 8 × 10 inches, any 5 megapixel or higher digital camera would produce results equaling 35 mm film. However, if enlargements are needed for court displays or to later view details or items within a digital photograph image, one would need a digital camera of 11 megapixels or higher. An 11 megapixel digital camera can only deliver enlargements that equal 35 mm film of up to 16 × 20 inches. Consider that most all ISO 100

35 mm films can be enlarged to well beyond 32 × 40 inches with minimal loss of resolution. The bottom line is that digital cameras with at least 5 megapixels can perform as well as 35 mm film if the film rating is ISO 100 to 200 and enlargements beyond 11 × 14 inches are not needed.

THE DIGITAL SENSOR

While digital cameras retain many of the mechanical elements familiar to film photographers, the most notable change is the replacement of film with an electronic sensor. The sensor resides where the film plane previously existed, positioned behind the shutter of the camera. As previously mentioned, the sensor is simply a silicon-based light detector, which may be either a CCD or CMOS chip. The sensor itself consists of small picture forming elements or *pixels*. Each pixel acts as a light recording medium and is directly related to the effective resolution of the photograph. Most camera manufacturers will advertise their cameras via the pixel count of the sensor. For example, a 12 megapixel (mp) camera serves to indicate that the sensor consists of 12 million pixels.

IMAGE RESOLUTION

Image resolution refers to the amount of detail that is present in an image. Several factors can affect the resolution of a digital image:

- Camera resolution (number of pixels)
- Optics and focus
- ISO setting on the camera
- Duration of the photographic exposure

The camera resolution as discussed affects the resolution of a digital image. Consider a digital image that is 4″ × 6″. If the contents of the image were defined by 100,000 pixels, many of the elements within the photograph would lack definition, as there would not be a sufficient number of pixels to define the boundaries of subjects within the image. As the number of pixels contained within a finite space is increased, the boundaries between objects within the photograph become better defined. The number of pixels within a given photograph is typically referred to as pixels per inch, or PPI. Naturally, the higher the PPI, the higher the resolution of the image.

It is important to note that pixels are square in geometry, thereby limiting the rotation of images in postproduction to 90° increments. If an image is rotated 45° and saved, the resulting pixels would be diamond shaped, resulting in a loss of image resolution due to the interruption of continuous pixels.

SENSOR SIZE AND OPTICS

The physical size of sensors may vary. In the early stages of digital photography, camera sensors were small in size compared to the 35 mm format of film. This created a problem in the sense that SLR type cameras were no longer optically compatible with older lenses that were designed for the 35 mm film format. The images formed by these lenses on the plane of the sensor were larger than the actual size of the sensor, which resulted in an apparent magnification of the image. The effective magnification was approximately 1.5–1.6× the focal length of the lens, depending on the camera. For example, if you used a 60 mm macro lens meant for a camera with 35 mm film on a Nikon camera with a small format CCD sensor, it would be the equivalent of using a 90 mm lens. For most photographers this meant having to buy additional lenses that were optically corrected for the smaller sensor size. Camera manufacturers have since introduced digital sensors that approximate the physical size of 35 mm film. Cameras bearing these sensors are termed "full frame" and have a restored optical compatibility with older lenses. Currently, full frame sensors tend to be available in higher end cameras while small format sensors are popular in consumer grade cameras.

While it is not unspeakable to use lenses intended for a 35 mm recording medium (film) with small camera sensors, the converse can result in various image aberrations. For example, if you were to use a lens that is optically corrected for small CCD on a full frame camera, the image projected on the full frame sensor will be smaller than the size of the actual sensor. The resulting image may appear clipped and may display vignetting, an underexposure at the edges of the photograph. Further, these images will not make use of the effective resolution of the sensor. The actual visible portion of the image will be formed from some lesser number of pixels than the total for the full frame sensor, in essence decreasing the resolution of the image (Figure 4.10).

The APS-C sensor covers an area of 370 mm^2 and can be found in many of the small format Nikon DSLR cameras. The APS-H sensor found in most Canon DSLR cameras is slightly larger, covering an area of 548 mm^2. The full frame format is the equivalent of 35 mm film and covers an area of 864 mm^2 (Figure 4.11).

When lenses are not properly paired with the size of the sensor being used, the resulting photographs may be affected. For example, if a small format sensor is paired with a lens intended for use with a full frame camera, the image projected onto the recording plane would be larger than the size of the sensor. This results in an effective magnification, which may also be referred to as a "crop factor." In Nikon cameras that use an APS-C sensor, the crop factor will be 1.5× the focal length of the lens. For example, if an older 60 mm lens is used on a Nikon camera with an APS-C sensor, the crop factor makes the lens equivalent to a 90 mm focal length lens. In Canon cameras that use an APS-H sensor, the

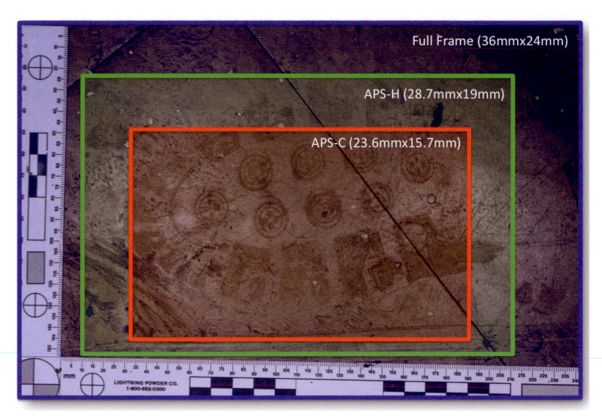

FIGURE 4.10
The relative sizes of sensors found in popular DSLR cameras.

crop factor for a 35 mm camera lens will be 1.6× the focal length of the lens. Contrariwise, if a lens that is corrected for a small format sensor is used on a full frame camera, the image projected on the imaging plane will be smaller than the size of the sensor.

COLOR REPRODUCTION

When a photograph is taken, light passes through the lens elements of the camera and through a filter with a specific color array before reaching the sensor. This filter is termed the *Bayer filter* and it is responsible for generating color in the final image. A Bayer filter typically consists of red, blue, and green filters distributed in a ratio of 1:1:2, respectively, for each pixel. The number of green filters is generally higher in proportion to red and blue to mimic human vision, where the human eye has its peak sensitivity in the green spectrum.

Color contrast filters in general serve to transmit light of the same color and block light that is complementary. As the camera shutter opens, the sensor is

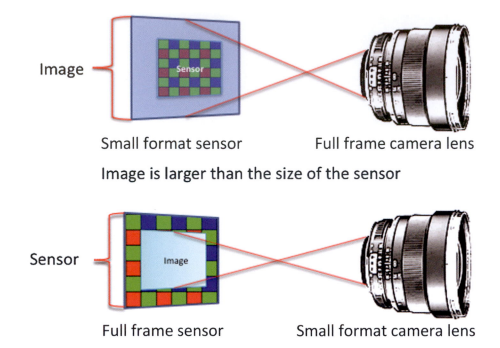

Image is larger than the size of the sensor

Image is smaller than the size of the sensor

FIGURE 4.11
Lens projection of the image vs. sensor size.

exposed to red, green, and blue (RGB) light that is transmitted through the Bayer filter and onto the sensor. The resulting raw image will therefore consist of these three colors, which must undergo further processing to render a colorful reproduction of the scene being photographed. The process of constructing a full color image from the Bayer filter colors is generally referred to as *demosaicing* or *Bayer interpolation*. The specifics in camera processing algorithms that are used in demosaicing may vary among camera manufacturers, but the process typically involves the averaging of both light intensity and color that is detected across each pixel elements of the sensor. For example, a pixel with a green filter will detect only green light. The RGB values for that green pixel requires additional color data from neighboring pixels that are detecting red and blue light.

The Bayer filter is composed of red, blue, and green filters in a proportion of 1:1:2, where there will be more green filters than blue and red. Green filters are present in a higher quantity to mimic human vision, which is very sensitive to green light. Cameras sensors are not capable of producing color images. The Bayer filter provides a means by which color in a scene can be reproduced by the camera. As illustrated in Figure 4.12, as light enters the camera it passes

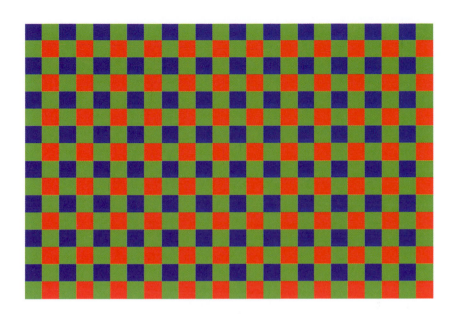

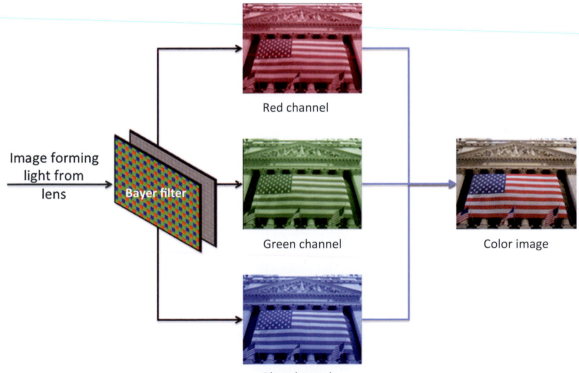

FIGURE 4.12

A typical Bayer color filter array.

through the color filter array before reaching the sensor. Each pixel will construct an image based on the intensity of light for each color channel, creating an image that will be a mosaic of red, green, and blue colors. Demosaicing is the process by which each pixel averages color data from neighboring pixels to generate a full color photograph.

IMAGE FILE FORMATS

Once an image is captured, the camera will generate an image file based on the settings selected by the photographer. There are currently three file formats that are commonly used by photographers to store digital images: JPEG, TIFF, and RAW file formats.

The JPEG (Joint Photography Expert Group) format is perhaps the most common type of image file encountered in digital photography. Practically every commercially available imaging device from cell phone cameras to professional DSLR cameras utilizes this file format. JPEG uses a compression algorithm that reduces the image file size by deleting pixel data from the raw image. This type of compression is also referred to as *lossy compression*. The photographer can often select the degree of compression through the camera settings menu, where low, medium, or high quality image settings can be selected. A high-quality image setting would retain the most amount of the raw image data. While it is not often a concern to the lay user, the law enforcement professional should be aware that the image data deleted by the camera in the JPEG compression process is not retrievable.

When a JPEG image is opened in picture-viewing software, the file must undergo a decompression process to restore the pixels that were deleted from the original image. The picture-viewing software will typically employ an *interpolation* algorithm to restore deleted image pixels. During the interpolation process, the picture-viewing software identifies areas in the image file where pixels were deleted by the camera and then identifies the color and intensity of pixels surrounding the deletion. The software then averages out the values of these surrounding pixels and creates new pixels to fill in the deletions. This process occurs for each pixel that was deleted from the image until the entire picture is restored. This process does result in artifacts, often referred to as JPEG decompression artifacts, which can affect the detail of the final image. The extent of perceptible detail artifact in the image depends on the degree of JPEG compression used when taking the photograph. If a low-quality image is taken, more pixels are deleted during the compression process than if a high-quality picture was taken. In turn, there are fewer pixels available to the image-viewing software to average when restoring deleted pixels during decompression process. This results in more detail artifacts as well as a loss in image resolution during the reconstruction of the image (Figure 4.13).

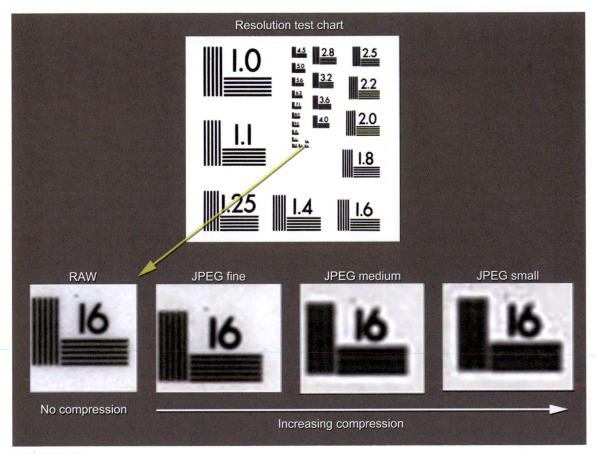

FIGURE 4.13
A resolution test chart.

These charts can be used to measure the ability for a camera to resolve individual lines in the chart based on the optics and camera setting used. The chart was photographed using a Nikon D300 camera equipped with a 60 mm macro lens. The initial photograph was recorded in RAW format. Each subsequent image was recorded using the JPEG file format while increasing the level of compression used. As can be seen, the fine lines in the chart are well resolved when using RAW format. The lines of the resolution chart are also slightly resolved with the JPEG fine settings; however, between JPEG medium and small, image resolution and detail are progressively lost as a result of increased compression.

TIFF or Tagged Image File Format is another type of image file that can be generated by digital cameras. This image format can generate images that are uncompressed, use *lossy compression* or use a *lossless compression* algorithm. In lossless compression, the camera uses an algorithm that reduces the size of an image file by shortening repetitive pixel data. As imaging software opens the file, it will be able to restore the compressed data to its original form. The TIFF format has its advantages over other file formats in that it is also capable of storing additional color data. For example, where a JPEG file can store 8 bits or data values for each color channel (red, blue, and green), the TIFF format can retain up to 16 bits per color, for a total of 48 bits. An image bearing 8 bits per channel is capable of producing images consisting of approximately 16 million colors, which are referred to as a true color images. If a TIFF image is captured in 48 bits, this will produce an image capable of generating billions of colors, or deep color images. Having that much color depth available has its advantages in both the postprocessing and printing of images. Deep color images can provide more dynamic tonal range that can be used to better reproduce the color and color intensity of the scene being photographed during postprocessing.

The RAW file format is typically an uncompressed file format that represents the data as captured directly from the sensor. These files are generally devoid of any in-camera processing such as hue, sharpening, and color effects. The RAW file format is also considered the equivalent of a digital negative. Like a film negative, the RAW file cannot typically be used as an image itself, but rather it is used to make a final image that is saved as a TIFF or JPEG file.

One of the issues surrounding the RAW format is the lack of standardization across camera manufacturers, although an international standard exists (ISO 12234-2:2001) for the format. Because of this lack of standardization, RAW formats can have various file extension names. For example, the Nikon extension for a RAW file is the NEF or Nikon Electronic Format. Likewise the Canon equivalent is CRW for Canon Raw. Practically each camera manufacturer will have different RAW extensions for their cameras that generate RAW images. Because of the proprietary nature of RAW, these file types are not typically supported by generic viewing software, often limiting the photographer to manufacturer-supplied software that may have limited processing capabilities. The RAW files therefore have to be converted to a more common file format such as TIFF or JPEG to postprocess. The proprietary nature of RAW has also given rise to issues regarding archiving and long-term usability of these image files. Because the RAW format can be specific to each model of camera manufactured, over time the format may find limited software support, if any, as camera models become discontinued and software platforms are updated. To circumvent this issue, Adobe Systems, the developers of Photoshop, have attempted to introduce the DNG format or "digital negative" file. DNG is currently offered as an open source file format that aims to eventually become a universal RAW. The goal of the DNG format is to retain the usability of RAW images long after the camera model that took the image has been discontinued.

USE AND SELECTION OF FILE FORMATS

As digital camera technology progresses, more features are becoming available to photographers on inexpensive consumer-grade DSLR cameras. One of these features is the ability to capture an image in two file formats such as JPEG and RAW. The JPEG file format by itself is not recommended for evidentiary photography because of the potential for detail artifacts that may interfere with the subsequent analysis of a photograph. However, it is fine to use these images for quick viewing or dissemination to parties who may not necessarily need to analyze the detail in a photo. For physical evidence documentation or any photography where a detailed analysis may be needed, the best file format to utilize is currently the RAW format or uncompressed TIFF.

REFERENCE

Highton, S. (2003). *Ask the VR photography experts*, Found at: www.vrphotography.com/data/pages/askexperts/pano/filmvdigpanos.html.

Photographic Exposure

CONTENTS

ABSTRACT

The many facets of police work require a good working knowledge of photographic principles to properly capture quality images that may aid in the investigation and prosecution of crimes. Exposure involves using the inner workings of light, intensity of light, shutter speed, aperture, and lens to achieve a photographic image that is useful. In addition, a working knowledge of depth of field will help the photographer capture crisp details in the image or keep the focus on a particular item within the photograph.

KEY TERMS

Aperture
Depth of field
Exposure
Exposure values for digital cameras
f-stop
f-system

INTRODUCTION

The rigors of police photography demand that the photographer make pictures in all conditions of light. Photographs must be made of subjects that are far away or of objects that are no more than a few inches from the camera lens. To do this, the light that enters the camera must be controlled.

The adjustable camera was designed so that the photographer could control the light that is recorded on film or a sensor chip. The focusable lens allows the camera to focus sharply on objects 3 feet away or at infinity. The adjustable shutter permits light to be let in for as little as 1/1000 of a second or for many minutes.

In addition to adjusting the focus and the shutter, the photographer can control the amount of light that enters the camera at any given moment. The photographer can let in as little light as a pinhole or as much light as the diameter of the lens allows by changing the aperture, or diameter of the opening. The mechanical device that allows the photographer to adjust the aperture is called a diaphragm. Usually, the diaphragm is an integral part of the lens system. On cameras that have detachable lenses, the diaphragms are a part of each lens and not a part of the camera itself.

Letting just enough light into the camera to expose the film or sensor is called exposure. With a simple camera, the photographer decides whether there is enough light for an exposure. If there is not, one does not take a picture or one takes a picture with a flash. An adjustable camera, however, allows the photographer to photograph under many different conditions. For basic exposure, the photographer need be concerned with only two settings: aperture and shutter speed. Aperture controls the intensity of light that is let inside the camera, and shutter speed controls the time that it spends inside the camera. A formula for setting an adjustable camera might look like this:

$$\text{Intensity} \times \text{Time} = \text{Exposure.}$$

EXPOSURE

Exposure is the amount of light that is allowed to reach the film or sensor by controlling the variables of aperture and shutter speed. Light meters quickly, accurately, and conveniently measure light in almost any photographic situation and help to determine the appropriate aperture and shutter speed combination. The development of light meters makes it possible for contemporary police photographers to use illumination from any direction such as the back, side, or front or even diffused through the atmosphere. Light can also be used to produce many different aesthetic effects.

Even the highest quality-camera and lens register only some of the many different tones the human eyes can see. Some tones, and therefore some detail, are lost in photographs. Thus, in every situation one must choose between tones to emphasize and tones to neglect.

Accurately measuring light with a light meter dictates how to set the aperture and shutter to get both the best detail the film can register and the desired aesthetic effect. Most cameras have built-in light meters. If a police officer is to become a professional, he or she must act like a professional photographer and learn how to use a light meter so photographs can be obtained that will be a credit to them in a courtroom. The police officer may discover that it is an advantage to use a hand-held meter because of its greater accuracy and versatility.

There is an old photographer's maxim: "Expose for the shadows and develop for the highlights." That is, if you must choose between over- and underexposure, it is better to overexpose to bring out the detail of the shadow areas than to underexpose. It may be possible to correct for some degree of overexposure by working with the image on the computer.

INTERNATIONAL STANDARDS ORGANIZATION (ISO)

Another factor affecting the exposure of an image is the International Standards Organization (ISO)/Americanl Standards Association (ASA) setting. The ISO setting of a camera allows the photographer to control the effective light-gathering capabilities of the sensor, directly tying the ISO number to the overall exposure as well as the exposure time of a photograph. Starting from ISO 100, subsequently increasing ISO numbers (e.g., 100, 200, 400, 800) can be used to increase the exposure by a factor of 2. Therefore, increasing the ISO from 100 to 200 can double the amount of light in the exposure. If the f-number for a given exposure remains constant, the shutter speed can be quickened, reducing the overall exposure time required for the photograph. Likewise, maintaining a constant shutter speed, the f-number can be increased, which also increases the depth of field in the image. This can be particularly helpful in low light conditions; however, as the ISO is increased from 100 to 3200, ISO noise progressively increases and appears as grainy, textured, multicolored artifacts in an image. Furthermore, ISO noise decreases the resolution in a photograph.

In a forensic setting, ISO noise can negatively affect the value of evidentiary photographs because of the decrease in resolution. The photographer should always be aware of the maximum usable ISO on the camera being used; this can vary depending on the manufacturer and grade of the camera. Older cameras may have a maximum ISO of 3200, where significant grain can be noted in the photograph. Newer cameras may use advanced noise reduction algorithms that can correct ISO noise in the image, extending the usable ISO range of these cameras well up to 6400 (Figure 5.1).

Automatic ISO

When film was used, the ISO/ASA was constant for the roll of film selected. With digital cameras, the photographer can vary the sensor ISO number directly in the camera. Automatic ISO selection is available in some digital single-lens reflex (SLR) cameras and functions similarly to the program or automatic exposure modes. When a camera is set to program/automatic exposure mode, the internal light metering system adjusts the aperture and shutter speed based on existing light conditions to obtain a nominal exposure. Similarly, when using automatic ISO, the camera can be set to vary the ISO number based on a minimum shutter speed selected by the photographer. As the camera light meter detects less light, the camera boosts the ISO to obtain the desired exposure. This is particularly helpful when handholding a camera in low light conditions and when flash photography is not desired. The minimum shutter speed required for stopping motion is approximately 1/60 of a second (higher for fast motion). The automatic ISO can be set so that the camera maintains a shutter speed of 1/60 s by varying the ISO. The photographer

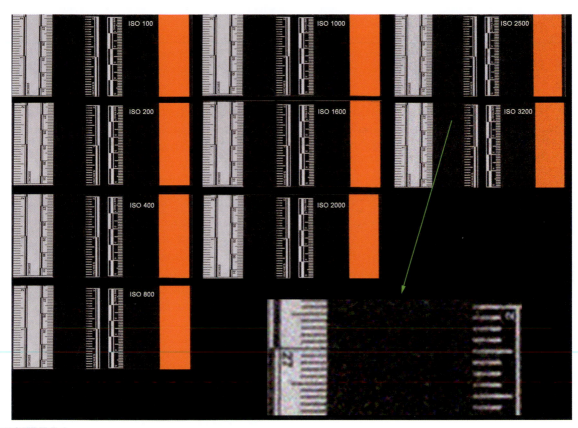

FIGURE 5.1
A series of photographs taken with Nikon D300 camera with a 60-mm lens. In each photograph the ISO was increased from 100 to 3200. The degree of ISO noise can be seen in each photograph, which progressively increases as the ISO number increases. The green arrow points to a magnified section of the photograph taken at ISO 3200, depicting the croma-noise and grain typically associated with the use of high ISO numbers.

can also set the maximum ISO used by the camera, which is helpful when the maximum usable ISO of the camera is known.

EXPOSURE METERS

It is almost impossible to make a good print from a badly exposed image, but making a good print from a good image is a simple process. It is important, therefore, that the image be uniformly exposed. A good exposure meter, when properly used, is the best insurance a photographer can carry to be sure of uniform exposure.

While most cameras have built-in metering systems, photographers may find it beneficial to have a hand-held light meter as a backup. This is especially true when using lenses without camera metering capabilities. Many lenses, especially large telephoto lenses (e.g., 500 mm) have a fixed f-number with no coupling mechanism for the camera's internal metering system. A hand-held exposure meter can be used to accurately calculate exposure with such lenses.

The photoelectric type is the most accurate exposure meter available. This instrument measures the intensity of light and indicates the light value of a scene on a scale. Calculator dials attached to the meter are designed to compute the correct exposure rapidly by considering the light value in relation to the film speed. The problem of transcribing light values into terms of exposures is simplified, and direct readings in numerous combinations of f-stop and shutter speeds suitable for photographing the scene are shown on the calculator dials.

From experience, it is recommended that the Luna PRO line of exposure meters be used for police work. The Luna PRO is exceptional in that it is a system exposure meter. By means of instant-lock-on attachments, it makes refining measurement techniques possible not only in camera work on location and in the laboratory but also in enlarging or in photomicrography. Figure 5.2 shows a Luna PRO analog meter (digital versions also are available). The Luna PRO is so easy to use that, within a short time, its operation will become almost automatic.

FIGURE 5.2
Luna PRO meter.

Choosing a Meter

The most important part of the exposure meter is the photoelectric cell. It is a simple device that takes in a certain amount of light and emits a current in proportion to the amount of light falling on it.

The first practical exposure meter came about as a result of the invention of the selenium barrier-layer photocell, which was incorporated in the earliest Weston meters and in many others until very recently.

The barrier-layer cell is self-generating—that is, it emits current in proportion to the light falling on it and does not require batteries or other outside sources of current. Some meters today have two cells, a normal cell for average illumination and an attachable "booster" cell for making readings in dim light. With the introduction of the cadmium sulfide photoconductive cell came a great breakthrough for exposure meters. The cadmium sulfide cell does not generate any current; it merely changes its resistance according to the light falling upon it. The more light it receives, the more current passes through it. But the current must be provided from an outside battery, a new type that is very small, has a long life under small loads, and whose voltage is quite constant until it is finally exhausted. Some meters (such as the Luna PRO) incorporate a cadmium sulfide cell and a small battery as their basic elements. In general, a push-button switch is provided so that current is drawn from the battery only when a reading is being taken. Under these circumstances a single battery will last up to a year and, in some cases, longer.

Although the Luna PRO has been highly recommended for police work, the photographer may wish to experiment with several of the many meters on the market. The Luna PRO, with its system attachments, is a versatile meter, however, and should not be overlooked when making a choice between meters.

Using a Meter

The principle of operation of most exposure meters is basically the same. The exposure speed (ASA/ISO number) and the light value reading are set on the calculator dials. Numerous combinations of exposure then are shown opposite each other as pairings of f-stop and shutter speed. To use the meter:

1. Set the calculator dial on the ISO/ASA rating of the camera. Once this is set, it need not be changed as long as that rating is used on the camera settings.
2. Direct the meter at the scene to be photographed and obtain a light value reading. Usually this reading is taken from or near the camera position. The reading should be taken from a position that includes only the area to be covered in the photograph. Hold the meter near eye level with the photoelectric cell directed at or near the center of the scene. Do not hold the meter so that light from the sun, auxiliary lights, or large highly

reflective surfaces can directly reach the cell. Avoid including more sky than necessary by directing the meter slightly downward. Be particularly careful not to obstruct or interfere with light that could reach the cell.

3. Set the light value reading on the calculator dial. Then all that remains is to select the desired combination of f-stop and shutter speed from those indicated on the dials (on the Luna PRO, set the light value reading on the yellow triangle at the bottom of the meter).

Proper Exposure

There are many more shutter speeds and aperture numbers on the meter calculator dials than are found on any one make of camera. These calculators were designed to make the meter convenient for use with every standard type of domestic and foreign camera by including practically every f-stop and shutter speed found on them. Select and use only those combinations that are marked on your camera and disregard the others. Remember that intermediate shutter speeds cannot be obtained by setting the index between two marked speeds on the shutter housing. However, should the meter indicate a diaphragm setting that is not marked on the lens, the index may be set between two marked f-stops for an intermediate setting or it can be set to the nearest f-number.

Figure 5.3 shows the face of a light meter set for a film rating of ISO/ASA 400. The meter was set while pointed at a subject that gave a reading of f/8 at 1/60 of a second. A camera shooting the same subject would give a good, even exposure if set at f/8 and 60. Other combinations of exposure are available with this reading: f/4 at 250, f/5.6 at 125, f/11 at 30, and so on.

Any combination of exposure settings can be used for a given reading, depending on the effect desired by the photographer. For instance, an action photograph of a speeding car can be shot at f/2 at 1/1000 of a second; a nonmoving subject can be photographed at f/32 at 1/4 of a second for a sharp image (a tripod would be a necessity for an exposure longer than 1/30 of a second).

Incident and Reflected Light

Light values can be measured by either of two ways: as incident light or as reflected light. An incident light reading is taken by holding the light meter in front of the subject and pointing it back at the camera. With the Luna PRO and other meters, an opal white bulb must be placed over the light cell before taking an incident light reading. Reflected light is read by pointing the light meter toward the subject, slightly downward, and taking the reading.

There is considerable controversy regarding the subject of determining light values as to whether the reflected or incident method is superior. Each method has certain advantages and disadvantages. The incident method is especially

FIGURE 5.3
Luna Pro meter set at ISO/ASA 400, reading f/8 and 1/60 second.

useful when the intensity of illumination is very low. It is extremely accurate in measuring the intensity of light falling on the subject. On the other hand, the photographer is more interested in the amount of light that is reflected from the subject. Black velvet absorbs a high percentage of incident light, whereas a sheet of white paper reflects perhaps as much as 85%. Obviously, the light-reflecting quality of the subject must be carefully considered when determining exposure by incident light readings. Some meters are manufactured specifically for reading incident light values. These meters are certainly just as capable of accurate readings as those reading reflected light. Either type is reliable, but both must be used with intelligence.

Cautions and Techniques for Meter Use

The ISO/ASA setting of most meters is connected to the aperture dial. A change in the ISO/ASA reading will change the aperture reading, while the reading for speed will remain the same.

Because a light meter averages light values, it cannot guarantee 100% accuracy, particularly in situations in which there is a bright sky, snow, or a beach. On a bright day the meter should be aimed downward to measure the light reflected from the ground and not the light from the sky. When the ground is highly reflective, as when it is covered with snow or when the photographer is over water, readings should be taken of lighted areas and of areas in shadow. The aperture should be set midway between these readings.

An 18% gray card, available at any camera supply store, is often useful for taking readings of reflected light. The palm of a hand may substitute for a gray card in many situations.

Spot Meters

At times, the photographer will want to meter only a small part of a scene. A spot meter measures reflected light in a very small section of the scene before it. Ordinary light meters measure light over an angle of 30°–50°, whereas a spot meter can measure at an angle of 1° or less.

A spot meter is particularly useful when the exposure is based on one important tone in a scene. Backlighted areas, shadowed areas, bright highlighted areas, and extreme changes in illumination can affect the accuracy of a reading from an ordinary light meter. A spot meter can accurately read each area so that an exposure that compensates for these extremes in illumination can be calculated.

Spot meters are handy to have in those instances where extreme changes in illumination occur, but they should be considered an optional piece of equipment for the police photographer. The cost of spot meters may be prohibitive for the amount of actual use to which they are put in police photography. An ordinary light meter can be used to measure different parts of a scene, and an average of the readings can be taken. The photographer can also bracket exposures to make sure certain areas of the scene are properly exposed. Bracketing, in this way, allows multiple shots of one scene to be taken and then merged through software such as Adobe Photoshop. Some exposure meter manufacturers produce light meters that double as spot meters. While the cost may be high, they should still be considered. In addition, some digital SLR cameras have built-in spot meters.

THE "f" SYSTEM

There have been at least a half-dozen systems to mark the opening of the diaphragm, but most cameras now use the "f" system. The diaphragm opening, which is called a stop, is usually marked in numbers on the exterior of the lens.

The "f" system is the relationship between the diameter of the lens opening, or aperture, and the focal length of the lens. The "f" indicates the speed

Table 5.1 f-Stop Exposures

	f-Stop										
	1.4	**2.8**	**4**	**5.6**	**8**	**11**	**16**	**22**	**32**	**45**	**64**
Fraction of focal length	1/1.4	1/2.8	1/4	1/5.6	1/8	1/11	1/16	1/22	1/32	1/45	1/64
Exposure ratio	1/4	1/2	1	2	4	8	16	32	64	128	256

of the lens or, in other words, the amount of light the lens lets through in proportion to its focal length. Some years ago, a photographer would more or less guess the size of the lens opening and then guess the exposure that would be required. In 1881, members of the Royal Photographic Society of Great Britain worked out a system of apertures based on a sequence of ratios so that aperture and exposure time could be controlled scientifically. They began with a unit of one as an aperture of f/4. The ratio that was worked out gave each succeeding stop an area just one-half of the previous one. Each numerical stop, as the stops become smaller, lets in half as much light as the preceding one.

The "f" system is used in most of the world today. Table 5.1 shows the common f-stops in use today, the fraction of the focal length that each represents, and the ratio of exposures.

METHODS OF REGULATING TIME

The oldest method of controlling the amount of time of exposure was to have a light-tight cap on the lens that was removed by hand and replaced after sufficient time had elapsed.

Inexpensive box cameras were usually equipped with a single metal plate attached to a spring. When a lever was pushed, the spring rotated the plate, allowing light to enter for about 1/50 of a second. These mechanical devices, which are used to control the amount of time the light is allowed to pass through, are called shutters.

Many higher-quality cameras have a complicated device that allows exposure times of from 1 s to 1/4000 of a second. This is indeed a wide range. In addition, they have provisions for time and strobe exposures. Many modern digital cameras have a self-timing feature that delays the opening of the shutter for several seconds and enables the person to take his or her own picture. This type of shutter, which is usually in the lens, is called a compur shutter or a leaf shutter.

CONTROLLING INTENSITY

The diaphragm of a camera or camera lens is graduated into measurements of the intensity of the light that it lets pass through the lens. The measurements, called f-stops, are standardized and are usually printed or engraved on the lens barrel as follows: 1.2, 2, 2.8, 4, 5.6, 8, 11, 16, 22, 32. Confusingly, an f-stop with a larger number, such as f/16, lets in less light than one of a smaller number, such as f/5.6.

Each f-number indicates that the diaphragm is allowing twice the light that the next higher number would let pass through the lens into the camera and half the light that the next smaller number would let pass. That is, f/11 is twice as bright as f/16 but only half as bright as f/8. While learning about aperture, photographers would do well to think of f-numbers as fractions: just as 1/4 is smaller than 1/2 but larger than 1/8, so is f/4 larger than f/5.6 but smaller than f/2.8. Stop f/1, then, lets in 1024 times as much light as f/32!

CONTROLLING TIME

The shutter on an adjustable camera can be set so that, once it is released, it will stay open indefinitely or for as little as 1/1000 of a second. In between these extremes are various fractions of a second, for example, 1/15, 1/30, 1/60, 1/125, and 1/250 of a second.

On the camera setting, these fractions are engraved or printed as whole numbers: 15, 30, 60, 125, and 250. The fractions of a second may vary from camera to camera; some cameras are marked 25, 50, 100, 200, indicating that shutter speeds of 1/25, 1/50, 1/100, and 1/200 are available to the photographer. Also, short shutter speeds of 1/500 and 1/1000 of a second are not available on all cameras. The letter *B* on a shutter setting means bulb exposure; with this setting the photographer can open the shutter and hold it open indefinitely. The letter *T* means time exposure; the photographer can open the shutter on a timed setting and walk away from the camera. When the photographer returns and trips the shutter again, it will close.

The use of long exposure times can have practical applications in police photography, as seen in cases where luminol is used. Luminol is a colorless liquid that produces a light-emitting reaction, or chemiluminescence, when it comes in contact with blood. The reagent is typically prepared just before use and is delivered via a spray so that large areas of a crime scene can be tested with relative ease. The luminol reaction releases a blue-while light (~425 nm) that must be visualized in complete darkness. Because the light emitted by luminol can be weak, any ambient light can obscure the luminol reaction. In homicide cases where it is suspected that blood was cleaned from the crime scene, it may become necessary to use luminol to detect blood that has been diluted past a point where it can be visually detected. The photographic documentation requires the use of long exposures, for example, 30 s, to document any chemiluminescence.

Testing areas with luminol and the photographic documentation of luminol reactions should be performed simultaneously. Since luminol is used to detect blood that is potentially very diluted, the first treatment with luminol typically provides the most intense chemiluminescence. As subsequent sprays are made, blood becomes more diluted and the intensity of the chemiluminescence gradually diminishes. If blood has been diluted past the sensitivity of the luminol ($\sim 1 \times 10^{-6}$ dilutions) because of continuous spraying, chemiluminescence no longer occurs. This scenario may also prove deleterious for any subsequent serology and DNA testing. For this reason, careful planning and systematic testing coupled with simultaneous photography is recommended.

When using luminol, an area to be tested should be identified and the camera should be set up such that the area to be tested is within the camera's field of view. The camera should be set on a tripod and equipped with a shutter release cable. A wide-angle zoom lens can be used; these lenses provide practical flexibility when framing the field of view. The camera can be set with the following parameters:

- Manual exposure mode
- Aperture of f/5.6
- Shutter speed of 30 s
- ISO 400

Once the camera has been set up, the room should be completely darkened and the test area treated with luminol using a minimal amount of spraying. If chemiluminescence is noted, the photograph can be taken immediately, photographically capturing the reaction.

Because luminol photography is performed in complete darkness, any chemiluminescence will be devoid of context with the scene. Two methods can be used to overcome this. First, an external flash unit can be used to illuminate the scene at the end of the 30-s exposure. This can be done by attaching the flash unit to the hot-shoe of the camera and aiming the flash at the ceiling. The flash output should also be stopped down by one or two exposure values. A test photograph can be taken in complete darkness to determine how much of the scene is illuminated by the flash when it is stopped down. These photographs will be purposefully underexposed, however; enough of the scene should be visible so that the luminol reaction will have some context with its surroundings. If the exposure appears too bright, the chemiluminescence may be overpowered by the flash and may not be visible in the photograph. The flash output should, therefore, be adjusted. The camera should also be set to "rear curtain" or "second curtain flash" mode, which will fire the flash at the end of the 30-s exposure. The idea here is that the camera will capture the chemiluminescence during the 30-s exposure in complete darkness. At the end of the exposure, the flash will illuminate the scene, which will put the luminol reaction in context.

FIGURE 5.4

This photograph depicts a luminol reaction obtained from the bathroom of a homicide scene, where attempts were made to clean blood from the scene. Careful inspection of the bathtub with good lighting revealed the presence of dilute bloodstains. Subsequent treatment with luminol revealed chemiluminescence on the bathtub floor, drain, and a bucket that was in the tub. The photograph was captured in the darkened bathroom using a tripod-mounted Nikon D3x camera equipped with a 24- to 70-mm lens. The exposure was set to f-5.6 for 30 s. The camera also was set to "rear-curtain flash," the light from the flash itself was attenuated by a −1.5 eV so as to not overpower the luminol reaction.

A second option involves taking the 30-s exposure of the luminol reaction then, without moving the camera, taking a second exposure with lights on. The two images can then be superimposed using Adobe Photoshop to create one image that will incorporate the scene and areas where blood was detected with luminol (Figure 5.4).

Other techniques that utilize long-exposure photographic documentation include ultraviolet imaging, documentation of laser light used in ballistic trajectory reconstruction, and painting with light.

COMBINING CONTROL OF INTENSITY AND TIME

The aperture and shutter speed work together to provide the film with an accurate amount of light. Which shutter speed and aperture the photographer chooses depends on (1) the amount of available light and (2) the depth of field required by the subject matter of the photograph. Depth of field will be discussed in the next section.

When shooting outdoors in daylight, the photographer can divide the intensity of light into five categories: bright sunlight, hazy sunlight, cloudy bright, cloudy dull, and cloudy dark. If the aperture is set at f/11, a different shutter speed will be required for each category of light. Cloudy dark skies require the longest exposure, and bright sunlight requires a short exposure. Conversely, if the shot is only at 1/125 of a second, the aperture must be adjusted for variations of light intensity.

In practice, however, the photographer must choose the best possible combination of aperture and shutter speed for the light conditions and the subject matter. A photograph of a moving object always requires a fast shutter speed to capture the object. The photographer who wishes to photograph a moving car will shoot at 1/250 or 1/500 of a second and adjust the aperture according to the light available. When photographing still objects, though, depth of field becomes the most important consideration when choosing exposure.

DEPTH OF FIELD

The art photographer often takes pictures in which one object: a model or a flower, for instance, is in sharp focus while the foreground and background are a blur. The effect is pleasant and suggests a painting. But the police photographer is not concerned with art; the facts must be presented, and to do so, details must be clearly represented. The distance from the closest clear object in a photograph to the farthest clear object is called the depth of field, and the police photographer must always strive to obtain the greatest depth of field possible in every photograph (Figure 5.5).

Fortunately, depth of field increases as the lens aperture decreases; to get greater depth of field, the photographer stops down, or uses a smaller f-stop (e.g., f/22). Thus, for most police photography, the photographer will use the smallest possible aperture and adjust the shutter speed accordingly. It is no exaggeration to say that the smaller the aperture is, the better the picture will be.

The technique of using small apertures for greater depth of field does have its limitations. When the photographer focuses on an object close to the camera, the depth of field will be less than for objects farther away, so the focus on nearby objects must be more accurate than for distant objects. Also, as was the case of the speeding car in the preceding section, and is for any fast-moving object, a fast shutter speed is required, and a small aperture may therefore be impossible. The photographer must then be extremely careful to focus accurately on the moving object.

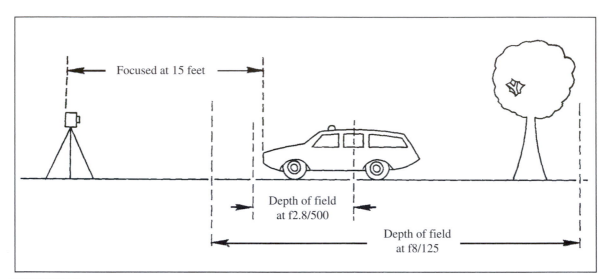

FIGURE 5.5

Depth of field illustration.

MORE ABOUT FOCUS

Incorrect exposure, resulting in imperfect images, may be corrected on a computer—faulty focusing cannot. Improperly focused photographs seldom appear in the courtroom because they are unusable. The most important thing a photographer can do is to focus correctly on the subject before snapping the shutter (Figures 5.6 and 5.7).

When focusing, it is good to remember that the closer a subject is to the camera, the farther the lens must be from the sensor. This is more easily seen with a bellows-type camera that becomes elongated when the lens is focused on an object far away. Most digital SLR cameras have screw-type lenses that are focused by turning the lens as one would a screw. The lens moves closer to or farther from the film when it is turned, but the change of distance is not as obvious as it is with a bellows camera. Most autofocus lenses have a switch that allows for manual focus. It is sometimes necessary to switch the lens to manual when making fine focus adjustments or in situations where the autofocusing device is trying to focus on something else (such as taking a photograph of a fingerprint on a window pane).

Many police photographs are taken at night, making focusing difficult. Whenever the photographer cannot accurately focus on the subject, the focus should be set at infinity and the smallest possible aperture should be used (thus insuring depth of field). In such cases, it may be wise to increase the camera's ISO setting.

FIGURE 5.6
First shot (left) taken at f/2.8. Second shot (right) taken at f/11. Notice all four numbers are in focus at f/11.

PHOTOGRAPHING MOVING OBJECTS

When a subject is in motion during exposure, its image on the sensor moves. Even when the duration of exposure is only 1/1000 of a second, the image moves a small fraction of an inch during this time. However, the movement at 1/1000 is only 1/10 as far as it is at 1/100 of a second.

The photographer must determine just how much image movement can be tolerated before it becomes objectionable; then the shutter speed must be regulated accordingly. It is necessary to visualize how the image will be used to determine what constitutes "objectionable" blurring of the image. An image that is to be used as a small print will permit considerably more blurring than one that is to be enlarged. In addition, if a print is likely to be examined through a magnifying glass or enlarged on a television monitor, the image must be sharper than is necessary if the print is to be viewed from a distance.

Unusual circumstances may make it impossible to obtain great degrees of sharpness of a moving object. In such cases, it is necessary to decide whether it is more important to take a picture even though the subject is somewhat blurred than to leave it unphotographed. When it is imperative that a sharp image of a fast-moving object be obtained, it is possible to use the "follow-through" method of keeping the camera constantly trained on the object and following it until after the exposure is made, rather like shooting a duck. Of course, this method completely blurs the background but provides a sharp image of the object itself, even at relatively slow shutter speeds. This technique is commonly used by sports photographers making images of cyclists and race cars.

FIGURE 5.7
First shot (top) taken at f/2.8. Second shot (bottom) taken at f/16. Notice that the truck, ball, body, and goal are all in sharper focus at f/16.

Although it is not always possible to do so, the photographer will achieve better results if he or she can choose the direction of movement. An object moving toward or away from the camera will not be as blurred as an object crossing the camera.

MANUAL CAMERAS

Before the digital and electronic age of photography, 35-mm SLR cameras were operated manually. The photographer had to set the aperture, shutter speed, and focus all by hand. Unless the camera was equipped with a motor drive, the photographer had to crank the lever to wind the film for each shot. Batteries in manual cameras were used for the metering system and usually nothing more. With their metal bodies and gears, these cameras were rugged and could be operated without battery power. If the photographer found him or herself without battery power for the internal metering system, photographs could still be made. With experience using a manual camera, photographers could usually make accurate estimations as to what the aperture and shutter speed settings should be in a given situation. A simple exposure method, called the f/16 system, or Sunny 16 method, works very well when a photographer has no means of measuring available light for a photograph. Here is how it works:

1. Set the aperture at f/16. This will insure good depth of field.
2. Set the shutter at a speed closest to that of the ISO rating of the camera being used; for example, if the camera ISO rating is set at 200, the shutter speed may also be set to 1/200.
3. Focus the lens.
4. Correct underexposure or overexposure on the computer. No exposure meters or estimating are needed.

Police photographers should not rely too heavily on today's automatic camera features. If a battery goes dead in an automatic camera, nothing is going to work. It is imperative that extra batteries be taken along on a photo shoot. Some police photographers take along a backup manual camera in case something happens to their regular primary camera. Today's automatic cameras—with their plastic bodies, vinyl gears, and electronic components—are neither rugged nor do well in inclement weather. In fact, the camera could easily "short-out" in rain, leaving the photographer with no means of taking photographs. It is wise to have back-up cameras and batteries.

AUTOMATIC CAMERAS

Automatic cameras are of three basic types: shutter priority, aperture priority, and fully automatic. Cameras with shutter priority automatically set the aperture, but the photographer must select a shutter speed first. A photoelectric cell is activated on shutter priority cameras when the photographer pushes slightly on the shutter release button or some other mechanism specific to the camera. A display in the viewfinder indicates whether there is enough light for the pre-selected shutter speed. If there is not enough light, the photographer selects another speed and tries again.

Aperture priority models automatically set the shutter speed after the photographer has selected an aperture. This system gives the photographer far more control over depth of field.

Fully automatic cameras use advanced electronic circuitry to determine exposure and automatically set aperture and shutter. Many fully automatic cameras allow the photographer to manually override these features for shutter priority and aperture priority, although most digital cameras are fully automatic with no manual override capability. As was discussed in Chapter 2, the police photographer should select a camera with manual override capability.

CAMERA EXPOSURE MODES

A photograph may also be referred to as an exposure, whereby the light-recording medium of the camera is exposed to light for a given length of time. There are several factors that affect the exposure of photographs, including shutter speed, lens aperture, and ISO. With the exception of ISO, a camera's exposure modes can be used to control the camera's mechanical variables, such as the aperture and shutter speed, to control exposure. The exposure modes of an SLR camera include

> shutter priority;
> aperture priority;
> manual mode; and
> program mode.

Most digital cameras contain internal light meters, which are used to determine the proper exposure based on the intensity and amount of available light.

Shutter Priority

Shutter priority mode allows the photographer to control the length of an exposure by directly dictating the length of time during which the shutter element of the camera remains open. While the camera is in shutter priority, the camera adjusts the exposure by automatically controlling the diameter of the lens aperture. In this mode, it's important for the photographer to understand that a shutter-speed setting of 1/60 s or faster will freeze motion under most circumstances. Conversely, a shutter speed slower than 1/60 s can lead to motion blur if the camera is not mounted on a tripod. Long shutter-speed settings have their utility in crime scene documentation. Dark, poorly lit outdoor scenes can be properly exposed using slow shutter speeds. Very dark scenes can be adequately illuminated using a combination of long shutter speeds and a handheld flash positioned at various locations within the exposure frame, a technique that is referred to as "painting with light." In addition, blood enhancement techniques, as with the use of luminol, require long exposures to capture chemiluminescent reactions.

Aperture Priority

In aperture priority mode the photographer can select the camera's aperture setting while the camera selects the shutter speed that will produce an optimal exposure for the selected aperture. Aperture priority is the preferred mode for crime scene photography since it allows the photographer full control over the depth of field of each exposure. It is important to note that in most SLR cameras, when a flash is attached the shutter speed is usually fixed to 1/60 s. Because a change in aperture either doubles or halves the light reaching the sensor, with a fixed shutter speed, these changes also affect the exposure of the image. High aperture settings can produce dark, under-exposed images, whereas low aperture settings can produce overexposed images.

The aperture refers to the physical diaphragm present in the lens element of the camera, whose physical diameter can be controlled by the photographer. The degree to which the aperture diaphragm is open or closed is indicated by the f-number, also known as the f-stop. This number is inversely proportional to the diameter of the aperture diaphragm, that is, a high f-number indicates that the aperture diaphragm opening is smaller than that with a low f-number. The lowest achievable f-number (widest aperture diaphragm opening) signifies the speed of the lens. Control over the aperture diaphragm allows the photographer to directly control the amount of light that reaches the camera sensor and hence exert some control over the exposure of the image. Low f-numbers correspond to wide aperture openings and therefore allow more light to enter the camera. Conversely, high f-numbers correspond to smaller aperture openings, allowing less light into the camera. This generally leads to longer exposure times in the absence of additional lighting (such as a flash unit or flood lamp).

Aperture and Depth of Field

In addition to controlling overexposure, the f-number can affect the depth of field in an image. Depth of field refers to the range of distances along the axis of the lens that are in focus for a given exposure. For example, if the camera is placed perpendicular to an evidence item that has some depth to it (shell casings, footwear impression, etc.) using a low f-number (2.8–3.5), only the area on which the lens is directly focused on will appear clear in the image.

The background will be out of focus. The degree to which the background (or foreground) can be brought into focus is varied by increasing the f-number (closing the aperture diaphragm). As the f-number is increased, more items along the axis of the lens come into focus. Depth of field should always be considered when taking close-up photographs using a macro lens. If the subject is focused at infinity (beyond the focal length of the lens), depth of field is generally not a concern.

Keep in mind that increasing the f-number also decreases the amount of light that enters the camera. Photographs taken with high f-numbers could potentially result in underexposed photographs and may require longer exposure times. The correct exposure time (shutter speed) can be determined through the use of the in-camera exposure meter and vary depending on the lighting conditions. Exposure times may be quickened by illuminating the subject with additional lighting from white-light sources such as flood lamps or a camera flash. If the proper exposure time is determined to be longer than 1/60 s, a tripod must be used and the camera should not be handheld. Photographs taken with a handheld camera at exposure times greater than 1/60 s typically exhibit motion blur.

Manual Mode

In manual mode, the photographer can vary both the aperture and shutter-speed settings to obtain a nominal exposure. A nominal exposure can generally be determined with the use of the camera's internal light meter. The aperture can be set to achieve an optimal depth of field; the shutter can then be varied for an optimal exposure. Exposure bracketing is recommended when utilizing manual photography. Activating the exposure bracketing in most modern digital cameras allows the camera to take three to five photographs in rapid succession while varying either the shutter speed or aperture (the photographer decides which) within a range of three to five steps from the nominal exposure. Also of note, in manual mode, the shutter can also be set to "bulb," where the shutter can be held open indefinitely with the use of a shutter release cable.

Program Mode

When a camera is set to program mode, the camera automatically adjusts both the aperture and shutter-speed settings to obtain an optimal exposure. These settings are generally based on the cameras light metering sensor readings and the ISO setting selected. While this setting is good for simple "point and shoot" photography, it is generally not recommended for crime scene or evidence photography. While the camera is in program mode, the photographer does not have the ability to vary the aperture and shutter speed settings to adequately document an item of evidence and the depth of field issues that may arise.

EXPOSURE VALUES FOR DIGITAL CAMERAS

Digital cameras operate on the same principle of light intensity and time as film cameras. The charge-coupled device (CCD) or complementary metal-oxide semiconductor (CMOS) merely serves as the "film" for digital cameras. Almost all higher-end digital cameras have an exposure compensation mode that allows the photographer to make adjustments to the automatic exposure feature of the camera. This compensation is sometimes referred to as the exposure value (EVs), which is measured in steps, typically between [+]2.0 through [−]2.0 EV in half- or third-increment steps. For instance, if strong sunlight is coming from behind the photographer, he or she must either change position or decrease the exposure by about [−]0.7 or [−]1.0 EV. On the other hand, if strong light is behind the subject being photographed, the EV should be adjusted to about [+]0.7 or [+]1.0 EV. Positive EVs increase the brightness of a photo, whereas negative EVs darken it. One of the advantages of digital cameras over film cameras is the ability to view photographs immediately. If the recorded image appears too dark, reduce the EV [−]. If the image is too light, increase the EV [+]. Fill flash may have to be used in some situations. The use of fill flash is discussed later in this chapter.

Most digital SLR cameras have an auto exposure (AE) mode that automatically sets the proper exposure according to existing lighting conditions. There are three types of AE systems: programed mode; aperture priority mode; and shutter priority mode. In programed AE mode, the camera automatically picks the best shutter speed and aperture. In aperture priority mode, the photographer chooses an aperture value (f-stop) and the camera picks the appropriate shutter speed. In shutter priority mode, the photographer selects the shutter speed and the camera automatically selects the appropriate aperture setting (f-stop). If the photographer needs good depth of field, he or she should select aperture priority and set it at the highest possible f-stop value.

The ISO rating can be manipulated on digital cameras. Manufacturers of digital cameras have tried to equate the ISO (ASA) of digital cameras to those of film so that photographers switching from film to digital cameras would not have to relearn exposure. By default, most digital cameras have the ISO set at 100. The ISO on digital cameras determines the overall light sensitivity. The ability to change ISO settings without having to change the CCD (as one would have to do with film) is one of the advantages of digital cameras over film cameras. However, if the ISO is set too high on a digital camera, the result might be what is called "noise." Noise is something like grain on high ISO film. To minimize noise, one should avoid exposure of more than one half second and keep the ISO value below 400. On the other hand, if the ISO is set too low, a phenomenon known as "blooming" might result. Blooming is a visual effect caused by overexposing a CCD to too much light and causes distortions of the subject and/or color. Exposure on digital cameras should not be controlled by manipulating the ISO in lieu of aperture priority or shutter speed priority. In general, one should adjust the ISO on digital cameras only as a last resort after aperture priority and/or shutter speed priority settings have been adjusted.

EXPOSURE WITH FILTERS

Many filters decrease the amount of light that reaches the sensor, so exposure must be adjusted accordingly. This is not a problem with automatic cameras because the through-the-lens metering will compensate.

For cameras not using a through-the-lens metering system, the photographer must know the factor of the filter being used. The filter factor is a figure that tells the photographer how much more light is needed for correct exposure. A filter factor of 2, for instance, means that the exposure should be doubled. For an exposure that would be 1/125 at f/16, the photographer would double the exposure and shoot with the filter at 1/125 at f/11 or 1/60 at f/16.

Some filters are marked with figures such as 1X, 2X, and so on. These are not filter factors. A filter marked 2X, for example, means the aperture should be opened up two stops. Before using any filter, the photographer should read carefully any directions that come with it.

Flash Photography

CONTENTS

ABSTRACT

Very often police photographers have to introduce artificial light when available light is too low or nonexistent. In most instances, artificial light is added by means of an electronic flash. Light can be manipulated in several ways with the camera. It can be produced as a single flash, helping to fill in shadow areas; it can be used with multiple flashes, illuminating several parts of the scene at one time; and it can be used to decrease shadow by bouncing the flash illumination off a reflective source.

KEY TERMS

Bounce flash
Fill-in flash
Flash meter

Guide numbers
Multiple flash
Painting with light
Photoflash
Strobe
Thyristor

FLASH

Whenever photographers go inside to shoot photographs or work outdoors at night, they must be concerned with making use of available light or creating light to suit their needs. Although the available light may be sufficient to shoot with a wide aperture, photographers may wish to "stop down" (larger f-stop number) for a clearer, more focused image. In this case, the available light may not be enough. No matter what the desires or limitations may be, police photographers eventually, more often than not, need to create light. To do so, they merely add a piece of equipment—an electronic flash—that gives, on cue, a satisfactory amount of light for the short period during which the shutter is open.

The principle of flash (synchroflash) photography is essentially nothing more than igniting a flashlamp at the proper time so it burns at peak brilliance while the shutter is open for exposure. When there is no movement in the scene being photographed, the shutter may be opened before the lamp is ignited, and closed again after the light has completely expired. In such cases, it is a very simple matter to synchronize the action of the shutter with the firing of the lamp. However, when a fast shutter speed is necessary, an extremely sensitive and accurate synchronizing mechanism must be used. This mechanism is usually an electrically or mechanically operated device that trips the shutter after the lamp, and tripping the shutter must be accurate to approximately the thousandth of a second (1 millisecond) to ensure correct synchronization at faster shutter speeds. If the shutter opens too early or too late, only a small portion of the flash is used, resulting in underexposure of the film.

Electronic Flash

Electronic ("strobe") flashes have been around for more than 100 years. Electronic flash units have come a long way, and today there is an electronic flash unit for everyone's taste. Most DSLR cameras have built-in or integrated flash units along with a mount shoe for external flash units.

A typical flash unit consists of a power source (alternating current (AC) or battery), one or more energy-storing capacitors or condensers, a triggering circuit, a flash tube through which the stored energy is released as a brief flash of light, and a reflector that directs the light toward the subject. The duration of the flash from a strobe unit is intense and very short, making it excellent for stopping action and minimizing the effect of camera movement.

The quantity of light produced by a strobe unit is determined by the watt-per-second rating of the power supply, the size of the flash tube, and the size of the reflector. A large energy charge in the power supply produces a brighter light than a smaller charge; a large flash tube produces a brighter light than a small tube. The size, shape, and surface texture of a reflector greatly affect the light output. A large reflector yields more light than a small one, a bowl-shape reflector yields more light than a flat one, and a polished reflector yields more than a matte (dull) finish reflector. An average reflector increases the light output of a flash tube by 10 times, about three f-stops, by directing the light forward (Figure 6.1).

Strobe units use one or more of the following power sources: penlight batteries, nickel–cadmium (ni-cad) batteries, high-voltage batteries, and AC (house). Penlight batteries are inexpensive and provide up to 300 flashes per set. Penlight batteries are not rechargeable, but they are not expensive, either. Ni-cad units are more expensive than penlight-powered units, and they must be used at least once a month or their capacitors deform, causing very long recycle times and possibly preventing the unit from recharging at all.

Many two-piece units operate using high-voltage batteries, which are heavy and expensive, but give very short recycling times and provide around 1000 to 1500 flashes before having to be replaced. High-voltage batteries cannot be recharged, and they wear down even when not in use. These units are usually more powerful than others, and more expensive.

Some penlight-powered units, most ni-cad units, and high-voltage battery units can be operated with AC (house) power, which provides an almost infinite number of flashes without recharging or replacing batteries. Recycling times are usually slightly longer when using AC power.

FIGURE 6.1
Sunpak electronic flashes.

Most strobe units have ready lights that indicate they have recycled and are ready to flash again. On many units, however, the ready light comes on at less than full charge. Because the output of a unit is controlled in part by the amount of energy stored in the capacitors, the light output of a partially charged unit is less than a fully charged unit. If the unit's ready light comes on when it is 70% charged, the unit puts out half as much light as when fully recycled. Therefore, the exposure will be one full stop underexposed. This can be corrected on the computer, or, if foreseen by the photographer, the aperture may be stopped up one full stop to compensate.

For flash photography with an electronic strobe unit, the camera should be set on "X" synchronization. Cameras with focal-plane shutters may have a maximum shutter speed that functions with the strobe (usually 1/60 or 1/125 of a second). The maximum allowable shutter speed should be noted and not exceeded.

Automatic strobe units save time and trouble. Instead of determining the flash-to-subject distance and then using the guide number to figure out which f-stop to use, photographers just set a predetermined f-stop on the lens and proceed (see the instructions with the automatic unit to determine the correct f-stop to use). Automatic units have a sensor that reads the light reflected from the subject and alters the flash duration to produce the correct exposure. Flash durations as short as 1/50,000 of a second are possible with some automatic units.

The latest improvement in automatic electronic flash technology has been the development of "dedicated" flash units that are mated electronically for electronic DSLR cameras. Besides the large synchronization contact on the hot shoe, dedicated flash units have one or more additional contacts to match corresponding hot shoe contacts on the camera for which they were designed. When a dedicated flash unit is mounted on the hot shoe of a matching camera and turned on, the camera's shutter speed is set automatically to the correct synchronized speed. Some dedicated flash–camera combinations also set the correct lens opening and operate with the camera's internal metering system.

Some units have thyristor circuits that save power, recycle in a very short time, and permit as many as 400 flashes between charging with ni-cad units. The principle involved is that it takes a certain amount of power to produce a 1/1000-second flash. It takes much less power to produce a 1/50,000-second flash. When a subject is at the maximum distance of an automatic unit's range, the flash duration is the same as the flash duration with the unit on manual (nonautomatic) setting. If the subject is closer, the sensor in the unit cuts the flash short to reproduce the correct exposure. If the flash duration is less than the unit's maximum (usually 1/1000-second), the thyristor circuit saves the excess power that would otherwise have been wasted.

Flash Meters

Flash meters are often used by studio photographers. They are similar to an ordinary light meter, but are designed to read the brief, intense burst of light from an electronic flash. Ordinary light meters cannot record the burst of light from an electronic flash quickly enough. Flash meters were once very expensive and "out of reach" for all but professional studio photographers. The cost of flash meters has decreased significantly with new technology. For instance, the Shepherd and Prolux flash meters can be purchased for less than $300.

As with spot meters, flash meters are handy to have in police photography but should be considered optional. When police photographers are experienced in calculating flash exposures, the perceived need for a flash meter may be lessened. However, because the cost of flash meters has decreased significantly in recent years, the purchase of this type of meter would greatly reduce the amount of time spent at a crime scene calculating exposures. As with combination exposure and spot meters, flash metering capabilities may be built into one exposure meter. Gossen (LUNA-PRO) and Minolta also manufacture exposure meters that can measure flash bursts (Figure 6.2).

FIGURE 6.2
LUNA-PRO digital flash meter for flash, ambient, and reflected light.

Artificial Light

In Chapter 4 it was noted that photography involves controlling, recording, and creating light. Much of the police photographer's job requires that artificial light be created, because many auto accidents and crimes occur at night. A flash may be required at many accident and crime scenes.

Two types of flash are used by photographers: strobe and photoflash. Photoflash refers to any kind of flash created by an instantaneous ignition of a flashbulb that, once used, is discarded and replaced by a fresh bulb for the next shot. The more common strobe refers to a recharging unit with a flash tube that flashes thousands of times before requiring replacement (Figure 6.3).

Single Flash

Most cameras come equipped with an integrated "pop-up" flash and/or a shoe or bracket to which a flash or strobe is attached when needed. They are also built with an electric input that, when connected to the flash, synchronizes the flash to the shutter. Because of the convenience of attaching a single flash directly to the camera and shooting, most amateur photographs are made with a single flash at the camera. Such pictures are characterized by flat lighting on the subjects and harsh black shadows in the backgrounds. When the flash originates very close to the lens, the eyes of persons in the photograph may appear red in color images, otherwise known as the *red-eye effect*, and it can be most disconcerting. The "red eye" is actually light being reflected off the retina. Some cameras with a built-in integrated flash decrease the red-eye effect by allowing the flash to illuminate before the shutter is open, thus allowing the iris of the person's eyes to contract before the picture is taken.

Objectionable effects of single-flash lighting can be minimized or overcome by several methods, the simplest of which is to detach the flash from the camera. If the flash must remain on the camera, it should be covered with some kind of diffusion material, such as a white handkerchief, cheesecloth, or frosted cellulose acetate. Diffusion, however, reduces the intensity of the light, and exposure must be increased accordingly (Figure 6.4).

OFF-CAMERA FLASH TECHNIQUE

One of the best methods for using a single flash is to detach the flash from the camera and direct it at a surface other than the object being photographed. The light then bounces off the surface (a wall or ceiling) and provides soft, even illumination for the subject. This technique is called *bounce flash*, and it works best in a low-ceiling, white or off-white room. It is ineffective outdoors if there are no surfaces to reflect the light.

Bounce flash is so widely used that some strobe and photoflash units are made to tilt while remaining attached to the camera. Photographers

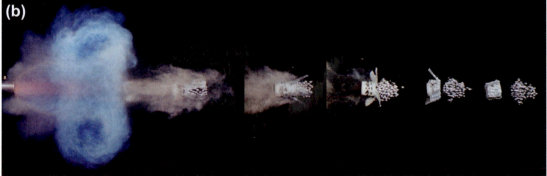

FIGURE 6.3

High-speed strobe photographs. *Courtesy, Andrew Davidhazy, Rochester Institute of Technology.*

should, however, learn to hold the camera in one hand and direct the flash with the other.

Adjustments in exposure must be made for bounce flash because the light must travel farther. This is discussed in the section Exposure for Bounce Flash later in this chapter (Figure 6.5).

FIGURE 6.4
This camera is equipped with a hot shoe for attaching the flash. Conscientious photographers rarely use the shoe.

FIGURE 6.5
Bounce flash technique.

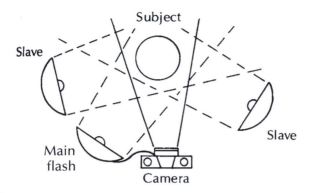

FIGURE 6.6
Use of multiple flash.

If the flash needed for a photograph comes from more than one source, the light is more even and it creates fewer harsh shadows. Multiple flash is accomplished by stringing together a number of flashes or by purchasing slave units that flash automatically when the main flash goes off. Slave units are inexpensive devices that attach to the hot shoe of a secondary electronic flash and "sense" the main flash unit when it discharges. Most slave units are so sensitive they can activate 100 feet away in direct sunlight. It should be noted that many cameras have prebursts of light from built-in strobes to reduce the red-eye effect. If such a camera is used with a slave flash, the slave flash discharges prematurely when it senses the preflash from the camera strobe.

Multiple flash is particularly helpful for shooting outdoors at night when bounce flash is impossible. Ten units can be used to illuminate an entire parking lot (Figure 6.6).

PAINTING WITH LIGHT

Painting with light is a film camera technique that simulates multiple flash, but requires only one flash unit. It can be used only with subjects that are absolutely stationary. Here is how it works:

1. Two people are generally required for painting with light; one walks around with a strobe unit while the other remains at the camera.
2. With the shutter of the camera locked open (a T or B setting) on f/22 (for maximum depth of field), the photographer holds his hand over the camera lens to keep out stray light.

3. The person with strobe in hand walks to the first position from which a flash would be fired, instructs the photographer to remove his hand from the camera lens, and then fires the flash. The photographer then replaces his hand over the lens.
4. The person with the strobe walks to a new position and repeats the process again and again until the entire area to be photographed has been illuminated.

When painting with light, the person who carries the strobe must be careful to remain outside the field of view of the camera, or she may appear as a ghost, not once, but several times in the finished picture. Also, the photographer must take care that nothing moves while the process is taking place, or the evidentiary value of the photograph is lost. A photographer could, using the painting-with-light technique, fill an entire parking lot with the same automobile photographed over and over again.

Digital cameras may not perform well using the painting-with-light technique. Long exposures may result in "noise" on the finished photograph. Noise is speckled images created by extended periods of exposure. Some high-end digital cameras are capable of prolonged exposure and may have a feature to decrease noise on the photograph. If a digital camera is used for painting with light, the photographer should act quickly while firing the strobe to decrease the chance of noise in the photograph (Figure 6.7).

FILL-IN FLASH

Many photographs taken in daylight could be improved by using flash as fill-in. Many areas in daylight are in dark shadows (e.g., the underside of a car or the area under the hood) and need fill-in flash to appear on the finished photograph.

It may appear ridiculous, at first glance, to observe a photographer using a flash when taking a picture in bright sunlight. Actually, it is just as sensible as using two or more lights when taking any interior view or a portrait; one is the key light and the other is the fill-in. Working in bright sunlight, the sun is the key light and the flash is the fill-in. It is often desirable to reduce or otherwise change the lighting contrast of a subject in bright sunlight. When the sun casts deep shadows on the subject, it is quite difficult to obtain both the highlight and shadow detail in the image. By filling the shadow areas with a flash, the contrast is reduced to obtain good detail in all parts of the subject and make a much more pleasing picture. Synchro-sunlight is a method of using supplementary illumination synchronized with sunlight for the purpose of obtaining better shadow detail in all types of outdoor photography.

FIGURE 6.7
Difference between photos taken at night with a single flash (top) and painting-with-light technique (bottom).

The outdoor flash can do an excellent job of lighting a difficult shot, if handled properly. It can also produce a crude, overilluminated effect of having been shot at night with a single flash. The challenge is to balance two extremes of exposure on a single image, each in itself providing the correct exposure for the image. These two extremes are the normal daylight exposure for the highlights and the

FIGURE 6.8
Photo showing use of fill-in flash for good contrast.

normal flash exposure to light the shadows. Thus, a flash exposure and a sunlight exposure must be balanced harmoniously during the instant the shutter is open to achieve a pleasant result. Naturally, the ratio between flash and sunlight varies according to subject matter and the particular effect desired. Whether the shadows are to be eliminated or merely subdued must be determined by the photographer, and the flash and sunlight balanced accordingly (Figure 6.8).

EXPOSURE FOR FLASH

The primary consideration when figuring exposure for flash is the distance of the subject from the flash. In daylight photography, the distance between the subject and the camera makes little difference to the exposure; with flash photography, the distance from flash to subject is crucial.

Many electronic flash units have sensors to measure available light on a subject and they adjust the power of the flash illumination automatically. Autoexposure flash units judge the exposure correctly in most cases because most scenes contain a lot of middle tones. Auto flashes are designed to emit enough light so a scene is reproduced as a middle tone. However, not all photographic situations fall into a "normal" flash area. Some scenes are dark whereas others are bright with harsh shadows. It is important for the police photographer not to become overly reliant on automatic-exposure flashes. In the absence of a flash meter, the ability to calculate flash exposures manually for any number of photographic situations is of benefit to the police photographer.

The Inverse Square Law

Because the light created by a flash moves away from the flash source, it seems to dissipate or to disappear. The light from a single flash illuminates a subject 20 feet away only slightly, but at 10 feet the single flash is adequate and at 5 feet it is too bright. Why?

As the flash is moved away from a subject, the light must not only travel farther, but it also must spread out more. A single flash 1 foot from a subject provides a square foot of light, but a flash 2 feet from the same subject provides 4 square feet of light. If the subject being photographed has a surface area of 1 foot, it is plain that it will be illuminated by four times as much light at 1 foot than at 2 feet. This is called the *inverse square law*. Inverse means fraction and square means a number multiplied by itself. An object illuminated at 20 feet is five times as far from the flash as one illuminated 4 feet from a flash. Five squared equals 25; the inverse is 1/25. Therefore, an object 20 feet from the flash receives only 1/25 the light it would at 4 feet, so the photographer must adjust the camera accordingly.

Guide Numbers

Correct exposure for flash is determined with the use of mathematical formulas that have been greatly simplified by the manufacturers of flashbulbs and strobes, who have worked out guide numbers and tables for figuring exposure. For every combination of shutter speed and film speed, there is a guide number that represents the product of the flash-to-subject distance multiplied by the f-stop.

Guide numbers for flash units are often greatly inflated by the makers of these units and must be tested carefully by the photographer and, in many cases, reassigned completely. Frequently, strobes are not working at peak power and do not produce as much light as they should. Here is how to arrive at a guide number for a strobe flash:

1. Set up a subject exactly 10 feet away from the flash. It is suggested that large f-stop numbers written on an 8 × 10-inch gray card be used.
2. Place the camera on a tripod.
3. Attach the strobe unit to the camera in the position used normally.
4. Make a series of exposures at half-stop intervals (e.g., f/5.6, 6.7, 8, 9.5, 11, and so on).

5. Examine each photo image through the digital light-emitting diode screen and select the image with the best exposure.
6. Multiply the f-stop by 10 (the distance used in the test); this is the guide number for the strobe unit. If the picture with f/8 was the best photograph, then 8 × 10 = 80, so 80 is the appropriate guide number.

When the proper guide number has been determined, the flash-to-subject distance can be used to determine the proper f-stop. Divide the guide number by the distance from flash to subject for the correct f-stop. For instance, if the guide number of the flash is 80 and the distance from flash to subject is 20 feet, then 80/20 = 4; f/4 is the correct f-stop.

Exposure for Bounce Flash

Whenever the photographer bounces the flash to provide even light, the flash travels farther than the flash-to-subject distance, and the exposure must be adjusted accordingly. This exposure is determined by adding the flash-to-ceiling distance to the ceiling-to-subject distance, then dividing the guide number by the total two distances, and then increasing the exposure indicated by approximately two f-stops. For instance, if the guide number of the flash is 80 and the distance from the flash to the ceiling is 5 feet and from the ceiling to the subject is 5 feet then 80/10 = 8 plus an increase of two f-stops would indicate f/4 as the proper f-stop. The photographer may wish to "bracket" exposures to make sure a properly illuminated photograph is obtained. In the example, the photographer would make three exposures: one at f/8, one at f/5.6, and one at f/4. Although this is a very useful method, it does require some experience to estimate the distances and reflective ability of the surfaces of the room. Obviously, dark surfaces reflect less light than those painted white, and require additional exposure.

Exposure for Multiple Flash

When automatic-exposure flash units are used for multiple flash, they should be set on manual mode. The sensor on an automatic flash is designed to produce properly exposed pictures, assuming it is the only source of flash.

In multiple-flash photography, one flash is usually used as the main light. The camera exposure is based on the light from the main flash unit. Secondary flash units are used to fill in shadows, illuminate the background, or to add rim lighting to the subject. The light from a secondary flash unit is not as great as that from the main flash unit. Lighting ratios are used to compare the brightness of the main light to the fill light. To calculate the exposure, set the camera lens to the f-stop given by the flash's calculator dial for flash-to-subject distance. The fill flash and any other secondary units are positioned so they illuminate the subject less strongly than the main flash. For example, if the main flash unit is 5 feet from the subject and the exposure is f/11, set the lens aperture to f/11. If fill lighting is to be two f-stops less than the main light source (4:1 ratio), position the fill flash at a distance that produces an f/5.6 exposure. If the fill and main flashes are of equal power, the fill flash distance in this example is 10 feet.

EFFECT OF FLASH ANGLE

With sufficient practice, compact flash units can be used to control the level of detail seen in a photograph. When the flash unit is affixed directly on the hot shoe of the camera, there is a tendency to illuminate the subject of the photograph with direct lighting. Subjects with reflective physical properties such as glass, glossy painted surfaces, or finished wood may exhibit specular reflections when photographed in this way. Also referred to as *hot spots*, this effect in a photograph can result in an overexposure of the image in the center of the photograph, with the periphery of the image darkened. The effect of darkened edges in the photograph is referred to as *vignetting*. Care should be taken when photographing physical evidence in this manner because specular reflections can "wash out" details in the physical evidence (Figure 6.9).

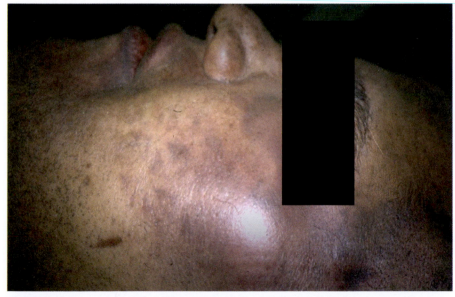

FIGURE 6.9

This photo shows the effects of using direct illumination from a flash unit on a reflective surface. In this case, the victim of an assault had a patterned contusion on his cheek, presumably from footwear. A photograph taken of the pattern with the flash unit attached directly to the hot shoe of the camera resulted in a specular reflection from the cheek, essentially overexposing the patterned abrasion and diminishing its visible detail.

The flash unit can also be attached to the camera via a flash cable accessory. In this manner, the photographer can vary the position of the flash unit in virtually any angle or distance with respect to the evidence. Specular reflections can be avoided by placing the flash unit at an angle of approximately 45° relative to the lens axis. In addition, if the flash unit is positioned at oblique angles to the evidence, the topography of the evidence is emphasized. Textures or patterns present on the physical evidence can be highlighted in this manner (Figures 6.10 and 6.11).

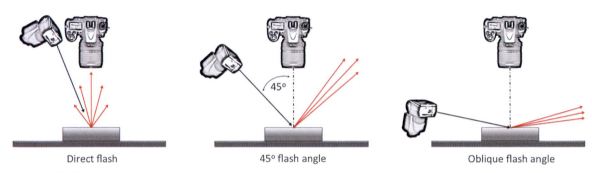

| Direct flash | 45° flash angle | Oblique flash angle |

FIGURE 6.10

This photo illustrates the various flash angles that can be used with an off-camera flash unit. If the flash is positioned next to the camera and is aimed directly at reflective evidence, light may reflect back directly into the camera lens, creating specular reflections in the photograph. Specular reflections are best avoided by positioning the flash unit at a 45° angle relative to the axis of the camera lens. If the flash unit is positioned at an oblique angle relative to the evidence, texture and patterns on the evidence may be enhanced in the image.

FIGURE 6.11

These photos illustrate how patterned impressions can be enhanced simply by varying the angle of an external flash unit. These images are of a footwear impression on sand. The camera was positioned on a tripod over the sand and leveled with the ground using a digital inclinometer. (a) The footwear impression was photographed using ambient light, which revealed some of the tread pattern. (b) The footwear impression was photographed with the flash unit placed on the hot shoe of the camera and aimed directly at the impression. The details of the footwear impression were not recorded in the photograph in this manner. (c) This shot was photographed by holding the flash at an oblique angle with the impression. Because the impression consists of raised and depressed areas, angling the flash low to the ground casts light across the impression, creating highlights and shadows that reveal the tread design of the footwear that formed the impression.

Crime Scene Photography

CONTENTS

ABSTRACT

One of the most important duties of a police photographer is to document a crime scene. Crime scene photographs can be used not only to document the scene as found by police but also to help determine events leading up to, during, and after a crime. They may also aid in solving crimes and obtaining a conviction in court. One useful tool is perspective grid photography. Also known as photogrammetry, perspective grid photography allows measurements of a crime scene area to be measured using a camera. This chapter details the photographic steps to take to capture images dealing with individual crimes such as homicide, suicide, sex offenses, and arson and documenting injuries to victims and suspects.

KEY TERMS

Alligatoring
Arson
Autopsy
Homicide
Perspective grid
Photogrammetry
Reflective ultraviolet photography (RUP)
Sectoring
Sex offenses
Suicide

INTRODUCTION

Photographing the scene of a crime is very important despite whether the case eventually comes to court. In fact, few photographs end up being used in the courtroom. Photographs are not taken for courtroom presentation alone; they help the police in many ways. When a suspect is being questioned, a photograph of the crime scene may be used to refresh his memory. The guilty party may sometimes confess when confronted with relevant photographs. Often, detectives must take a suspect around the city to show him, for instance, the homes that he is suspected of having burglarized. By showing the suspect or suspects different photographs of these scenes, the investigators can save themselves many precious hours and the municipality many dollars. If the case should come to court, the photographs can give both the judge and the jury the best possible idea of the crime scene as it was at the time of the crime.

It is, or should be, general practice for the police to photograph the crime scene immediately after a crime has occurred and before anything has been disturbed or removed. No one should be permitted to touch anything at the scene of a crime before it is photographed.

A GENERAL APPROACH TO PHOTOGRAPHING A CRIME SCENE

There are numerous aspects of a crime scene that need to be documented with images, ranging from large structures to minute pieces of physical evidence. Further, the scene must be photographed in such a manner that evidence items identified at the scene can be related back to specific locations. Each crime scene is different and requires various forms of photographic documentation. A crime scene is also an uncontrolled environment that can pose many challenges to photographers in terms of lighting and equipment needs.

Properly recording the crime scene ultimately occurs through a systematic method of documentation that includes not only photographs but notes and diagrams as well. This is necessary to adequately preserve the scene and the locations where physical evidence was found for future reference.

The goals of crime scene photography are three-fold:

- To record the condition and location of the crime scene.
- To document the original position, location, and condition of physical evidence within the crime scene.
- To document the details of physical evidence.

These goals can be accomplished by taking a series of photographs that are referred to as *establishing photographs*, *midrange photographs*, and *close-up photographs*. These series of images should be the standard regimen for any photographic crime scene documentation, regardless of the nature of the case. Establishing, midrange, and close-up photographs should create somewhat of a visual funnel effect for any one piece of evidence, where each photograph takes the viewer from an expanded view of the crime scene progressively closer to the evidence item being highlighted in an image. In this way individuals who were not present at the crime scene, such as investigators, attorneys, or jury members, can obtain a clear understanding of where a particular piece of evidence was located within the crime scene from a review of the photographs (Figure 7.1).

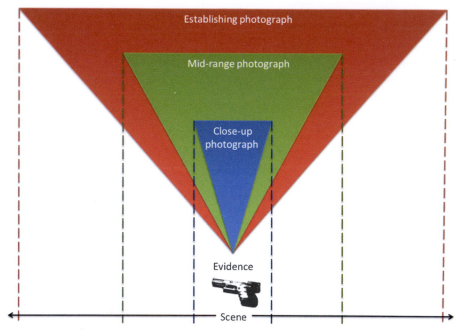

FIGURE 7.1

A series of establishing, mid-range, and close-up photographs should create a visual "funnel effect" for any one piece of evidence. These photographs should take the viewer from an expanded view of the crime scene progressively closer to the evidence item. This photographic documentation technique serves to preserve the context between evidence and the overall crime scene.

Establishing Photographs

The term "establishing photography" is derived from the film industry term "establishing shot," which refers to cinematography sequences that provide the viewer with a "feel for the scene" or indicate the location where the scene is taking place. This concept is not too far from the purpose of establishing photographs in crime scene documentation. Establishing photography, or "overall" photographs, are images that serve to capture wide-angle views of the scene that document the location, surroundings, and boundaries as well as the overall conditions of the scene. In the case of an outdoor crime scene, establishing photographs typically include images that relate the location of the crime scene to nearby roads, landmarks, or street signs. Areas that define the boundaries or perimeter of the established crime scene should also be included. If the crime scene is contained within a residence, photographs that identify the address and location of the scene should be taken. Establishing photographs of an indoor crime scene include wide-angle floor-to-ceiling photographs of each room in the residence. In addition to a wide-angle perspective, a series of establishing photographs should include some degree of overlap, as if to generate a panoramic effect. Establishing photographs can be achieved with the use of fixed wide-angle lenses or wide-angle zoom lenses.

Midrange Photographs

In addition to recording the general or overall appearance of the crime scene, photographs that depict the location, position, and conditions of physical evidence are required. In these instances a series of photographs can be used to not only preserve the appearance of physical evidence at the time of its discovery but also provide its context, that is, the location and position of the evidence as they relate to the overall crime scene. This is achieved through the use of *midrange photographs*.

The goal of a midrange photograph is to capture an item of evidence and its immediate surroundings in a manner that the evidence is in clear view, yet enough of the surroundings are present in the photograph such that the location of the evidence can be identified in an establishing photograph of the scene. These photographs aid in avoiding issues that may arise when only close-up images of physical evidence are taken coupled with establishing photographs. There is often not enough reference points in a close-up photograph to relate it to an overall depiction of the scene, resulting in a loss of visual context between the scene and evidence item.

Evidence is identified either within a scene or on the victim, so midrange photographs should be taken to establish a spatial relationship between the item of evidence and its immediate surroundings. A good midrange photograph should include the item of evidence and at least three additional points of reference in the field of view (landmarks, anatomic landmarks, field markers, furniture, etc.). Initial midrange photographs should not include any photographic scales because these images ought to depict the evidence in its original state without obstructing any surrounding areas or items. Once these photographs are taken, midrange photographs should be repeated with reference scales and evidence markers in place so that the item of interest can be clearly identified and distinguished from other items in the photograph.

Midrange photographs can be taken with the use of a "normal" lens or a wide-angle zoom lens. Using a wide-angle zoom lens such as an 18–55- or 28–85-mm lens that covers the normal range of focal lengths is very practical for taking both establishing and midrange photographs in quick sequence.

Close-up Photographs

Close-up photographs are used to document the detail and condition of specific physical evidence items. Examples may include the following findings:

- Hair and blood under the fingernails of a decedent
- Injuries on a decedent such as stab wounds, stippling from gunshot wounds, gunshot entry wounds, and ligature marks or other patterned injuries
- Patterned impression evidence
- Footwear patterns

- Fingerprints
- Ballistics evidence such as shell casings, bullets, bullet impact marks, and bullet holes
- Details of weapons such as knives and firearms found at the scene
- Bloodstains

Close-up photographs of evidence must be taken so that the area of interest fills as much of the frame of the photograph as possible, leaving enough space on two axes for the placement of a right-angle scale or two perpendicularly oriented straight scales. A reference scale should be present in all close-up photographs of evidence. Close-up photographs can be taken using a normal lens with a fixed focal length or a wide-angle zoom lens set to a normal focal length or higher. If the close-up image is taken for the purpose of comparison to a known object (examination-quality photograph) a macro lens with a fixed focal length should be used to minimize optical distortion (Figure 7.2).

SECTORING

At times, evidence such as pattern of bloodstains across a wall or indentation evidence across the side of a vehicle is distributed over a large area. The distribution of these patterns often needs to be photographed as a whole and coupled with photographs detailing the individual aspects of the pattern. In the case of bloodstain patterns, the appearance of the overall pattern can be just as important in determining the mechanism that gave rise to the pattern as the appearance of stains from the individual droplet within the overall pattern. Because of this, the evidence must be photographed in a way that the details within a pattern can be related back to the overall pattern.

One way to achieve this is by using the sector method, or sectoring. *Sectoring* is achieved by dividing a large area into zones (or sectors) so that both the overall pattern and the fine detail can be captured. A combination of both establishing and midrange/close-up photographs can then be taken in a manner that relates all the sectors. When documenting pattern evidence it is important to remember that scales should be placed in the same plane as the evidence. Also, photographs must be taken perpendicular to the evidence and scale (i.e., the plane of the camera sensor must be parallel to the plane the evidence is on). This is necessary to reduce any photographic distortion that would prevent comparisons made with the use of the photograph or extrapolating any measurement information from the photograph. To achieve this likely requires the use of both a tripod and an inclinometer.

FIGURE 7.2

An example of establishing (a), mid-range (b) and close-up (c) photographs detailing the position of a knife within a scene.

PERSPECTIVE GRID PHOTOGRAPHS

Crime scenes can be accurately measured using photographs (sometimes called photogrammetry). As long as a square or rectangle of known size is included in a photograph of a flat surface (such as road pavement or indoor crime scenes), measurements of every object appearing in the photograph can be made and a scale map or sketch can be prepared from the photograph. A square or rectangle can be made in advance (perspective grid) using a 1- or 2-foot^2 sheet of heavy cardboard or photo mat.

When using a perspective grid, position it so that the bottom edge of the grid is along the lower edge of the photographic field of view. The camera may be elevated somewhat to improve the accuracy of the grid measurements. In general, the higher the camera elevation, the more accurate the measurements will be. The focal length of the camera lens has no appreciable effect on the accuracy of measurements, so a wide-angle lens can be used (see Figure 7.3). Inaccuracy usually occurs when the surface is not flat. Surfaces (such as roadways) can slant and still be flat. Avoid uneven areas, particularly outdoor fields and indoor stairwells.

If a single photograph cannot show the entire area to be measured and mapped, two or more overlapping photos can be made, relocating the perspective grid for each photo. The individual maps are made and combined into a single final sketch.

There are a number of computer programs and applications (apps) that can assist the photographer in making measurements and sketches from photographs. PhotoModeler (www.photomodeler.com) is one such program; it allows diagrams of traffic accident and crime scenes to be prepared from photographs. This program can also provide detailed measurements from photographs. Magic Plan CSI is an app for tablets and smart phones.

HOMICIDE INVESTIGATIONS

One of the most difficult jobs that a police photographer may have is photographing a homicide. Most police photographers spend many hours learning how to photograph a homicide, yet have the good fortune throughout their careers of never having to put their learning to use. Others may have to do this job only once or twice, and though they have had little practice, they must carry out their task to the fullest extent of their training, talent, and intelligence.

The material below discusses the major points that should be stressed when covering a homicide; each angle mentioned should be photographed carefully. The photographer can use his or her discretion in taking any additional shots it is felt may help to solve a case. One should consider that these photographs cannot be taken again.

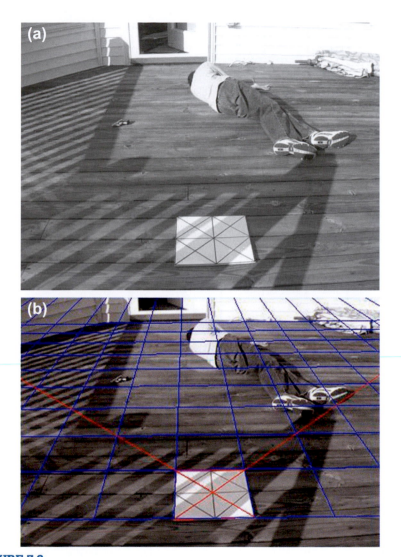

FIGURE 7.3

Perspective grid photography. (a) A rectangle or square (usually 1 or 2 ft) is prepared and placed in the photograph. (b) Extend the rear and far edges of the grid to rise beyond the left, right, and top edges of the photograph. Continue drawing lines to these "vanishing points" until the rows of "squares" cover the photograph area to be mapped.

In all murder cases it is essential that the photographer arrive at the scene as soon as possible. Nothing should be moved or any search made at the scene of a homicide until all photographs that accurately record the scene have been taken. On occasion, it is necessary for the medical examiner or coroner to examine the victim to verify death, but it usually is not necessary to move the body for this purpose.

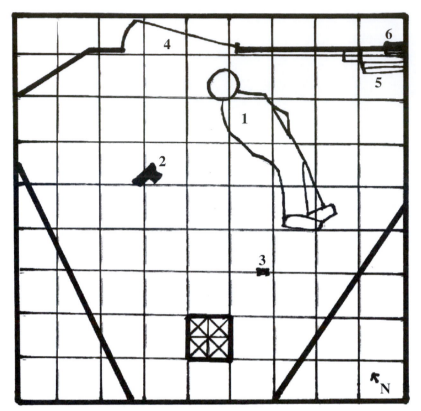

FIGURE 7.3   Cont'd
(c) Prepare an orthogonal grid map from the photograph. The two angular lines appearing on the sketch indicate the camera's angle of view. This example shows 1-ft squares.

Full coverage of the crime scene must be photographed, showing the body in relation to the other objects at the scene. If outdoors, several shots from different angles and an overhead shot of the body (Figure 7.4) and the weapon or instrument are usually sufficient, but any footprints, tire marks, or other marks that could assist in tracing the person responsible must be photographed as well. As has often been stated, it is better to take too many photographs than too few; this is especially true in a murder investigation; the photographer will not have another opportunity to return to the scene and take additional pictures.

Sometimes it is necessary to photograph injuries on the accused as well as on the victim; these injuries, as a rule, amount to scratches or other signs that indicate that the victim attempted to defend him or herself. Since the accused may be in custody and charged with the offense, the photographer can make arrangements to obtain the necessary pictures.

FIGURE 7.4

Taking an overhead shot of a victim.

The same photographs will be required if the crime scene is indoors, but the photographer may be handicapped by the size of the room and furniture or other objects that cannot be moved. These disadvantages can be overcome by using a camera arranged to take photographs from directly overhead. A fairly small camera, for example, a special camera with a wide-angle lens, can be adapted for use in this way. A long boom attached to the camera tripod, with the camera fixed on the end, is steadied against the ceiling; the exposure is made either by means of a long cable release or a remote-controlled shutter release. Some professional photographers use rubber grips to attach the camera to the ceiling, and others have obtained the same results with a clamp and a suitable attachment to a lighting fixture in the center of a room. Whatever method is used to obtain overhead photographs, the lighting that gives the best results without harsh shadows or "hot spots" is a flash bounced against the ceiling that acts as a large diffusing reflector. These overhead cameras are the only satisfactory means of photographing bodies in such places as elevator shafts, small bathrooms, and other small areas.

Having covered the scene, it is necessary to photograph anything that has any bearing whatsoever on the crime, such as blood spatter, signs of struggle, or indications of alcohol or drugs. Any mark of any kind should be recorded: a man once was identified by teeth marks on an apple he had bitten into at the scene of the crime. All outstanding peculiarities should be recorded, as in the case of a man who took off his shoes and socks so that he could use his feet to trigger a shotgun, the barrel of which he placed in his mouth.

Any signs of entry or exit must be recorded, as well as any fingerprints left at the scene. Because all of these photographs have to be taken before the investigating officers can search the scene or move the body, it is obvious that the photographer must work quickly. This can be done only if he has suitable equipment maintained in excellent condition and an adequate strobe unit for flash photography.

The first person to arrive at the scene of a homicide has the responsibility of determining whether the victim is dead. This is the only exception to the rule that nothing be touched. To ascertain whether the victim is actually dead, the officer should observe carefully whether the victim is breathing and then should feel for a pulse at either the neck or wrist. While doing this the officer should touch the body as little as possible and try not to move it out of the position in which it was found. The first duty of the police officer is to protect life and property. If there are any signs of life, first aid should be administered and the person should be taken to the nearest hospital.

If there is no sign of life in the victim, the police photographer should ask, "What will I have to photograph now so that I can convince a jury that this is the way the scene actually appeared?" All the officers at the scene should be instructed not to touch anything until the series of pictures is taken. The photographer should keep in mind that an important objective of these photographs is to accurately convey to other investigators and persons how and where this crime was committed.

Not all homicide cases will end up in court, but those that do require good photos from which courtroom presentations can be made. A Chicago detective, giving a talk on homicide photography at a convention, once stated, "On arriving at the scene of a homicide, always keep your hands in your pockets and survey the situation for at least ten or fifteen minutes. Figure out all the possible angles you would need and then begin taking your photographs." The photographer may not be given that much time to compose the work, but the basic idea of patience and thought before photographing should be kept in mind.

After taking photographs at the scene, the police photographer should attend the postmortem examination of the victim and take photographs as directed by the pathologist (see Figure 7.5). It is useful at this time to take photographs of the fully clothed body before it is stripped for autopsy. Prints of all the photographs will be required without delay by the investigating officers, particularly photographs of any fingerprints that may have been found. A number of copies of these are required so that a search can be made, and copies also are needed to send to other law enforcement agencies. Other prints are required for the purpose of house-to-house inquiries or for showing on television. All these requirements must be met by the police photographer with as little delay as possible, and the photographer should therefore standardize procedures and have ample assistance available to do so. This is one area where digital photographs are helpful, as prints may be produced from an inkjet printer very quickly. Photographs can also be sent to other agencies as an attachment in emails.

The police photographer may also have to take photographs during postmortem examinations in cases of death other than murder, including street accidents, accidents in the home, industrial accidents, suicides, drownings, and so on; also, cases in which an inquest must be held are instances in which photographs are taken during a postmortem examination. The photographs are usually required by the coroner at the inquest, although in some instances where there are proceedings either in civil or criminal courts, the photographer may be called on to give evidence.

An electronic flash can be used to light these photographs. An electronic flash that can be held away from the camera can direct the light in any direction, as needed.

In cases of serious assault, a charge of robbery, wounding, or causing grievous bodily harm usually follows. Photographs in these cases are required to show

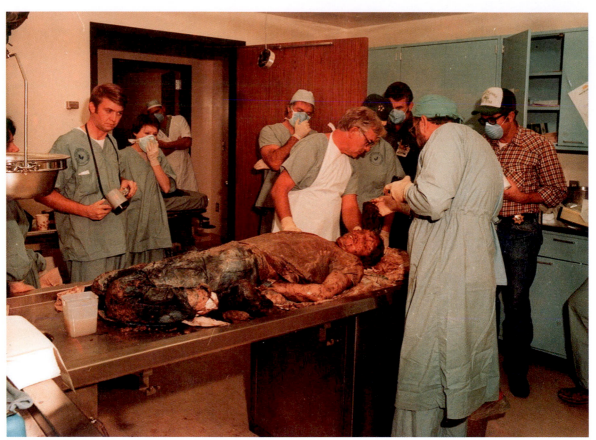

FIGURE 7.5
Photographing an autopsy.

the extent of the victim's injuries so the court can assess the violence of the assault. The hearing of the case may occur weeks or even months after the assault, and during that time the victim usually has recovered from the attack and (if they are fortunate) the marks from the injuries have healed. Without photographs it would be difficult for any court to realize from only a medical description the extent of the injuries. For this reason, arrangements must be made by the photographer to obtain photographs of the injuries. If the injured person is able to travel, is merely bruised, or has no wound covered with dressings, then perhaps the best way to obtain the photographs is to bring the injured person to a laboratory and take the photographs there. Remember that bruises are more apparent at about 24 h after an assault, and it is better to wait for a period of time to allow the bruising to develop than to take the photographs too soon after the occurrence of the assault. In addition, the victim is usually in a state of shock immediately following an assault, and a delay usually produces a more cooperative subject.

Wounds may have to be treated by a doctor as soon as possible and, of course, may be covered with dressings. There is no point in photographing any person covered with bandages because, however incapacitated the person may appear, there may be very little injury, if any, under the bandages.

The photographer should not, in any event, remove any dressings to obtain a photograph. If it is necessary to obtain photographs of wounds, this must be done by arrangement with, and in the presence of, a doctor. A telephone call will reveal when the doctor has directed that the dressing should be changed. There is normally no objection to the photographer being present when this is done so the necessary photographs can be obtained. Doctors are helpful in instances such as this because the photographs are useful to them when they appear in court to give medical testimony with respect to the wound or wounds.

Many victims with wounds are kept in the hospital, and the photographer is asked to work quickly to cause the patient as little discomfort as possible and to avoid the risk of infection. The same equipment as that suggested for use at postmortem examinations is ideal for this kind of photography. In these cases it is generally only necessary to show the extent of the wounds, so the photographer may need to take only a few pictures. The photographer should be guided by the doctor in this case.

How to Photograph a Homicide Scene

The police photographer is always under a great deal of pressure from the coroner and others at a homicide scene. They may wish to rush the body to the morgue. The police photographer must not allow these pressures to interfere with the work. Later, these same people will want photographs that were taken properly. Views should be taken of the entire scene, showing the location of the body and its position in relation to its surroundings. To photograph a homicide:

1. Start by taking an overhead shot of the victim. Try to get as high above the victim as you possibly can for this shot. You may have to improvise. If you can obtain a stepladder, that will suffice. Stand as high as you can on it, then shoot straight down on the subject and try to avoid shooting from any angle other than vertical (see Figure 7.6). A shot from an angle or a long shot of the subject will be distorted.

2. If the body is in such a position that you can circle it, your first shot should be from the head to the feet, then go clockwise to the subject's right arm and take another shot. Then move down below the subject's feet and take a shot from the feet-to-head position. For your last clockwise shot, move to the subject's left arm and take a picture from that angle. If this scene is outdoors you should have no problem taking these shots because you will easily have enough room to operate. But

FIGURE 7.6
Overhead shot, indoors.

you may find that most homicides are committed indoors, where you will have a limited amount of space in which to work. Be sure to document where photographs were taken on the crime scene sketch (see Figure 7.7).

3. After you have taken shots of the general scene and shown the location of the body in relation to its surroundings, begin to take close-up shots of the body and its immediate surroundings. In step two, you took photographs of the general views and the full-length shots of the body. Now move in closer, taking pictures of the head, body, arms, hands, legs,

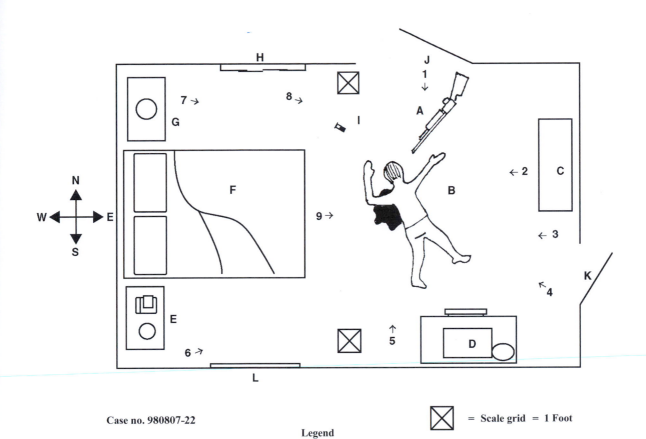

Case no. 980807-22

⊠ = Scale grid = 1 Foot

Legend

1–9	Photo positions. Photos 4 & 9 overhead shots.
A	Shotgun.
B	Body, face down position.
C	Chest.
D	Desk with chair.
E	Right bedside table with phone & lamp.
F	Bed.
G	Left bedside table with lamp.
H	Closet, sliding doors.
I	Spent shotgun shell
J	Doorway to hall.
K	Doorway to bathroom.
L	Window.

FIGURE 7.7
Crime scene sketch showing the position of the camera for each photograph.

and feet. Be sure to take specific photographs of the wound marks (see Figure 7.8). These can be very important photographs for the police later on in the courtroom.

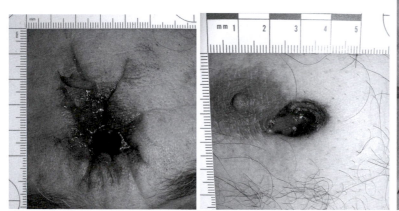 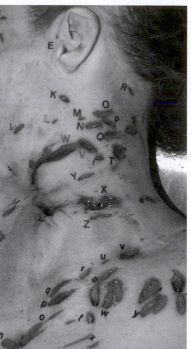

FIGURE 7.8
Close-up photographs of gunshot and stab wounds.

4. If a gun was used in the homicide, be sure to take photographs of any bullet holes in the furniture, walls, floors, or any other place where the bullet might have landed (Figure 7.9). Always take close-ups of the bullet hole itself.

5. Next, look around the vicinity of the crime; if you find any weapons, objects, or instruments that were used to perpetrate the crime, be sure to take close-up shots of all of them.

6. If it is possible, use a tripod to take all of these shots. This is a good example of shooting to get fine detail in your photograph, so try to take these photographs at f/16 or f/22. The speed can be obtained from your light meter reading, or use the aperture priority mode so the camera can automatically make the appropriate speed adjustment. If you are using a tripod, you can use any speed, depending on what your light meter calls for.

7. After you have taken the above shots and before the body is removed, you should mark the outline of the body and any other objects that are related to the crime. When this is completed the body can be removed. After the body is removed, begin taking again all the shots that you took before the body was removed. One of the major reasons for this is

FIGURE 7.9
Homicide details (clockwise). (a) Bullet hole in a door, (b) unmoved weapon, (c) the place from which the weapon was taken, and (d) a close-up of the weapon.

that once the body is gone, there is less confusion at the scene. Second, repeating the same shots with the marked image insures one good photo out of two shots of the same scene. Show the marked outline of the body in relation to the furniture if indoors or to other objects if outdoors.

8. Be sure to photograph the entire inside of a home. If the murder happened upstairs in a bedroom, photograph all other rooms upstairs, especially those adjacent to the crime scene. Be sure to photograph every ingress and egress to the homicide scene. The best shots that you can take of a room are usually those taken from the corners of the room. Take at least one photograph from each corner of the room. Be sure to include a perspective grid or similar measuring device in the photographs.

9. If the crime happened in a bathroom, which may be rather small, put a wide-angle lens on your camera and shoot with it. This is a good example of a situation in which you will probably have to shoot at f/22 or f/32. Remember also that if you have to use flash in the bathroom scene, you may have to put a handkerchief or two over your flash unit because bathroom tile and fixtures reflect a great amount of light.

10. The next step is to photograph anything that might have fingerprints on it. If the objects are movable and you can take them into the crime laboratory, it is much better for the fingerprint specialist to photograph the object in the lab because a better job can be performed there than at the scene. If it is impossible to bring the object into the laboratory, however, you will have to photograph fingerprints or any other evidence at the scene of the crime.

11. In a clockwise fashion, photograph the exterior of the building, usually from distances of about 75–100 feet away. Start with a shot of the driveway and front of the house, and move in a clockwise fashion, photographing views from each side of the house. Include a view of any backyard or garage. Be sure to show all possible entrances and exits that the perpetrator may have used.

12. Take photographs showing the landscaping, shrubbery, fences, buildings, and all surrounding homes to show what kind of a neighborhood it is.

13. Take some shots from the front of the house looking down the streets from both sides of the home. Of course, you should include the driveway and all other routes of access to the home.

14. Take some shots from the rear of the house, showing all possible ways the intruder may have entered the house from the rear, and go out to the next street.

15. If this develops into an important case, aerial photographs can be taken later, showing the house where the homicide occurred and its surroundings.

The homicide may have been committed in a small room. Always treat the small room as you would a bathroom and use a wide-angle lens. The courts usually admit wide-angle pictures of room interiors because they often provide photographs that cannot be obtained in any other way. Be sure to draw sketches as you work to show exactly where you were when each of the photographs was taken. Perspective grid sketches are particularly helpful to show camera positions, especially if the grid is placed in the same location in front of the camera for each shot.

Lighting for a Homicide Scene

Achieving proper lighting is the biggest challenge facing police photographers. Unlike a professional studio photographer, who has a relatively fixed lighting arrangement, a police photographer frequently works outdoors at night where a flash does not provide enough light. Indoor photography, day or night, is easy by comparison.

There are several ways to attack the problem of lighting for outdoor photography at night. The photographer can:

1. "Paint with light."
2. Use a large strobe unit.
3. Use three or more strobe units as slave units. The strobes may be connected with cords to the main strobe, or they can be rigged with slave attachments.
4. Use photoflood where house current is available. The type of light bars that video cameras use can be set on tripods or improvised stands and aimed at the subject. Be sure to check the white balance on the camera if using artificial light other than an electronic flash.
5. Bracket shots at different exposures and use high dynamic range processing in Photoshop or other software program (see Chapter 12).

The photographer should practice shooting outdoors at night and keep a record of everything photographed so that when he or she must actually photograph a scene, a record of what was done correctly or incorrectly can be referred to.

Homicide Photography Summary

When photographing the scene of a homicide, the photographer should reproduce what his eyes are seeing and relate this to other people. The photographer has to show the manner in which the homicide occurred, views of the room with the body in it, all the rooms surrounding the crime scene, and all routes of ingress to and egress from the crime scene. The photographer must show whether there is any evidence of a struggle and try to show what was happening in the room before the crime. Obvious evidence such as drinking glasses and bottles and any trace evidence such as cigarette butts, blood, or broken glass should be noted.

Also, take direction from the investigators on the scene, who may have noticed things of possible importance that should be photographed. The circumstances of death can be illustrated by various views of the body, including close-up shots of the wounds and bruise marks. Finally, the photographer must photograph the weapon and the place from which it may have been taken.

SUICIDE SCENE

The investigator often determines whether the act is a suicide, a homicide, or an accident. Of the many investigations to be performed by the police, one of the most difficult is a suicide. Suicide victims typically wound themselves with a knife in the throat, wrist, or heart region, or with a gunshot through the temple, forehead, center of the back of the head, mouth, chest, or abdomen. Although some wounds, such as a knife wound in the back or cuts on the palm of the hand, tend to suggest a crime other than suicide, neither the position and depth of the wound nor the seeming difficulty of self-infliction should exclude suicide as an explanation.

How to Photograph a Suicide Scene

If there is any doubt as to whether a death may be a result of suicide, the scene should be photographed in the same manner as a homicide. It may not be determined until several days, weeks, or months later whether it was a suicide; if the case should turn out to be a homicide, you will have photographs. A good rule is to treat every death investigation as if it were a homicide.

Suicide by Shooting

Photograph both the entrance and exit wounds. Place identification alongside each wound as well as a ruler for measuring. The entrance wound is almost always larger than the diameter of the bullet. In close and near contact wounds, the hairs surrounding the entrance wound usually will be singed and the skin will be burned to a reddish- or a grayish-brown color. Also, if the shot was fired from a range of less than 8 inches, a smeary black coat of powder residue may be evident. If possible, photograph close-ups of the wound to show these various discolorations (Figure 7.10). If the victim was shot through clothing, infrared photography (see Chapter 10) may record a better pattern image.

Suicide by Hanging

Strangulation by hanging is a common form of suicide. However, the investigator must not assume that a victim found hanging committed suicide. Auto-erotic deaths may be unintentionally self-inflicted.

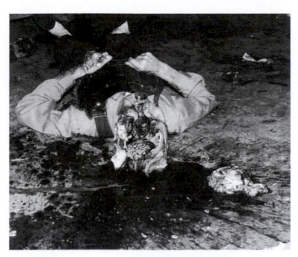

FIGURE 7.10
Suicide by shooting.

Photograph the subject at a distance from four views, showing the full body. Then move in close and show the knot, bruise marks, and the discoloration of the body (Figure 7.11).

Suicide Scene Photographs Summary

A suicide case should be photographed as though it were a homicide, but the photographer should not assume that it is one or the other. Careful work is important because, should the death be determined a suicide, the victim's insurance company may need to see photographs of the deceased before settling a claim.

SEX OFFENSES

The crime of rape may be taken as typical of the class of sex offenses. The purpose of the photographic subjects listed below is to offer useful information related to signs of any struggle; indications of the victim's efforts to resist, such as bruises; and evidence of the presence of either or both parties at the scene.

Scene of the Crime

A photo of the locale itself may be important to show that the cries of the victim could not be heard or to illustrate the fact that the nature of the place would make it an unlikely meeting place for ordinary social purposes. Photographs that show the remoteness of the scene from general traffic or from the nearest dwelling may be useful. Four views diagonal to the purported scene

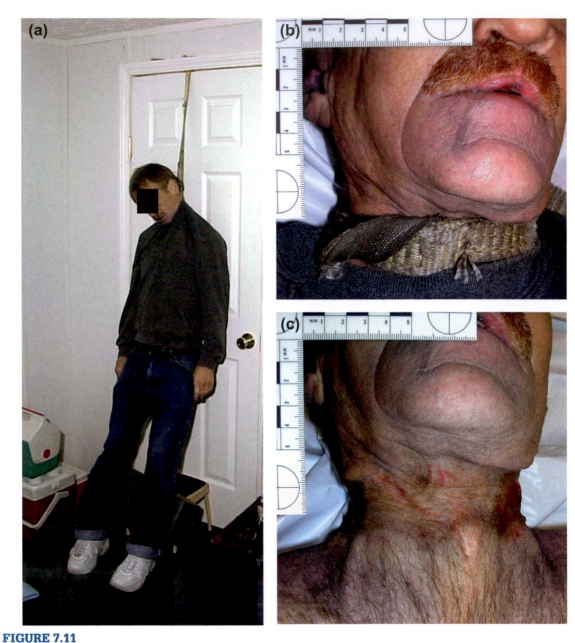

FIGURE 7.11
Hanging death showing position of the body at the scene (a), close-up of the knot (b), and neck injury (c).

of the crime should be taken. A single photograph in a case like this may be misleading. For example, a view of the scene may show it as a desolate and uncivilized area, while a slight change in the position of the camera may show that the spot is very near another dwelling.

Positioning the camera at an improper height above the ground may also create misleading photographs. For example, suppose the scene of an alleged sexual offense is a deep hollow in a park; if the camera is placed close to the ground near the brink of the hollow, the resulting photograph will create the impression that no hollow exists. This is because the farther bank blends with the nearer bank, creating the impression of level ground. The proper way to take such a picture is to raise the camera sufficiently to include both the hollow and its nearer and farther banks. From this level, a correct view of the surroundings is obtained.

Photographs of stains or marks should also be taken at the scene of the crime. When photographing blood stains, it is permissible to use contrast filters and/or illumination from an alternate light source. Selecting the proper filter often enables the photographer to bring out marks that are practically invisible to the naked eye, particularly if used in conjunction with illumination from an alternate light source. After the stains have been photographed, specimens should be carefully preserved for submission to the medical doctor or other specialist whose duty it is to identify them and prepare photomicrographs for use as evidence.

Additional shots of special features such as foot and tire impressions; broken branches; buttons; torn clothing or other personal property; used matches and books of matches; disturbances to rocks, foliage, and other natural features; and displacement of objects from their normal positions should be taken.

An indoor crime scene may also contain evidence of a struggle, which should be photographed. Fingerprints, if found, should be photographed with a fingerprint camera, macro lens, or close-up lens attachments.

Photographs of the Suspect

An examination of a suspect by a physician and the assigned investigator may reveal evidence that links the suspect to the scene. It is desirable to photograph such evidence in the position in which it is found. The suspect's body may show evidence of a physical struggle, such as scratches or bruises. Foreign hairs, pollen granules, or fibers may be discovered by the physician. The garments of the suspect may reveal blood, semen, or traces of grass stains or mud. Because semen fluoresces, it may be shown more easily by ultraviolet photography and/or illumination by an alternate light source. Trouser cuffs, pockets, or folds in clothing may contain weed seeds or soil. Similarly, if the crime occurred indoors, materials peculiar to the premises may be found on the suspect's person or clothing. Identifying marks on the suspect's body, such as tattoos, scars, and other features that may support the victim's description of the perpetrator, should also be photographed. When photographing physical evidence, include a data sheet and a ruler.

Photographs of the Victim

Evidence of resistance to the criminal act may be particularly important in sex offense cases involving adult victims. Thus, marks and discolorations of the body in general; the condition of specifically affected parts of the body; and the presence of foreign hairs, fibers, and biological fluids are significant. Traces associating the victim with the crime scene, such as those described in the preceding section, are also important in some cases to corroborate the victim's account of the occurrence. Permission from the victim or from the parents or guardian if the victim is a minor, preferably in writing, ordinarily is obtained before photographing the person of the victim. It is recommended that the victim's physician, a forensic nurse, or a sexual assault nurse examiner be present when such photographs are taken.

In child physical and sexual abuse cases, photographs should always be made of the victim's injuries. Child Protective Services social workers may also request such photographs in their investigations of child abuse. Such photographs are usually made at a hospital or Department of Social Services offices. If parents are suspected of causing the injuries to their child, social services workers are empowered to take emergency legal custody of the child and can provide legal permission for photographs to be taken by a police photographer. Bruises, lacerations, and especially bite marks, should be photographed with a small scale or ruler in the photograph. Including a scale will enable forensic odontologists and pathologists to accurately match the perpetrator's teeth or the instrument that caused the injury. In addition, at least one photograph of the injury should include an 18% grayscale card. With digital photographs, injuries can be made to look worse than they really are by manipulating contrast and brightness using Adobe Photoshop. Including a grayscale card will ensure that the injuries, especially bruises, are rendered in their proper colors (Figure 7.12).

One photographic technique, reflective ultraviolet photography, has been used by dermatologists during examinations to detect cancer and fungi growth on skin. This technique can also be used to document injuries on skin up to 9 months after they have visibly healed (Aaron, 1991). Reflective ultraviolet photography can be useful in child abuse and assault cases if injuries have faded or disappeared visually (see Figure 7.13). This technique is discussed more fully in Chapter 10.

Another technique involves a feature found in Adobe Photoshop called infrared filter. Photoshop uses a complex algorithm to convert color digital images into black and white images that emulates near-infrared photography. While not a true infrared photograph, anything red in the photo will appear much darker, which makes it ideal to enhance bruises and lacerations on a victim (see Figure 7.14).

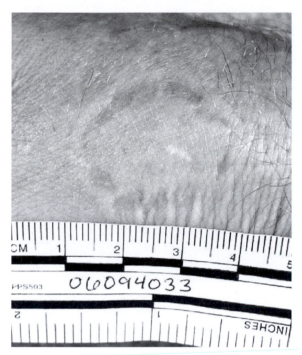

FIGURE 7.12
Bite marks should be photographed with a scale or ruler.

BURGLARY AND BREAKING AND ENTERING

The burglary investigator should always try to take photographs with the thought of how the pictures will help to prove that the suspect was the one who committed the crime. However, most of the pictures of a burglary will be used mainly to assist a detective in solving the case. Rather than take a suspect around the city to show him some of the homes that were broken into to refresh his memory, detectives can show him photographs to help him recall whether he was involved in any of those burglaries. A good set of burglary photographs can save the detective a great deal of work and time.

Photographs also are necessary for the prosecutor's office to successfully argue a case. Many cases are lost because the prosecutor does not have the right kind of evidence to use in court. The prosecutor's objective is to show that a particular crime was committed and that the accused perpetrated the crime. The prosecutor must establish the elements of the offense and produce evidence associating the defendant with the crime scene and events. Photographs can help establish these elements.

For example, in a burglary, the elements of breaking and entering would suggest photographs of the exterior of the building with close-ups of a window

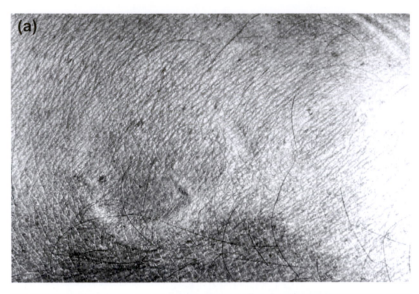

FIGURE 7.13
(a) Injury revealed by reflective ultraviolet photography and (b) photograph of the buckle that caused the injury.

showing where it was "jimmied" open. Views of a ransacked room or a rifled safe would aid in showing the intent of larceny. Photographs of footprints and fingerprints could link the suspect to the scene (see Chapters 9 and 11).

Photographing a Burglary

It is up to the officer taking the pictures to decide how many to take. For a routine burglary, usually six to eight shots should suffice. In planning a series of photographs, the elements of the offense can dictate the type and number of photographs

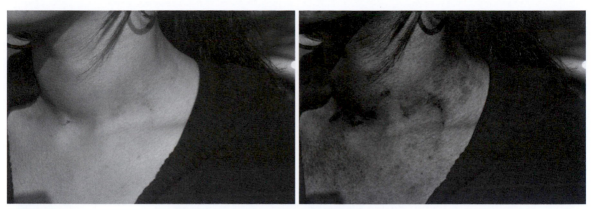

FIGURE 7.14
Visualization of neck injuries to victim enhanced using Adobe Photoshop infrared filter.

to be taken. When photographing a burglary the photographer should include (at least) the following shots in the set, photographing in color if possible.

1. The exterior of the building in which the burglary occurred.
2. The point of entry. Just as in the homicide case, begin with a distant shot, working in to get close-up shots to show the forcible entry (see Figure 7.15). Many times the house or building must be examined carefully to find how the criminal entered. Look in the window wells of the basement and check all doors, windows, and other openings (Figure 7.16).
3. Each room in the house or building that is disturbed should be photographed. Use a wide-angle lens, if available. Take shots from all four corners of the rooms that were ransacked. Usually two pictures, one from each diagonal corner, suffice in a burglary case.
4. Take shots of all furniture or items that show evidence of being disturbed. If the articles cannot be taken to the laboratory, then photograph each article at the scene. The lab technician will check each article taken to the lab for fingerprints and will photograph each article. When this is done, be sure to identify it's origin, the date, and your name on each item. Get in the habit of identifying any item you are working on.
5. If you can determine how the criminal left the house, photograph the exit.
6. When a burglar is in a house, many times he will be surprised by someone. In his haste to leave the house he may leave something behind, such as a hat, gloves, scarf, cigarette butts, or burned matches. Most of these articles are usually found at the scene and should be photographed.
7. All available physical evidence, such as fingerprints, footprints, tire prints, heel prints, and tool marks and tools, should be photographed.

FIGURE 7.15
Interior (right) and exterior (left) views of a point of entry.

8. If the merchandise that was stolen is recovered, it should be photographed. If any merchandise is recovered later from the suspect's home or apartment, it should be photographed where it was recovered.

9. Ask the victim whether any photographs of the property that was stolen exist. Often, people will photograph items of value for insurance purposes or may have family photos showing the stolen items in the picture. These are helpful in describing stolen property and also attest to the fact that the article was in the possession of the victim.

ARSON SCENE INVESTIGATION

Arson is probably the most difficult crime to identify and prosecute because the evidence, especially the materials used by the arsonist, are usually destroyed by

FIGURE 7.16
Close-up showing "jimmy marks" on a window.

the fire. A photographer should go to the scene of every fire. He should be one of the first persons to arrive at the scene so that photographs of the scene may begin before the arrival of fire trucks. All photographic equipment should be ready and photographs should be taken immediately. The entire progression of the fire should be photographed, taking factual pictures and leaving the sensational photographs for the news media.

How to Photograph a Fire in Progress

One of the best methods of taking photographs of fires is from a distance, with a camera that is equipped with a telephoto lens. The use of a telephoto lens avoids emphasizing one part of the fire over another. Pictures taken from a distance with a telephoto lens often reveal important details that would seem insignificant in a picture taken at close range. Also, the smoke does not fog a telephoto lens at a distance.

As a rule, conditions will not be ideal. Look over the entire scene and try to identify the best position for photographing (preferably a high position). With the availability of large snorkel ladder trucks, the photographer may be able to shoot the scene from above.

While the fire is burning, be sure to photograph as many of the spectators as you can. Most arsonists get satisfaction from watching the fires they started and

FIGURE 7.17
Photographs taken with a telephoto lens showing suspicious action in the vicinity of a fire.

they may be in the crowd. If you photograph all the spectators of a fire, and print them so that most of the people are recognizable, you can compare the photographs of one fire with another. A particular spectator noticed at many of the fires being investigated might indicate a suspect whom you could question to further investigate whether he is an arsonist (Figure 7.17).

After the fire is extinguished, take exterior shots of the scene from diagonally opposite corners of the building. Also climb up a ladder and take more pictures of the ruins to show the extent of the fire. The immediate vicinity of the fire should also be photographed to show the location of the building in relation to other buildings in the neighborhood. In major fires it is advisable to shoot some photographs after the fire from high adjacent buildings or even from a helicopter. Today most large cities, in conjunction with radio stations, have a helicopter that broadcasts traffic reports. It may be possible to make arrangements to have the pilot fly above the scene and so you can take these useful shots.

Photographs After the Fire

If the photographer for the fire department is not a trained fire investigator, the fire department should combine both jobs so that the individual who is the fire investigator is also the fire photographer. These jobs easily complement one another. If, however, the fire department has a photographer who is not a trained fire investigator and has another individual who does this work, then both should get together after the fire and go over the shots that they want. Nothing should be moved unless the chief investigator approves it. This is similar to police photography at a crime scene.

When the destruction is only partial, photographs of the interiors of every room should be taken, showing either damage by fire or smoke or evidence of a planned fire (Figure 7.18). These should be taken before any cleanup is started. Pictures taken with a wide-angle lens from two diagonally opposite corners of each room will show most of the condition in which each room was left by the fire. Sometimes, however, the photographer has to take pictures

FIGURE 7.18
Partial damage from fire. Top photo shows extensive damage to one room while bottom photo shows less damage to another room.

kneeling, sitting, or even lying down to photograph the ceiling. For this task, a pair of disposable coveralls or a Tyvek suit is almost as essential as a camera.

An indication of forced entry, such as a broken window or broken door locks, demands close-up photography because such things are often signs that the fire was started to conceal another crime. All clocks that have stopped should be photographed because the time shown may indicate the approximate time of the start of the fire.

After taking the photographs showing conditions immediately after the fire, photograph the debris being screened or sifted for evidence. Every step of this screening process should be photographed to show how the evidence was collected. This screening or sifting process may take days or weeks before it is completed. When the point of origin of the fire or explosion is located, close-up photographs of any bits of evidence uncovered should immediately be taken. After being photographed, such items should be turned over to the police laboratory (Figure 7.19).

FIGURE 7.19
Pour pattern of accelerant.

Equipment for Fire Scene Photography

The photographer must have a good tripod because there are many times when slower shutter speeds must be used. Also, because lighting is tricky at best when photographing a fire, a light meter is essential to arson photography.

Lighting is particularly troublesome when photographing burned interiors because it is difficult to sufficiently illuminate charred areas. Some photographers use floodlights and move them about during long exposures to produce the effect of "painting with light." Others find photoflash illumination suitable. In partially burned rooms where the ceiling is not blackened, "bounce flashing" toward the ceiling often produces good results. Bracketing exposures and using high dynamic range processing in Photoshop or Photomatix may also help (see Chapter 12).

Importance of Photographs during a Fire

The extent to which the investigator can conduct a preliminary investigation during the actual burning varies with the nature and severity of the fire. General observations can, of course, be made from an appropriate distance, and detailed examinations of the nearby areas can sometimes be made at this stage. Much of the information suggested below can also be obtained later from eyewitnesses. Using photographs and properly documenting the events of the fire will be invaluable later. Below is a list of some evidence that can be obtained from a fire and that can help win or lose a case.

Smoke and Vapors

The characteristics of the smoke, steam, or other vapors that emanate from a fire are useful indicators for determining the nature of the burning substances, including the accelerants used. In the following list, the color of the smoke is related to the most common incendiary agent that may emit it.

1. Steam and smoke. The presence of steam indicates that humid substances have come in contact with hot, combustible substances. The water present in the humid substance is evaporated before the substance begins to burn.
2. White smoke is given out by burning phosphorus, a substance that is sometimes used as an incendiary agent.
3. Grayish smoke is caused by the emission of flying ash and soot from loosely packed substances such as straw and hay.
4. Black smoke is produced by either incomplete combustion or the preponderance in the burning material of a product with a petroleum base, such as rubber, tar, coal, turpentine, or petroleum.
5. Reddish-brown or yellow smoke indicates the presence of nitrates or substances with a nitrocellulose base. Thus, smoke of this color can be emitted from burning nitric acid, nitrated plastics, film, or smokeless

gun-powder. A number of these substances can be used as accelerants (see Figure 7.20).

Color of Flame

The color of the flame is indicative of the intensity of the fire and sometimes of the nature of the combustible substances present. The temperature of the fire may vary from 500 to 1500 °C, with the color of the flame ranging from red, through yellow, and finally becoming a blinding white. Some accelerants may give off a characteristically colored flame. For example, burning alcohol is characterized by a blue flame. Red flames may indicate the presence of petroleum products.

Size of the Fire

The size of the fire should be noted at the time of arrival and at subsequent intervals thereafter. This information may be significant in relation to the time at which the alarm was received. An unusually rapid expansion of the fire is indicative of the use of accelerants, trailers, or some other method of physical preparation. A thorough knowledge about the construction of buildings is essential to the individual who wants to be an effective photographer of fire investigation.

FIGURE 7.20
Photograph of fire in progress, illustrating the direction and color of the smoke.

Direction of Travel

Because hot gases rise and fire normally sweeps upward, the direction in which a fire travels is predictable from a knowledge of the construction of the building. It is expected that the flames will rise until, upon meeting obstacles, they project horizontally to seek other vertical outlets. The extent and rate of travel in a horizontal direction depend primarily on the direction of the wind and on ventilating conditions, such as open doors and windows. The spread of fire in an unusual direction or at an exceptional rate should arouse suspicion as to the presence of accelerants or a prepared arrangement of doors and windows.

Location of Flames

The photographer should note carefully whether there is more than one apparent point of origin and should try to estimate the approximate location of each. Unrelated fires in different places are indicative of arson. The incendiary may, for example, arrange timing devices in different places, with the result that the separate outbreaks of flames are apparent.

Order of Searching

The area immediately surrounding the burned property should be thoroughly examined for evidentiary traces and clues. The doors and windows of the building should be studied for evidence of a break-in, particularly if the premises are normally locked during the period in which the fire took place. Tool impressions, broken window panes, and forced locks are obvious marks of such a break-in. The photographer then progresses to the interior, directing his or her observations to the charred remains of the fire, looking primarily for evidence of accelerants or other incendiary devices. Assuming that the burning has been extensive, the following order should usually be followed:

1. The outer shell of the remains.
2. The first open area or floor from the point of entry.
3. The first inner shell or wall of an inside room.
4. The general area suspected of being the point where the fire started.

Sketching and Photographing

A photographic record should be made of the destruction accomplished by the fire and of physical evidence uncovered by the search. The photographer should follow the order of the search, photographing each area of significance to the investigation before the search. Once located, the point of origin should be thoroughly photographed to show such things as the type and extent of "alligatoring," charring, and the remains of any incendiary device (see Figure 7.21).

FIGURE 7.21
Photograph of a pour pattern where accelerant was used to start a fire.

As each piece of evidence is discovered it should be photographed in its original condition and in its position when it is completely uncovered. In addition to the photographs a sketch of important areas should be made, showing the location of the various articles of evidence. As an aid to the construction of this sketch, blueprints of buildings maintained in the files of housing and building departments are particularly useful for giving the dimensions and other details of the structure.

If victims are found inside the structure, the scene should be treated the same as if it were a homicide. Photograph position of bodies thoroughly and document their location on a sketch (see Figure 7.22). Photograph items found near the body and document clothing remains. If clothing has been burned away from the body, look for metallic objects such as buttons, buckles, and zippers.

Problems and Cautions for Fire Scene Photography

The greatest problem the fire photographer will encounter is lens fogging produced by contact with heat and steam. The photographer must wait for the air to cool somewhat before attempting to photograph indoor damages. Smoke also forms a barrier that light sometimes cannot penetrate. Be careful when using flash units—they may explode in the atmosphere surrounding a fire.

FIGURE 7.22
Photograph of a fire victim showing the position of the body in relation to the room. Notice the characteristic "pugilistic pose" or "fighter's stance" of the body caused by heat drying of muscle tissue.

OTHER USES FOR CRIME PHOTOGRAPHY

Other uses of crime photographs include crime scene video recordings, surveillance video and still photographs, aerial photographs, and underwater crime scene photographs. There has been some debate regarding the usefulness of video recording of crime scenes. Some maintain that still photographs provide a much better understanding of the scene and lessens the chance that defense attorneys can find more to attack in court. Others maintain that a video of the scene provides additional understanding of the surrounding areas and relationships of physical evidence found at the scene. If the police photographer is asked to produce video recordings of a crime scene, the recommended procedure is as follows.

1. The video should have an introduction providing information regarding the date, time, type of crime, and location. In addition, the introduction should tell what the video depicts. This introduction can be in audio or with visual placards. Each scene should have an introduction as well. For instance, when the camera goes into a certain room, a visual placard or audio dub should state what room the camera is going into. Audio of others working at the scene should not be recorded.

2. The first part of the video should show the outside boundaries of the crime scene, overviews and surrounding areas. The camera then is moved inside the crime scene boundary.

3. Video the scene using a wide angle first then zoom into particular features and physical evidence locations. If the camera zooms into a particular area, return to wide angle before moving the camera to another location. Use slow panning and zooming. Ideally, the camera should be mounted on a tripod with dolly wheels to prevent unnecessary vibration and shakiness. If a tripod is not used, the photographer should try to keep the camera as still as possible while recording.

Video recordings may be used with witness and suspect interviews. For interview recordings, the audio must be turned on to record all that is said during the interview process. The frame should include everyone present in the interview room, so a wide angle may be more appropriate. The camera should be mounted on a tripod and not moved during the interview process. Most video cameras have a date/time feature that is imprinted onto the recorded media. This feature should be turned on and checked to make sure it shows the accurate date and time. As with crime scene videos, the interview video should have an introduction given by the lead investigator conducting the interview. This introduction should include the date, time, location, crime being investigated, and name of the party being interviewed. Miranda warnings should be video recorded to ensure that the suspect is providing voluntary information. If a break is taken during the recording session, the camera should be turned off. When resumed, an introductory statement should be made that nothing was done during the break to coerce the suspect into providing information.

Besides photographing scenes of crimes already committed, the police photographer may be called upon to photograph crimes in progress, such as "drug buys" (see Figure 7.23). Surveillance photography has long been used in police work to gather evidence and record meetings with offenders. Surveillance photographs can also be used to provide documentation for procuring search warrants (see Figure 7.24). Surveillance photography requires that images be clear, with recognizable persons and readable vehicle license plates. However, surveillance photography also may require that the photographer be hidden. The use of high-magnification telephoto lenses and higher-speed ISO settings are important in surveillance photography. A 500 mm or larger telephoto lens may be required to take clandestine photographs of individuals and places of "business." Most high-magnification telephoto lenses have a fixed f-stop, usually f-8, which requires faster ISO settings and/or optimum lighting conditions. However, since the police photographer cannot choose the time and place of surveillance, he or she must be able

FIGURE 7.23
Telephoto photograph of a drug buy in progress.

FIGURE 7.24
Telephoto photograph showing activity at a residence suspected of drug dealing. Notice the street sign included in the photograph to aid in identifying the location for a search warrant.

to choose from equipment and camera settings that will do the job. Other equipment essential to taking good surveillance photographs include a sturdy tripod, polarizing filters to fit the telephoto lens (particularly helpful when shooting through windows), and a "night-vision" scope attachment (see Chapter 10). Video recordings may also be used for surveillance photography, following the same basic procedures as crime scene and interview recordings. However, video recordings of surveillance situations may not be as good quality as still photographs. The best use of video surveillance is with banks and retail stores. Still, the quality of the video is sometimes poor and may require video experts to enhance physical features on the recorded images.

Aerial photographs may be required in documenting large crime scenes, such as aircraft crashes and areas burned by forest fires. Aerial photographs also are used to document areas surrounding a crime scene location. Aerial photographs have been successfully used to document areas where there may be suspected drug activities (e.g., sites growing marijuana or a meth lab). One of the main problems with aerial photography is the amount of haze that may be present in the air. For small amounts of haze, a haze or skylight filter on the lens can be used. The shutter speed should be high enough to record images without blur from vibration and movement but low enough for good resolution for enlargements to be made if necessary. An ISO speed of 200 is generally a good choice for daytime aerial photographs. Small particulate matter suspended in the air reflect blue light and cause haze. Using an infrared setting on the camera may help reduce these obstructions. Infrared film is not sensitive to blue light and may eliminate most of this atmospheric haze. Also, infrared can better document changes in soil conditions, plant materials, heat sources, and burn patterns than traditional settings. If aerial photographs must be made at night, the photographer should use a "night-vision" attachment. The quality will be poor, but images can be identified.

In some cases, underwater photographs may be required. This poses a particular problem for the photographer in that most bodies of water have low visibility because of suspended particulate matter. These particles reflect light from strobe units and may obscure what the photographer is attempting to show. In such a situation, the photographer should use a movie light rather than a strobe and set a slower exposure. This helps soften the reflectivity of particle matter and provide a clearer image. Using a digital camera offers the advantage of allowing the photographer to see immediately if the image is acceptable. Some departments may purchase small, disposable underwater cameras. Many of these cameras are film rather than digital and do not have the capability to bracket exposures. The diver should avoid using disposable film cameras unless the water is exceptionally clear (such as a swimming pool).

PANORAMIC PHOTOGRAPHY AND THREE-DIMENSIONAL IMAGING

In some cases panoramic photography may be used to provide a 360° representation of the crime scene. There are accessories in the form of motorized tripods and software programs that can help achieve this with the use of digital single-lens reflex camera. There are also dedicated camera systems that are specifically made for this type of photography, such as the Panoscan panoramic camera system (panoscan.com). Panoramic photographs can be converted into 360° rotatable images that can be used to demonstrate the overall appearance of the scene and can be zoomed to visualize details. These images are extremely useful for providing the viewer with an understanding of the crime scene and make excellent court presentations. These images can further be embedded in digitized plan diagrams such that clicking on a specific location of the plan diagram of a crime scene can launch a panoramic photograph of the selected area.

Several companies including Leica Geosystems also have developed technologies that utilize lasers, which can be used to scan and record a crime scene. Similar to a total station, a laser scanner emits a pulse of light, which collects data regarding the distances and angles that exist between itself and objects that are within its line of sight. As laser light is reflected from objects in the scene, the distance and angle data are collected by the scanner and used to generate discrete points in a software environment. The laser scanner, which is mounted on a 360° rotatable base, collects thousands of discrete points from the scene and uses these to generate a *point cloud*. The point cloud appears as an image of the subject being scanned; however, this image is actually composed of thousands of data points. The point cloud also is displayed as an intensity map, the colors of which indicate the distance between the laser scanner and an object it is scanning. When the scan of a scene is complete, the point cloud data are essentially in the form of a three-dimensional map of the scene that is to scale, rotatable, and measureable within the software environment. The point cloud data can also be overlayed with a panoramic photograph taken from the same perspective as the scan. This serves to give the point cloud data color values that are representative of the actual scene as opposed to an intensity map.

The laser scanner in this example was used to document a ballistic trajectory reconstruction. The flight path of the bullet into the vehicle was approximated with the use of a trajectory rod (light blue), then the vehicle was scanned with the trajectory rod in place. The resulting rotatable scan was used to illustrate the entry path of a bullet into the vehicle from several perspectives. Figure 7.25(b) shows two different views of the same scan data: a rear view of the vehicle and a top-down 45° profile view. The red pole also visible in the scan image is a 1.7-m calibration standard that is used to verify the accuracy of the scanner.

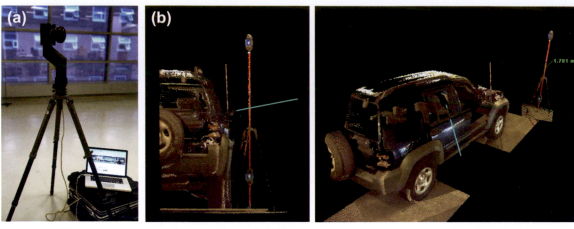

FIGURE 7.25

(a) Panoscan panoramic camera system that is used to generate 360° images of a crime scene. (b) Screen shots of point cloud data collected with a Leica ScanStation 2.

REFERENCE

Aaron, J. M. (1991). Reflective ultraviolet photography sheds new light on pattern injury. *Law and Order*, 21–32. November.

Motor Vehicle Incident Scene Photography

ABSTRACT

Taking photographs of motor vehicle crashes is challenging for police photographers. First, the environment may not be ideal for taking photographs. Photographers may find themselves taking pictures at night or during inclement weather. Second, there is usually a time factor involved in photographing the scene. Traffic patterns may be tied up as a result of the crash, and pressure is on the police to clear up the scene as quickly as possible. Photographers need to be aware of driver, passenger, and pedestrian viewpoints of a crash, and to record images detailing these perspectives. The driver's view may have been obstructed, so a photograph from the driver's perspective may help determine the cause of the accident. Debris may indicate point of impact in crash investigations, and photographic images with measurements need to be recorded not only for criminal investigation purposes, but also if a civil action is pursued at a later time.

KEY TERMS

Perspective grid
Skid marks
Tire impressions
Photographing viewpoints
Vehicle damage
Debris
Point of impact

INTRODUCTION

Motor vehicle incidents include traffic accidents, crashes, and crimes involving motor vehicles. The term "traffic accident" has lost favor with many police investigators. The term "accident" implies no one was at fault and the incident occurred by chance or by an act of God. Most police investigators prefer the use of the term "crash" to describe a traffic incident. This term implies the incident occurred as a result of someone's negligence in operating a vehicle or their criminal intention of crashing a vehicle. Regardless of the philosophical viewpoint, for our purposes we consider traffic accidents to include crashes, whether intentional or unintentional, resulting from negligence on the part of one or more drivers.

Traffic accidents happen very quickly. For the drivers and passengers of the vehicles involved in an accident, the short time in which the collision takes place can be traumatic and can influence the perceptions of all involved. Descriptions of the accident are not always accurate. Therefore, patrol officers who arrive at an accident scene must determine and record whatever evidence is available. The officers note the descriptions of the accident as told by the drivers, passengers, and other witnesses. Measurements are taken and weather conditions are noted. Also, if officers are equipped with a camera, photographs of the accident scene are taken.

With traffic accidents as well as costs on the increase, the importance of permanent, accurate, and unbiased records of an accident scene cannot be overstressed. Photographs, taken carefully, can provide a good part of the record of an accident. Measurements and other descriptions are also very important. Except for the minor details of an accident, a good photograph can capture many aspects of an accident scene that may be overlooked in the turmoil of the moment.

Photographs can be a great aid to the court, because they present physical circumstances of a case in a manner that is easily understood. Most people are visually oriented. A photograph of large or perishable evidence is accepted in place of the original. Items such as skid marks, footprints, or a body to show the location and type of injury should be included in the photographs. However, before the shutter is snapped, investigators should ask themselves: What will this prove? If the answer is "nothing," the photo should not be taken.

Police photographers must be qualified. They must know what they are doing and why, because the more important the picture, the stronger the attempt will be to discredit or disprove it in court. Commercial photographers are usually unsatisfactory for several reasons. In addition to being expensive, they may not know police photography requirements, they are often reluctant to appear in court, and they may not keep records to ensure the photograph can be admitted into evidence. If a commercial photographer is used, officers should direct the photographer to take the type of picture needed, and to record exposure and other related data. Remember, these photographs are not for publicity; they are evidence, as is the sketch of the crime scene. As valuable as they may be, investigators should not depend on photographs alone. They may be an important part of the case, but photographs alone do not constitute a complete investigation.

Pictures of the following subjects are often needed as evidence or to complete the records of a case: (1) general scene from the driver's viewpoint; (2) point of impact; (3) traffic control devices; (4) skid marks, showing length and direction; (5) condition of roadway at the location, showing defects, position of cars, victims, and parts of vehicles after impact, indicating points of collision; (6) view obstructions or lack of obstructions; (7) blood, flesh, hair, fabric threads, scrape marks, and the like, which are frequently present in hit-and-run cases; (8) tire prints; (9) footprints; (10) defects in the vehicles involved, such as a missing headlight; (11) trucks lacking turn signal indicators; (12) the roadside, showing the kind of environment; (13) sagging springs of an overloaded vehicle; and (14) the license number of the vehicles for identification.

Photographs, however, usually do not show measurement or dimensions. The photo may be exposed incorrectly, blurred, or otherwise impaired. The accident sketch, therefore, is as important as the record of the investigator's intricate, personal examination of the scene. However, use of the perspective grid photographic mapping technique allows accurate measurements to be made with a photograph. The basic procedure is to include a rectangle of known size in the photograph of a flat surface, such as road pavement, that permits mapping of objects on that surface. The rectangle may be a sheet of paper, a legal pad or a 2-foot-square grid made for this purpose. Chapter 7 explained in detail how perspective grid photography can assist with making quick, accurate measurements and preparing scale sketches of accident and crime scenes.

When photographing the scene of an accident, the usual limitations of color, lighting, and contrast affect the choice of lenses, filters, and flash. It is essential to obtain extreme definition and clarity in photographs for presentation in court, so that points of importance—such as the position of vehicles, point of impact, parts of damaged vehicles, and so on—are defined clearly. Combined with these desirable properties, the photograph should have the absolute minimum of perspective distortion possible.

When photographing the scene of an accident, the objective is to include all possible details that have a bearing on the cause of, or reason for, the accident. Experienced police photographers can obtain a reasonable estimate of the exposure required. With today's wide range of automatic digital cameras, it is almost impossible for a person to get a bad exposure. Even with less expensive or cell phone cameras, it is simple to obtain a well-exposed photo.

The viewpoint from which the photograph is taken is important. By directing the camera in a slightly different direction, obstruction of vision at a crossroad, for example, or the visibility of a sign may be magnified or minimized, giving a false impression.

When photographing the approach to the scene of an accident for the purpose of showing obstructions to the view of the driver, the camera is held at the eye level of the driver of the approaching car. This gives a true picture of what the driver sees when approaching a crossroad or rise, such as a hump-back bridge. In the latter case, the camera held down or at normal eye level or higher would give a false impression of the amount of obstruction created by the bridge, being excessive in the first case and minimized in the second. The photograph should also be taken in line with the travel of the driver's body relative to the road if a photograph representing the driver's view is to be produced. In the case of a pedestrian witness, the camera should be at the eye level of a pedestrian to give an effect of what the witness saw. Markings of the first impact should be recorded carefully to assist in establishing responsibility for the accident.

There is a rather important point to make about the type of lens used to take the photograph. A normal lens (such as 50 mm) is the best choice for this purpose because, when the scene is located completely and pleasingly in the viewfinder, the photograph shows normal perspective. A too-distant viewpoint, minimizing distances in depth, or a viewpoint too near, exaggerating these distances, cannot be obtained using the previous method. Such photographs are obtained by using, for example, a long-focus or telephoto lens and a short-focus or wide-angle lens, respectively.

Color images should, of course, be made to take photographs. This is especially important when multicolor road signs are involved in a case. Or, if an incorrect filter is used, the clarity of the signs may be falsified to give the impression of clarity where none existed or an impression of obscurity when the sign is perfectly clear. The best practice when photographing an accident scene is to use a normal lens to focus on the main object, then stop down the diaphragm to the smallest possible aperture. This last phase is determined by the presence or absence of motion at the scene. If persons or objects are moving about the scene, then the aperture must be such that the exposure is sufficient to record these moving objects reasonably free from blurs. For car interiors, expose for the shadows and/or use fill flash.

BASIC CONSIDERATIONS

The police officers control the accident scene. They must ensure that no one moves the vehicles involved in the accident until all the needed photographs and measurements have been taken. Many weeks or months may pass before the case comes to court, and officers must be prepared with careful records that cover any detail of the accident that might be needed by the attorneys in court.

The entire scene of the accident should be photographed, with all the vehicles in the position of collision and, later, with the vehicles removed. An overall view should be taken along with four different angles, one each from the north, south, east, and west. While photographing an accident scene, the photographer should ask herself: Does this view, angle, or position be of any value to me later, when I am called to testify in court?

In addition to taking all the necessary photographs, the photographer should draw a diagram that shows all the distances from the camera to the object photographed. All material objects should be measured. Everything should be documented.

PERMISSION TO PHOTOGRAPH

Although some people may object to being photographed at the scene of an accident, the police photographer has the right to photograph any evidence available at the scene of an accident on public property.

Private property (such as a shopping center parking lot) may pose a problem to the police photographer. Technically, the security officer is responsible for investigations concerning accidents on the property. Permission to photograph may, however, be obtained in writing from the owner, who is often willing to cooperate. If necessary, a search warrant, which takes the place of the owner's written permission, may be obtained.

VIEWPOINTS WHEN PHOTOGRAPHING ACCIDENTS

The viewpoint from which each photograph is taken can make a great deal of difference in the story the picture tells. A shift of only a few inches can, for instance, hide a stop sign behind a bush, although it may have been visible from the road. Obstructions to vision at a crossroad are relative to the position of a driver; the nature of such obstructions may be maximized or minimized in a photograph merely by moving the camera a few feet. Thus, it is very easy for the photographer to give a false impression that would not be helpful in conducting an investigation.

When photographing the approach to the scene of an accident, the photographer may wish to show any objects that obstruct the view of the driver. The camera should be held at a distance above the ground that approximates the eye level of the seated driver. The distance above the ground varies from vehicle to vehicle and with the physical height of the driver. The photographer may have to squat to photograph the view from a sports car, or stand on top of a ladder in the case of photographing the view from a large truck. Any appreciable variance from this position creates a false impression of the driver's view. The camera should, of course, be pointed in the driver's direction of travel. When photographing what a pedestrian saw, the camera should be held at the eye level of the pedestrian.

WORKING IN POOR CONDITIONS

Accident photography is nearly always done outside. In addition, because bad weather, darkness, and glare are often causes of accidents, the photographer must work in poor conditions.

1. At night: Taking pictures in the dark is a very difficult job. Even with the largest flash, most of the flash is not reflected. Foreground areas are overexposed and the background is underexposed. The photographer can get good results at night using the multiple-flash method, such as painting with light or strobe and slave (see Chapter 6). Focusing in the dark, although difficult, can be accomplished by shining a flashlight or spotlight at the object on which to be focused. The camera should be on a tripod to aid in this process. If this is not possible, the lens should be focused at infinity; most objects are then in focus. Photographing license plates at night can be very difficult. The flash unit must be held at a distance from the camera so that glare from the highly reflective plate is directed away from the lens. Three shots of a plate, with the flash unit 5 feet, 7 feet, and 13 feet from the camera yields good results.

2. At dusk: Shooting at dusk should be done with a combination of available light and flash.

3. Bad weather: The Rochester, New York, Police Department has a novel approach to the problem of protecting photographic equipment, and preventing cameras and flash units from shorting out during rain or heavy snow. Before leaving the car, police photographers cover the camera

tightly with a clear plastic bag from which they suck out the air. In Shaker Heights, Ohio, police officers use a large golf umbrella, which they carry with their photographic equipment. The electronics in digital cameras are very susceptible to moisture and "short out" if subjected to excessive moisture. Photographing a scene during snowfall or rainfall may pose a problem for the photographer. Snow and raindrops distract from the photograph. During periods of snowfall or rainfall, the photographer may place the camera on a tripod and use a slower shutter speed to soften or eliminate the image of snow or rain.

4. Daylight: Unlike most outdoor photography, the subjects of accident photography cannot be posed, nor can the photographer manipulate the camera to get only the most well-lit angles or wait for the sun to move for better lighting. When shooting the shaded side of a car, the underside of a car, or the interior of a car, a flash should be used to bring out details that are otherwise hidden in shadow. The photographer should cover the flash with a double thickness of handkerchief or a diffusion attachment when shooting inside vehicles, or the shots will be terribly overexposed. Automatic strobes must be used carefully, because daylight may throw the flash sensor off its proper exposure.

BASIC RULES FOR ACCIDENT PHOTOGRAPHY

Photographing an auto accident is something that must be done correctly the first time. All photographs must be obtained in a few minutes and nothing must be omitted. The accident photographer must be doubly careful to record everything, because the omission of a key photograph could misrepresent the case.

When arriving at the scene, the photographer should reconstruct the accident in her mind; then, using the proper equipment, take photographs of the scene are following these basic rules:

1. Work quickly. If any of the drivers, passengers, or bystanders at the accident are injured, they should receive the police officer's attention first. Then, all the necessary photographs should be taken so that the vehicles may be moved if they are obstructing traffic.

2. Avoid unnecessary surroundings. Objects that are not pertinent to the case should not be included in photographs of the accident. If only a small portion of a photograph is of interest in the case, decide whether it needs to be taken. This discernment is similar to a witness who rambles on with minor details that are of no importance to the case. Whenever possible, a series of photographs of a traffic accident scene should be taken from several different camera viewpoints that give an effective presentation of the entire scene without showing too much

of the surrounding area. People and animals should be avoided in the photographs unless they are involved in the case or serve some useful purpose, such as showing the size or location of objects. Living creatures always attract the attention of the observer of a photograph and, if they have no purpose in the picture, their presence weakens the effectiveness of the photographic evidence.

3. "See" through the driver's eyes. Photographs should be taken from the eye level of each driver. If there are witnesses, photographs should be taken at their eye level, from the spot where they were standing.

4. Determine shot angles. Shots should be taken from the four points of the compass and 25 feet from the vehicle. Additional shots, from 100 feet, show the approach and terrain. If only a few shots can be taken, they should be at a 45° angle from the front and rear of each vehicle. This allows two sides of a vehicle to appear in one photograph.

5. Take close-ups. From a distance of 8 to 10 feet, shots should be taken of the damaged parts of each vehicle. Different perspectives of the damage may be obtained by photographing each damaged area from two angles.

6. Tie the shots together. Some order of photographs must be established from the photographer's notes so their order assists in telling a story. The photographer must be prepared, with the aid of the photographs, to tell a court exactly how the accident occurred.

7. Practice. Photographers must practice the craft so they need to worry only about how to tell the story in pictures, not how to operate the camera.

8. Remember the chalk. Before any bodies are removed from the ground, they should be outlined with white chalk or bright, colored spray paint. If a vehicle must be removed, its four wheels should be outlined with chalk or paint. It is a good idea to chalk a white arrow that indicates which direction is north, for inclusion in each photo.

9. Be certain. If there is any doubt about whether to take a shot, take it. It is a good idea to take at least 20 to 30 pictures, because too much evidence is better than not enough.

10. Use a perspective grid. If measurements are to be made and sketches drawn of the accident scene, be sure to include a perspective grid in the photograph (see Chapter 7).

WHAT TO PHOTOGRAPH

The following is a list of what should be photographed at a crash scene.

1. All vehicles in their original positions; officers have the authority to prevent any movement of vehicles until photographs are taken (Figure 8.1).

2. Victims who have been thrown from vehicles (Figure 8.2).

FIGURE 8.1
Vehicles shown in original position.

FIGURE 8.2
Victim thrown from a vehicle. Notice the use of paint to outline the body.

3. Debris, which is the best indication the photographer has of showing where the first impact occurred (Figure 8.3).
4. Vehicle license plates, which should be clear in at least one photograph of each vehicle.
5. All skid marks and tire marks. Patches of oil or water, if present, should be included in these photographs. Tire marks will be straight and are caused by braking. Skid marks deviate from the general line of travel and are usually made by the front tires (Figure 8.4).
6. Any marks in soil or soft berm made by vehicles that have gone off the road, which may give an indication of the speed of the car.
7. A close-up of marks made in macadam roadways to indicate the texture of the road.
8. Photographs of the vicinity of the accident that do not include the accident scene itself; these should be noted carefully for reference points.
9. Well-thought-out photographs of a hit-and-run scene. The investigator of a hit-and-run accident has only part of the evidence and must make a case from the best photographs the photographer can take.
10. Vehicle interiors, which show the position of bodies, whether seat belts were in use, items inside the vehicle, and, in some cases, the

FIGURE 8.3
Skid marks and debris showing place of impact.

FIGURE 8.4
Skid marks and gouge marks in pavement.

speedometer, which may have stopped on impact and might show the speed of the vehicle (Figures 8.5–8.7).

HOW TO PHOTOGRAPH AN AUTO ACCIDENT SCENE

There is a five-step procedure that provides adequate photographic coverage of most automobile accidents. The following deals with an accident at an intersection, but it applies equally well to any vehicular accident.

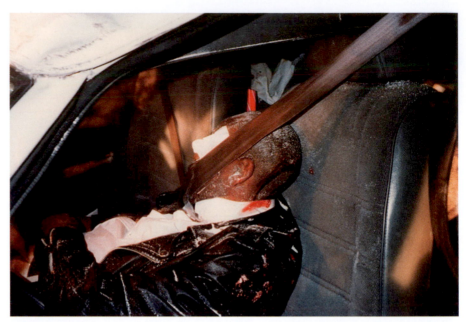

FIGURE 8.5
Interior shot showing the position of a victim. Was the victim wearing a seat belt?

FIGURE 8.6
Interior shot showing items in the vehicle.

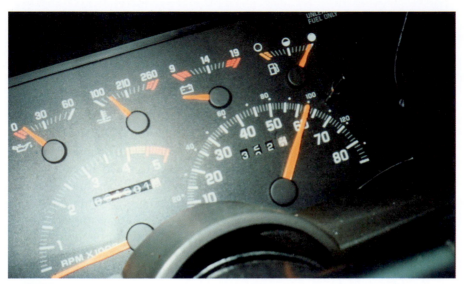

FIGURE 8.7
Interior shot of the speedometer showing the recorded speed at impact.

1. From a distance of about 100 feet, the photographer shoots toward the intersection to show how it appeared to the driver. Then, from the same spot, the photographer turns and shoots toward the direction from which the second car was coming. This establishes whether any obstruction could have prevented the first driver from seeing the second driver.

2. The photographer then moves up to about 25 feet from the probable point of impact and shoots again. This establishes what traffic controls were present and shows skid marks or lack of skid marks.

3. Next, the photographer takes these same basic three shots from the viewpoint of the second driver. The order is simply reversed. First, a shot is taken from the direction from which the second driver was coming, at 25 feet from the probable point of impact. Then, moving backward, the other two basic shots are taken from 100 feet.

4. These six basic shots, three from each driver's viewpoint, should be taken quickly, within 3 to 5 min. The overall scene, the probable point of impact, and the final locations of the vehicles and pedestrians have all been well covered. As soon as the photographic activity that interferes with the flow of traffic is complete, the photographer begins photographing each vehicle to illustrate damage. In the close-up views, the cars should be photographed from north, south, east and west. Close-up views of the car's damaged areas can give a good idea of the force of the collision. Color photographs show where one car's paint has been transferred to another, and also make it easy to distinguish the

damage under investigation from rusted areas or old damage. License plates should be photographed. Photographing shoe soles of a car's occupants can settle a possible dispute over who was driving if an imprint from the brake or accelerator pedal shows up on the sole of one of the occupants.

5. Any skid marks or tire tracks should be photographed head-on to show the direction in which the vehicle was traveling, and side-on to show their length. These photographs help determine the speed at which the vehicle was traveling and just when the driver perceived danger. To get the best views of the marks, it is usually advised to place the camera as high as possible. The Wyoming, Michigan, Police Department has devised a unique system for taking pictures from a high vantage point. Their photographic car is equipped with a wooden board mounted about 4 inches above the roof of the car. The tripod can be mounted easily, and photographs taken from this vantage point produce a good view of the tire marks. When photographing tire marks, great depth of field is desirable to ensure the entire length of the mark is in sharp focus. To acquire the greatest depth of field, it is best to set the aperture at the highest possible f-stop on the lens (i.e., f/22 or f/32). Using this exposure setting depends on the amount of light available. Under low-light situations, the photographer may use a focus-stacking process to ensure depth of field. Focus stacking is described in more detail in Chapter 9.

Hit-and-Run Accident Scene

Identifying the missing vehicle is, of course, the biggest problem in a hit-and-run accident investigation. Photography can make the task much easier.

1. Debris: Any debris possibly connected with the hit-and-run accident should be photographed at close range. For example, a photograph showing a paint fragment from the missing vehicle on another vehicle or on the pedestrian's clothing can mean the difference between a criminal's acquittal or conviction. All the debris in the immediate surroundings should be photographed to show the point of impact. Defense lawyers are very interested in seeing the point of impact in the auto accident.

2. Tire impressions: Even if tire impressions are to be reproduced by plaster casts, it is imperative to photograph them first. The camera should be placed on a tripod, with the back of the camera parallel to the ground. Remove the center column of the tripod and invert it to accomplish this. The photographer should select, when possible, a length of track that reveals any defects, such as cuts, that could help identify an individual tire. The photographer should always photograph, in sections, a length of tire track to equal the circumference of each tire.

3. Blood: The photographer should try to capture as much contrast as possible between a bloodstain and its background. If blood is difficult to see in a color photo, black-and-white images may be made with color filters to enhance contrast. If using a digital camera, the camera should be set to black-and-white or monochrome mode and, using a Kodak Wratten No. 25 (red) filter, the blood appears lighter than its surroundings. A Kodak Wratten No. 47 (blue) filter makes the blood appear darker. A photo of the trail of a pedestrian's blood can establish the direction the hit-and-run vehicle was traveling; the small drops of blood point in that direction.

Possible Murder or Suicide

There is nothing accidental about some fatal "accidents." It is always a good idea to photograph anything that appears suspicious. If, for example, a dead person is found behind the steering wheel of a car that has been in a serious collision and the driver shows few bruises and little bleeding, a photo could help show the driver was dead, possibly murdered, before the accident occurred. Often, especially when dealing with head-on collisions, it is wise to photograph the brake and accelerator pedals, the floor mats, and the soles of the driver's shoes. If the accelerator pedal imprint shows on the driver's right shoe and the floor mat impression on the driver's left shoe, there is good reason to suspect suicide. In any fatal accident, the interior of each car involved should be photographed thoroughly. Areas of deformation should be emphasized, particularly where there is any indication of occupant contact. Anything in the car's interior that indicates body contact, such as the steering wheel, the instrument panel, the interior of the doors, bent knobs, broken windshields, and so on, should be photographed.

Warning

It may seem immediately evident who the guilty party is in an accident. Nevertheless, police photographers must keep an open mind and not let any quickly formed opinions influence their approach in performing their job. If the work is done well, there will be plenty of solid evidence on which to base a sound conclusion.

Evidence Photography

CONTENTS

ABSTRACT

Although many photographers are able to capture images of overall surroundings, such as a crime scene or traffic crash scene, it takes specialized knowledge to capture images of small items of evidence or evidence that cannot readily be seen by the naked eye. This involves the use of macro- and microphotography. Macrophotography includes photographs taken at close-up range of 1:1 ratio or even closer. Taking macrophotographs requires specialized lighting techniques, such as axial lighting, vertical illumination, use of a beam splitter, oblique and grazing light, darkfield illumination, and backlight illumination. The use of a copy stand and copy lights or specially designed camera mounts may be required to properly record images of small items of evidence. Microphotography requires the camera be mounted onto a microscope for high-powered magnification or the use of a digital microscope. Microphotography requires the use of specially designed mounting systems for cameras and computer software if using digital microscopes.

KEY TERMS

Axial Lighting
Backlight Illumination
Beam Splitter
Bellows Attachment
Comparison Microscope
Copy Camera
Copy Stand
Darkfield Illumination
Data Sheet
Fill-Flash
Luminol
Macrophotography
Microphotography
Oblique Lighting
Reciprocity Failure
Ringlight Flash
Vertical Illumination

INTRODUCTION

Many valuable articles of evidence can be found at the scene of a crime. Each object should be photographed individually and in relation to other objects at the scene. Three purposes are served by this procedure: (1) a permanent record is made of the original appearance of the object; (2) the photographs can be used in place of physical evidence to supplement the case report; and (3) each article is preserved from unnecessary handling, which might cause the evidence to deteriorate or otherwise become altered.

Whenever possible, some or all of the evidence samples should be retained for photographs in the laboratory where the equipment needed for photomicrography and macrophotography is available.

As a general rule, a photograph should be taken at the scene of any piece of evidence that might deteriorate or change over time, or any evidence that cannot be moved from the scene or that might be damaged by handling. Objects that typically require individual photographs are tools, weapons, clothing, and contraband. Close-up photographs should be taken of wounds, bruises, scratches, and identifying marks on the body, and punctures in the skin of a narcotics addict.

EVIDENCE PHOTOGRAPHS AT THE SCENE OF THE CRIME

In addition to the overall shots of the crime scene, photographs should be made of items of physical evidence as follows:

1. Objects that serve to establish the fact that a crime has been committed (the corpus delicti).
2. Evidence relating to the manner in which the crime was committed (the modus operandi of the criminal).
3. Objects that might provide a clue to the identity of the perpetrator.
4. Objects that would connect a suspect to the crime (associative evidence).
5. Anything that has any bearing on the crime, such as blood spatters, signs of a struggle, or any indication of drinking or drugs. Any mark, no matter how slight, should be photographed.
6. Fingerprints found at the scene.

If a body is taken to the morgue, it should be photographed there as directed by the pathologist. The body should be photographed with any clothing that is on the body when the body is found, and then without clothing. If possible, take overall full body shots with scale or measurements. While the pathologist will measure the entire length of the body, they may not measure individual arms or legs. Arm and leg measurements may become important later if photographs are needed to reconstruct images for three-dimensional (3D) computer re-enactments. That may be difficult to accomplish after the body is buried. (see Figure 9.1).

The photography of evidentiary materials may necessitate additional photographic documentation of the evidence item. There may be facets of that evidence that require photographic documentation beyond what is necessary to establish the position and location of evidence within the scene. In some cases, it may not be possible to remove evidence from the crime scene for analysis in a controlled laboratory environment. These items may require analysis and

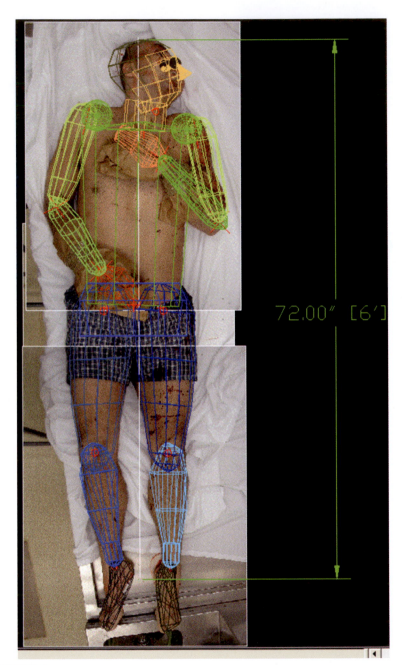

FIGURE 9.1

Photographs at the morgue may be used to determine body measurements for 3D computer scene reconstruction techniques. Here, three photos of the body were merged to create the total length so that computer wire measurements could be made.

sampling at the crime scene and therefore require photographic documentation that preserves the original condition and appearance of the evidence as it was found. Typical examples include fingerprint evidence, footwear impressions, tool marks, bloodstains, and bullet holes or impact marks, which can be present on walls, large non-recoverable surfaces, or fragile surfaces such as ceramic tile. In the case of fingerprint evidence, this form of evidence may require physical and chemical development at the crime scene that requires specific types of photographs at each stage of development. Furthermore, fingerprints need to be photographed in a manner that preserves the appearance of friction ridge detail. If fingerprint evidence is not properly photographed, later database searches and comparisons may not be possible. In other cases, fragile trace evidence such as hairs and fibers may need to be immediately documented and recovered due to its transient nature. Ballistic evidence such as bullet holes and bullet impact marks may benefit immensely from this form of documentation. Documenting the overall position and location of bullet holes is especially important in shooting incident reconstructions. Midrange photographs of bullet holes can further detail the bullet hole as an entry or exit hole in addition to documenting incident angle information. A series of close-up photographs may then be used to document trace materials transferred into the target such as blood, tissue, and fibers from clothing, where the midrange photograph serves as an evidence-establishing image at the crime scene.

As mentioned in Chapter 7 on crime scene photography, a systematic series of establishing, mid-range, and close-up photographs can be used to document the location of evidence at the scene. Likewise, this system of photographs may be used to record the details of physical evidence whether at the crime scene, the crime laboratory, or autopsy examination. Just as mid-range images provide details of the item of interest within the crime scene to provide context between an overall location and a specific evidence item, mid-range evidentiary photographs can provide context between a relevant feature of the evidence and the overall item. A close-up photograph can then detail that feature, further providing more detail (Figure 9.2).

Procedures at the Crime Scene

The item of evidence should be photographed at the crime scene using establishing, mid-range, and close-up photographs to document the position of the evidence within the scene. Once the location and position of the evidence are satisfactorily documented, all facets of the physical evidence should be photographed, being mindful of excessive handling. Depending on the nature of the evidence, this may require several photographs. Clothing items and weapons such as firearms and knives should be photographed from all sides to detail the condition in which the evidence is found. These close-up photographs of the overall evidence item should be taken with a fairly large image size to clearly show the

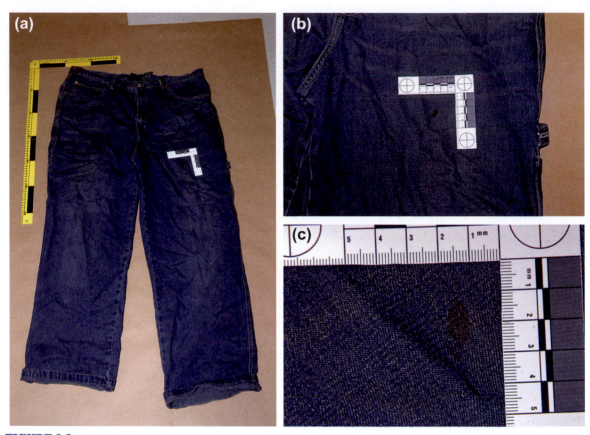

FIGURE 9.2

This series of photographs depict the manner in which a particular feature of an evidence item can be documented with photographs. In this case, jeans recovered in connection with a criminal event contain a bloodstain that needed to be documented in detail. The overall location of the bloodstain is documented with an establishing photograph of the jeans (a), while the mid-range photograph (b) depicts a closer view of the bloodstain and its immediate surroundings. A close-up photograph of the bloodstain (c) with an ABFO no. 2 scale further documents the appearance of the bloodstain in detail.

nature of the object and its identifying characteristics. A small ruler should be included in one of these close-ups and omitted in the other (some attorneys may object to the ruler and claim that it changes the scene) (see Figure 9.3a). Paper or plastic rulers that include room for the date, case number, department, and the officer's name can be purchased. (see Figure 9.3b). Any additional relevant features found on the evidence should be photographed in closer detail if needed.

EXAMINATION QUALITY PHOTOGRAPHS

Pattern impression evidence such as fingerprints, footwear impressions, tool marks, and bite marks are types of physical evidence that may be compared to

(a)

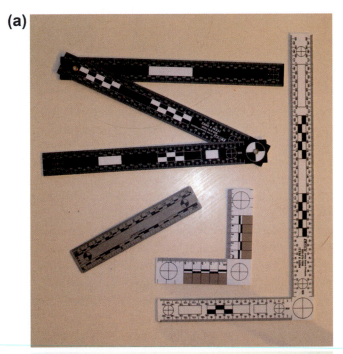

(b)

FIGURE 9.3

(a) Various types of measurement scales and (b) scale with case number written in pencil.

known objects in order to determine if the known object made the impression. These types of evidence may be encountered at the crime scene, in the crime laboratory, or at the morgue. Photographs taken of this form of evidence are termed *examination quality photographs*. The goals of examination quality photographs are to record the *fine* details of physical evidence to facilitate their use in the comparison process. Furthermore, these photographs need to meet certain requirements to be effectively used in a comparison. Some of these requirements include the following:

- The camera should be positioned so the sensor is parallel to the evidence.
- A normal macro lens should be used.
- The type of lighting used should provide maximum detail in the image.
- Illumination should be even.
- A right-angle scale should be used in the image.
- The subject should fill the frame of view completely.

- The subject should be in focus.
- The lens aperture should be set so there is adequate depth of field in the photograph.
- The photograph should be taken at full resolution.
- Uncompressed or lossless compression file format should be used.

The camera should be positioned so the sensor is parallel to the evidence to minimize optical distortion that can arise when photographs are taken at angles. When the camera is positioned at an angle to the evidence, one end of the evidence will be further from the sensor than the other, creating a perspective problem in the resulting image. Even at subtle angles, an effective size difference in the evidence can be created along the photograph that may affect any comparisons or measurement made from the image. Digital inclinometers or levels should be used to prevent this form of distortion. The level can be placed adjacent to the evidence (whether on a wall or on the ground) to establish any angle that exists. The level can then be placed on the camera so that the camera can be tilted to match the angle of the evidence. Proper leveling of the camera will also require that the camera be stabilized on a tripod or copy stand (Figure 9.4).

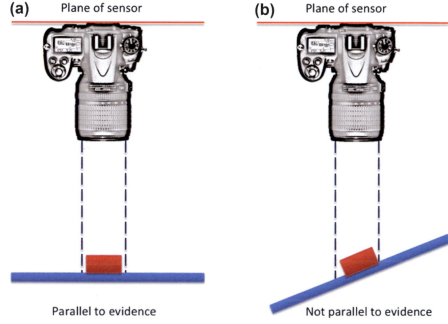

FIGURE 9.4
When taking examination quality photographs, care should be taken to ensure that the camera sensor is parallel to the plane of the evidence being photographed (a). When the camera is at an angle to the evidence (b), distortion may occur that could interfere with a comparison process or any measurement information that can be extracted from the photograph.

Macro lenses are also recommended for examination quality images as these lenses tend to be free of optical distortions that are common in wide-angle zoom lenses as a result of their components and manufacture. Barrel and pincushion distortion are common spherical aberrations observed in wide-angle zoom lenses. In barrel distortion, magnification occurs from the periphery of the lens toward the lens axis. This form of distortion can be seen in fixed wide-angle camera lenses or the full wide-angle setting of a zoom-capable lens. Conversely, in pincushion distortion, magnification occurs from the lens axis to the periphery of the lens. This form of distortion can be seen in either fixed focal length telephoto lenses or the telephoto setting of a zoom-capable lens. These forms of distortion interfere in a comparison process and can be mitigated with the use of normal (50–60 mm) macro lenses.

Some macro lenses are specialized for extreme close-up work and can focus at very close distances to the subject, capable of a 1:1 (one-to-one) reproduction ratio. A 1:1 image may be required for fingerprints and other forms of small evidence in order to fill the frame of the image with the entire evidence. Remember, camera lenses focus an image of the subject on to the camera sensor. The reproduction ratio basically relates the size of the actual subject to its image size on the camera sensor. When the size of the subject focused on the camera sensor is the same size as the actual subject, the reproduction ratio is 1:1 or "life size."

Filling the frame with the subject can be very important with certain forms of physical evidence. Filling the frame of the image and using high-resolution settings in the camera allows an examiner the ability to zoom into the image with minimal loss of image detail. Using the example of fingerprints, in addition to the overall pattern of the print and locations of minutiae, the thickness of friction ridges and position pores along the ridges may need to be measured. If the frame is not filled with the subject, as an examiner zooms in to areas in the print to examine fine detail, the number of pixels defining the area of interest may not be sufficient to resolve the sought details.

The file format used to take the photographs may also affect the resolvable detail. As previously mentioned, image files such as JPEG that use lossy compression can display artifacts when the images are decompressed for viewing due to the interpolation process used to restore deleted pixels. Because decompression artifacts can reduce the resolution in an image, examination quality images should be recorded in RAW of TIFF formats. Raw or TIFF formats can be either uncompressed or use a lossless compression algorithm. In the case of lossless compression, the decompression of the image for viewing results in the original image free of interpolation artifacts.

It is recommended, particularly if the evidence contains patterned detail, that several photographs be taken at various flash or lighting angles. For patterned

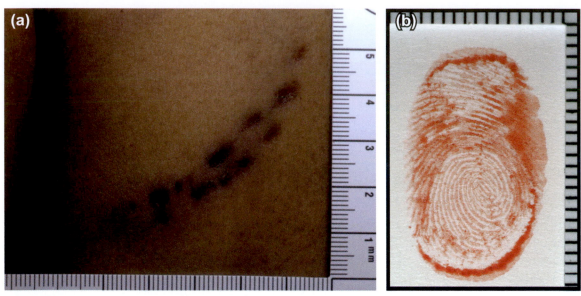

FIGURE 9.5

(a) Depicts an examination quality photograph taken of bite mark evidence. Because this mark may be compared to casts taken from a suspect's teeth, the photograph must be high quality and free from distortions that may interfere with the comparison, including lens distortion, file-format-related distortion, and distortion related to the position of the camera. In addition, because the bite mark is on a curved surface, the aperture of the camera must be adjusted so that enough depth of field is captured in the image. (b) Illustrates a 1:1 photograph of a bloody fingerprint. The right-angle millimeter scale visible at the edges of the photograph indicates that the image captured an area approximately 26 × 17 mm, the approximate dimensions of the camera sensor used, verifying that the image captured is 1:1 or life size.

impressions of an indented nature, the more oblique the flash source is to the subject, the more texture and detail will be revealed in the resulting photographs. For this reason it is advised to use an off-camera flash, particularly with evidence that has highly reflective properties or resides on a reflective surface. The use of direct lighting from a flash or other light source has the potential of creating specular reflection or "hot spots," which can reduce any visible details in the image by creating areas of overexposure (Figure 9.5).

DATA SHEET

A data sheet should be included for every evidence photograph. If a data sheet cannot be included in the photograph with the evidence, the data sheet should be photographed on the film frame prior to the evidence photograph. This procedure will help the officer recall what the following photograph depicts. The use of data sheets is becoming uniform throughout the country.

The data sheet should include the date, time, case number, location, and officer's name. Dates should be written in digits in the following order: month,

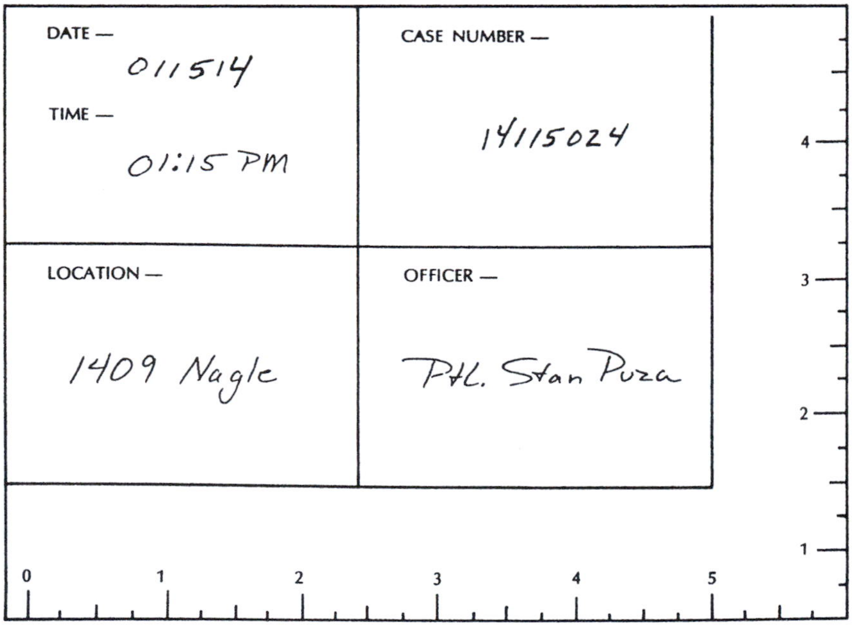

DATE — 011514

TIME — 01:15 PM

CASE NUMBER — 14115024

LOCATION — 1409 Nagle

OFFICER — Ptl. Stan Puza

FIGURE 9.6
Data sheet.

day, year. January is written as 01, February as 02, and so on, so that all months are written as two digits. In the same way, days should be written as follows: 01, 02, 03, etc. Years are abbreviated to the last two digits: 13, 14, 15, etc. Thus, every date will be composed of six digits: January 15, 2014 is written: 011514.

The time should be written in the following form: 01:15 PM, unless the department requires military time or a different format. Case numbers should signify logical representations. In small departments that handle less than a hundred cases a day, the case number can be written as the date plus a two-digit number, separated by a dash, indicating the number of the case for that day. The third case handled on January 15, 2014, would be written: 011514-03. This numbering system can also be used for mug shots.

The location should be given as the address where the crime took place. and the last space should be filled with the photographer's name.

Some cameras allow for the imprint of the date and time on the face of each photograph. Many digital cameras allow for a file to be saved for each digital image, which includes the date, time, camera serial number, and camera settings. This may be found in the RAW setting of most cameras. Such options may be beneficial in the absence of a data sheet and are particularly beneficial for use with crime scene and traffic accident photographs (Figure 9.6).

PHOTOGRAPHING BLOODSTAIN PATTERNS

Bloodstain patterns can yield much information to experts on the type of injury, force, and weapon in a homicide case. Photographing bloodstain patterns with a proper scale is essential for blood-spatter experts to determine this information. An excellent method for photographing blood spatters with proper sizing is to include a yardstick in the photograph. Photographs may be projected (using a digital projector) onto a wall in actual size (using the yardstick as a scale) and viewed in proper perspective and analyzed accordingly.

FOOTWEAR IMPRESSIONS

The imprints of shoes in soil are quite often found at or near crime scenes. Before reproductions are made by plaster casts or dental stone, the impression should be photographed. The camera, placed on a tripod, should be directed so that the camera axis is perpendicular to the plane of the impression; that is, the lens board and film should be parallel to the ground. It is imperative that the camera be in the same perpendicular plane as the impression to eliminate distortion. The use of a small level may aid the photographer by checking the level of the impression plane and duplicate this level indication on the camera. Many tripods include levels at the pan head. The height of the camera should be adjusted so that the whole impression is included in the film with a fairly large image size. A ruler placed at the side of the impression will indicate size. If a particular area of the impression contains any peculiar characteristics that may be helpful in identifying the foot or shoe, a closer shot should be taken so that this area (including the ruler) fills the picture and the desired information is given in clear detail. If the impression is deep (over 1 inch) the scale or ruler should be placed on the same plane as the impression. Carefully dig a trench adjacent to the impression at the same depth as the impression and place the scale into the trench to assure accuracy in measuring impression detail.

Oblique lighting (lighting that is low and to the side of the impression) is used when photographing impressions. The low light emphasizes the impression by creating shadows wherever there are ridges in the soil. Photographs made in daylight should be taken with photoflood, strobe, or photoflash placed obliquely to counteract the flattening effect of direct sunlight. Indoor shots and night shots should be made with photoflood whenever possible because this lighting can be easily controlled. Flash may provide too much light: if necessary, the flash may be cut by covering it with a handkerchief, or by using the bounce flash technique.

One method used to create shadow effects in footprints in light-colored soil or snow is to use black primer spray paint. Direct the paint spray at an oblique angle to the impression to create "shadows." A flash may not be required when this technique is used (see Figure 9.7).

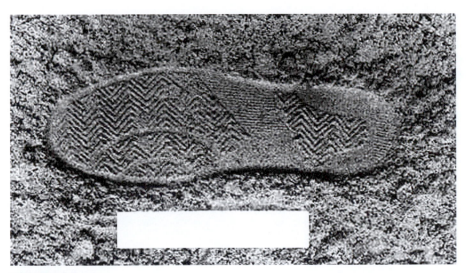

FIGURE 9.7
Shoe print in sand sprayed with black paint at an angle to "create" shadows.

CLOSE-UP PHOTOGRAPHY

Evidence of all kinds must be photographed close up to show details. The digital-single-lens-reflex (DSLR) camera is best for this kind of work because of its size and because parallax is avoided. A macro-capable lens will allow for accurate metering with the camera's built-in meter system. In addition, the photographer can add to a macro DSLR lens any of three powers of close-up lenses, or pair them as needed. The powers of close-up lenses are measured in diopters. A +4 diopter lens is the strongest. When two close-up lenses are used together, the stronger lens (the one with the highest number) should be next to the lens of the camera (see Chapter 3).

Close-up lenses simply allow the photographer to get closer to the subject. By adding a lens of +1 strength, one can get within 20–40 in of the subject; a pair of +3 lenses will reduce the working distance to about 6 inches, which would cover a field not more than 4 × 3 in.

Depth of field is practically nonexistent in close-up photography. There is no margin for error and focusing must be accurate within a fraction of an inch. It is best to use manual focusing rather than the automatic focusing system of the camera with close-up photography. Working distances should be measured from the front of the close-up lens to the front of the object being photographed. If the camera is on a tripod, a yardstick can be used to position it at a specific distance from the point of focus. Also, if the camera is pointed downward toward a flat plane, as when photographing footwear or tire impressions, a small level should be used on top of the camera to ensure that the lens is

FIGURE 9.8

Photo on left taken as a single shot. Photo on right taken as a series of six shots in focus stacking and combined into one image using Helicon Focus software. Note that the entire gun is now in focus using the focus stacking technique.

completely level to the photographed area. This will reduce distortion in the photograph. It is recommended that one use f/8 or f/11 for close-up photographs. These f-stops will provide the best resolution and sharpness compared to using a higher or smaller f-stop.

If depth of field is important to illustrate features in the photograph, a technique known as "focus stacking" may be used. Close-up photographs of 3D objects may not have enough depth of field to show all features of the object in focus. By taking several photographs of the same object in the exact position, slightly changing the focus on each shot, the images may be stacked using software and produce a single photograph with all areas of the object in focus. One such software program is called Helicon Focus (www.heliconsoft.com). The stacking technique may be used in a wide variety of applications, including photographs made through the microscope and general close-up photographs (see Figure 9.8).

Extension tubes or bellows can be used for large images at medium to close working distances. Bellows extensions are bulkier than tubes but are more versatile and, of course, more expensive. These units vary greatly, and generally are used with cameras that have focal plane shutters (Figure 9.9).

Basic exposure is subject to change with extension tubes or bellows, because they alter the lens-to-sensor distance. The light-transmitting capacity of a lens diminishes in relation to the length of the tube, necessitating a longer exposure

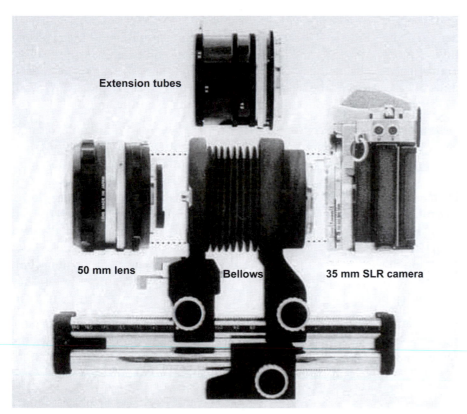

Extension tubes

50 mm lens **Bellows** **35 mm SLR camera**

FIGURE 9.9
Bellows attachment and extension rings for use with close-up photography.

for a given f-stop than the basic lens position requires. This obviously includes a reduction in the maximum "speed" of the lens.

The f-number is determined for the lens being used at about one focal length. If a lens is set at f-4, the opening of the diameter of the lens is 1/4th of the focal length. If the lens is placed on extension rings or a bellows attachment and extended from the film or sensor plane, the true f-number will change and an adjustment will be necessary to avoid underexposure. To determine the actual f-number when using extension rings or bellows, multiply the reproduction ratio by the indicated f-number and then add the indicated f-number to the product. For example, if you increased the lens-to-sensor plane distance with a bellows or extension ring to achieve a four-power magnification and the lens' indicated f-number is f-2.8, four is multiplied by 2.8, equaling 11.2, and the indicated f-number of 2.8 is then added to 11.2 giving a true f-number of f-14. The shutter speed should be adjusted to reflect f-14 rather than f-2.8 at four-power magnification.

Another problem is reciprocity failure. When the proper f-number has been determined and the lens is set at a small aperture, resulting in long exposure times (usually over 15 s), the resulting image may still be underexposed. One unit of light exposing the sensor for 60 s will not have the same effect as 60 units of light exposing the sensor for 1 s. This is the law of reciprocity. To avoid reciprocity failure, use wider apertures and shorter exposure times.

Determining the distance from lens-to-sensor plane for a desired power may also be a problem. If a "normal" 50 mm lens is mounted on a bellows or extension ring and a three-power magnification is desired, the reproduction ratio of three is multiplied by the focal length of 50. The 150 product means that the lens must be extended 150 mm from its normal position for a three-power magnification. By the same token, the magnification power can be determined by measuring the lens-to-sensor plane distance and dividing by the focal length of the lens. For example, if the lens-to-sensor plane distance using a bellows or extension ring is 170 mm and the lens focal length is 50 mm, the magnification will be 3.4 power. This may be useful information when a defense attorney asks, "What power magnification is this picture?"

A rigid camera support is essential for close-up work that usually requires slow shutter speeds or time exposures. When using bellows or extension rings, the camera may become very heavy, making it susceptible to jarring and vibration, especially during long exposures.

LIGHTING FOR SMALL OBJECTS

Special equipment is needed to light very small objects to enhance texture or to create special effects. Most close-up exposures require maximum illumination in places where shadows are cast by the equipment being used. Standard floodlights, if placed too near an object, are likely to light it too evenly and flatly; furthermore, if the evidence is perishable, heat from the floodlights may destroy it.

A 150-W miniature spotlight or an LED is a good lamp to use for lighting close-ups. A metal tube called a snoot can be added to the spotlight for a narrower beam. Illuminators and fiber-optic lights designed for stereomicroscopes and compound microscopes also work well with close-up photography. Ringlight electronic flashes are excellent for close-up photographs. Ringlight flashes are circular and attach directly to the camera lens (Figure 9.10).

Axial lighting, also called vertical illumination, is another technique for illuminating small items for photographic details. The principle of axial lighting involves a beam splitter to project light onto an object so that it reflects back directly toward the camera lens. The photographed object appears as if it is the light source-almost glowing. Excellent detail can be revealed through this technique. A

FIGURE 9.10

Ringlight flash attachment. The Sunpak ringlight flash attaches to the front of the camera lens for close-up flash photography.

beam splitter uses an optically flat glass mounted at a 45° angle to a light source. An LED flashlight or the white-light setting on an alternate light source (ALS) unit may be used. The light is projected horizontally onto the glass. The glass "splits" the beam of light, allowing one beam to be directed onto the object to be photographed (see Figure 9.11). The glass can be adjusted for the desired effect. Axial lighting may be troublesome for through-the-lens (TTL) camera meters, so several exposures may be necessary before the optimum image is obtained. Optically flat glass may be obtained from any glass supply house or a true beam splitter (5 × 7 in size) is available from most scientific supply companies such as Edmund Scientific.

MACROPHOTOGRAPHY AND MICROPHOTOGRAPHY

Macrophotography, also called photomacrography, is basically the same as close-up photography, although the lens is usually closer to the subject than in most close-up work. The photographer who frequently deals with macrophotography should have a permanent set-up with lighting and a floating table to minimize vibration.

Microphotography is photography that makes use of a microscope and is used to record minute evidence such as powdered debris, stains, hairs, and fibers. These photographs may also be referred to as photomicrographs. Microphotography is a specialized field and requires extensive knowledge and experience to obtain quality photographs through a microscope. To understand how photographs are made through a microscope, the operating principles of a

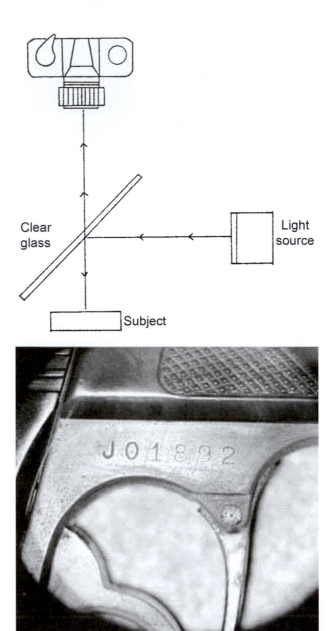

FIGURE 9.11
Diagram showing axial lighting technique (top). Photo of serial number taken by axial lighting technique (bottom).

microscope must be known. Basically, a microscope has two sets of lenses: an objective lens, which forms an image within the microscope tube, and an eyepiece (ocular) lens, which magnifies the image. For example, if a microscope objective lens is 40 power and the eyepiece is 10 power, the image seen by the human eye is magnified at a reproduction ratio of 400 times its actual size (400 power) (Figure 9.12).

Digital SLR cameras work well in microphotography. Most scientific supply houses supply microscope adapters for 35 mm SLR and digital SLR cameras. Adapters are simply metal tubes that attach to the camera body (without lens) and to the microscope eyepiece. The microscope lenses become the camera lens. Focusing the microscope should be performed while viewing through the SLR camera due to the difference in focal length with the attached adapter. The camera's TTL metering system may or may not work well with the microscope and because long exposures are usually required, several exposures may

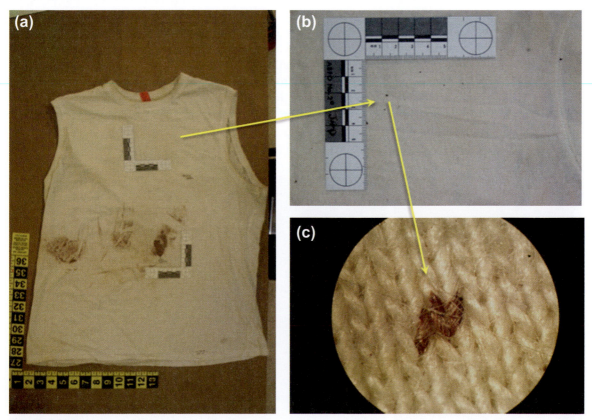

FIGURE 9.12

An example of bloodstain pattern evidence documented through the use of establishing (a) and mid-range photos (b) coupled with a photomicrograph (c) detailing fine blood spatter in the weave of a shirt.

need to be made to determine the best exposure. A good starting point using ISO 100 is 1/8 s. Remember, the white balance setting should be checked for the microscope's illumination source. Many microscopes are equipped with tungsten-halogen lamps, which will alter the color for daylight balanced images. Lower ISO speeds usually provide better detail than higher ISO settings.

Although Nikon and other camera manufacturers produce cameras made especially for microscope use, a standard digital SLR camera may be used with a proper adapter. Video camera adapters are also available from scientific supply houses such as Edmunds (Edmundoptics.com). Video cameras may be used with microscopes as long as the video camera's lens is removable. Because most video cameras and video camcorders have fixed lenses, they may not be used effectively with a microscope. However, many of the surveillance and security type black-and-white and color video cameras have threaded "C" mount lenses that can be removed from the camera body and attached, via an adapter, to the microscope. Sony's 8 mm EVC-X10 camcorder is a "C" mount camera that may be used with a microscope. Most dash-mounted video cameras in police patrol cars also have removable "C" mount lenses, and these cameras make excellent microscope cameras. A number of companies manufacture digital microscope cameras such as MiScope (www.zarbeco.com) which are very useful in police photography. Digital microscopes do not require a separate optical, compound microscope and are very portable (Figures 9.13 and 9.14).

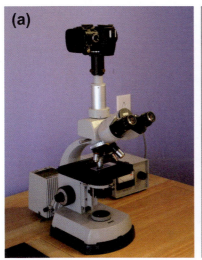 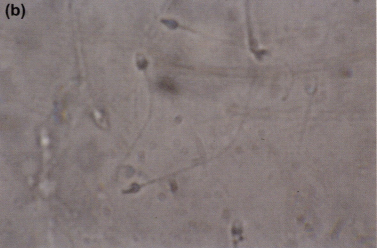

FIGURE 9.13
Camera mounted to a microscope (a) and a photomicrograph of sperm cells taken at 400× (b).

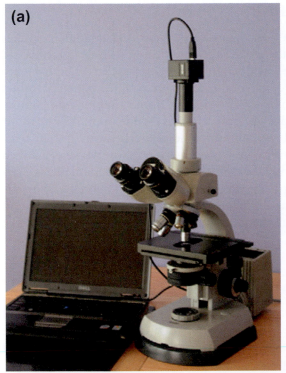

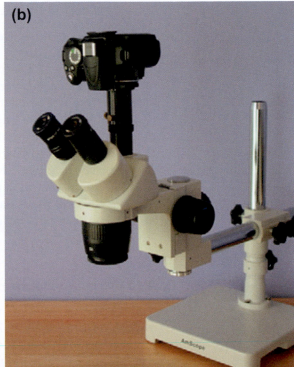

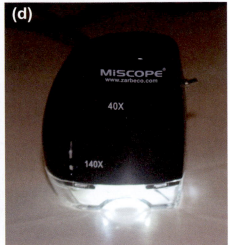

FIGURE 9.14

Digital camera mounted on a microscope (a). Digital SLR camera mounted to a stereo-microscope using a microscope lens adapter (b). A hand-held digital microscope attached to a computer using a USB cable (c). The MiScope digital microscope (d).

WOOD PHOTOGRAPHY

Criminal cases often involve wood as evidence. Very seldom are large pieces of wood recovered. Usually the wood is in the form of splinters, sawdust, or other small fragments. In the Lindbergh kidnapping case in 1935, evidence was introduced of a large piece of wood taken from an attic floor and a ladder made from it. This proved to be the downfall of Bruno Hauptmann, because the piece of wood in the ladder was proven to have come from the attic of his home. Large pieces of wood are helpful to the police because of their macro-characteristics. Small fragments of wood are found in burglaries, in which they are broken from a window, door frame, or furniture. Additionally, in cases of safe breakings, the wood packing between the inner and outer walls of the safe, which is used to insulate the safe, can be used as evidence. If the wood cannot be brought into the laboratory, it should be photographed at the scene with oblique lighting.

METAL PHOTOGRAPHY

Metal is replacing wood in many construction tasks, particularly in homes that have metal storm doors and windows. Metal should be photographed using the same procedure (oblique lighting) used for wood. The high reflectivity of some metals may make them difficult to photograph. Spray matte finishes, such as Calm, which can be purchased in spray can form at art supply houses, can be applied to the object to reduce reflection and glare (although some attorneys may object to its use), or reflectors can be used to subdue lighting. The use of polarizing filters may also help decrease glare. Cardboard covered with wrinkled aluminum foil and used as a light reflector can be used to photograph silvery objects; wrinkled gold foil should be used to photograph gold objects.

PAPER PHOTOGRAPHY

The impressions left upon a pad of paper by writing on an upper sheet that has been removed will sometimes provide a legible copy of the message written on the missing page (Figure 9.15). This kind of evidence is commonly found in connection with gambling investigations. The sheet bearing the original record of the bet will have been removed by the time the police officer makes the arrest. The officer must rely on the paper pad found in the defendant's possession to supply the needed corroboration.

There are two common methods for making indented writings visible. The traditional method uses oblique lighting or grazing lighting by directing a beam of light from the side (almost parallel to the plane of the paper), and the

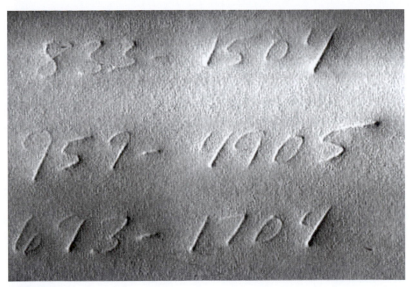

FIGURE 9.15

Oblique (side) lighting helps decipher illegible indentations on paper.

indentations can be brought into relief and the writing revealed. A sharper photograph may be made by placing the camera on a tripod or copy stand, setting the aperture at f-22 and exposure for 2 or 3 s with a handheld flashlight. The flashlight is continuously moved across the paper in a grazing fashion during exposure. A second, more recent, method is to use electrostatic imaging such as the electrostatic detection apparatus (ESDA). Electrostatic imaging involves applying an electrostatic charge to the surface of a polymer film that has been placed in close contact with the paper containing indented writing. The indented impressions are revealed by applying a toner powder (such as used with copiers) to the charged film. Photographs made using either of these two methods should be of high contrast to increase the readability of the indented writings. For this reason, digital photographs may be made more readable by using the black and white mode rather than color. When using side, oblique, lighting, it is sometimes impossible to obtain a satisfactory image of all the writing in one photograph, because different areas of the paper require different angles of illumination. In this instance, a series of photographs should be made and combined using PhotoShop or some other photo software program. Pairs of pictures made by lighting one from the right side of the paper and the other from the left side of the paper are helpful in some cases. By offsetting very slightly the two images obtained in this manner in PhotoShop, the writing can sometimes be made more distinct.

Illumination angles are also important in photographing folds, tears, and other imperfections and anomalies in paper. It may sometimes be important

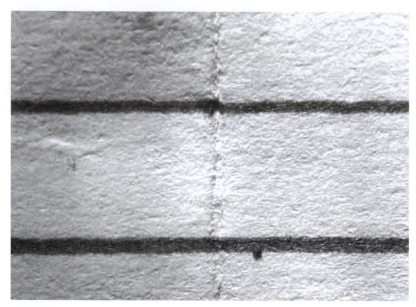

FIGURE 9.16

Two ink lines appearing on a sheet of paper that had been folded. Which line was added after the fold?

to know if writing was added to a document after the document was folded. A macrophotograph of the ink path across the fold line will usually show whether the writing was placed on the document before or after the page was folded. If the writing was added after the document was folded, the ink path will hesitate briefly at the fold line, leaving a small "blob" of ink on the fold (Figure 9.16).

The use of transmitted light is often useful in capturing details of paper, particularly watermarks. A light table or digital scanner may be used for this technique. If a digital scanner is used, leave the lid open and direct a lamp onto the document to allow the transmission of light. This scanning technique may also be used for recording the image of a paper watermark (see Figure 9.17).

When photographing fingerprints, handwriting, or other material on glossy paper surfaces, a polarizing filter may be used to reduce glare and reflections. Document examiners may use glass or plastic grids to measure handwriting angles and typeface alignment. These grids are placed on top of the document and photographed to show similarities or differences in angles and alignments. A polarizing filter may be needed to omit glare and reflection from flashes or other illuminating lamps when using transparent measurement grids (Figure 9.18).

FIGURE 9.17

Watermark photographed using a light table for transmitted illumination.

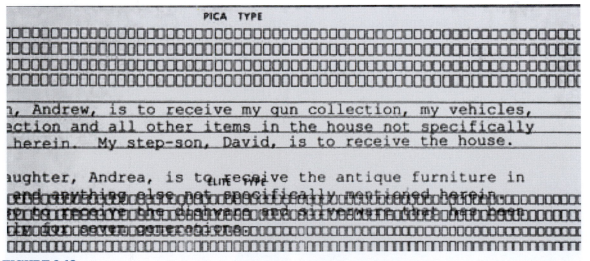

FIGURE 9.18

Glass typewriter alignment grid photographed using a polarizing filter to eliminate glare from the photoflood lights.

DUSTY SHOE PRINTS

It is particularly important to photograph any shoe impressions in interiors, such as on floors or countertops, because these cannot readily be reproduced in any other manner. Photographing dusty shoe prints can be a challenge for the photographer. Using a strong flashlight to graze across the floor where the print lies is one technique to try. With the camera mounted on a tripod, set the exposure to shutter priority at 3–4 s and expose while rapidly moving the flashlight back and forth in a grazing motion. This will capture all of the footprint area rather than a narrow beam (see Figure 9.19). When there is little contrast, it may be necessary to lift the print after photographing it. Rubber lifters, adhesive lifters, and electrostatic dust lifters may be used for this purpose. Once the print is lifted, it can be photographed in a more controlled lighting environment such as the lab.

TIRE IMPRESSIONS

The procedure for tire impressions is quite similar to that described for shoe impressions. A length of the tire track that shows a clear pattern should be shot several times close up to give maximum information. In each photograph, the full width of the impression should almost fill the frame. One of these should show the class characteristics that will identify the type of tire. Areas that reveal defects, such as cuts, may also serve to identify the individual tire.

It is also important to photograph, in sections, a sufficient length of each tire impression, if available, to provide pictures that correspond to the complete circumference of each tire. After photography, these same areas should be reproduced in plaster casts or dental stone.

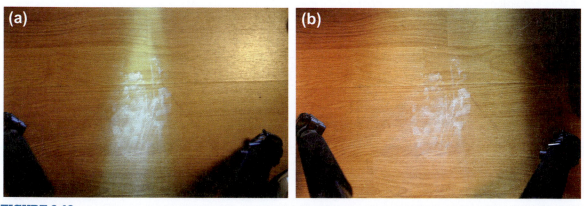

FIGURE 9.19
Dusty shoe print. First taken with stationary flashlight. Second taken at slower shutter speed with rapidly grazing light from the flashlight.

As in photographing shoe impressions, oblique lighting or black spray paint should be used to create shadows and emphasize the characteristics of the impression (Figure 9.20).

BLOODSTAINS

In homicides and serious assaults, it will sometimes be necessary to photograph in detail the pattern and color of bloodstains (Figure 9.21). The location, area, and tapering of the stains may indicate the positions and actions of the assailant or the victim.

Blood is often difficult to detect because the color of blood depends upon its age, the temperature, the time of year, and the material on which it is found. Blood may appear colorless, reddish-brown, green-brown, light olive green, or rose; the photographer cannot, therefore, look only for red spots. He should look in out-of-the-way areas for stains such as the bottom side of dresser drawers or table drawers that the suspect may have touched.

A portable ultraviolet light or an ALS is good for detecting bloodstains, as are the various presumptive blood-screening tests (e.g. Luminol, Phenolphthalein, Leuco-malachite Green, and Tetramethylbenzidine reaction tests). Further study of blood detection tests will aid the photographer immensely. Photographs of the stain should be taken both before and after the solution is applied.

The Luminol blood detection test requires the room to be darkened to observe the test's luminescent activity in the presence of blood. Photographing the Luminol reaction may be somewhat difficult, but the use of the "fill flash" technique should produce acceptable results. The fill-flash technique basically

FIGURE 9.20
Tire impression in grease made by a hand truck (dolly).

FIGURE 9.21
Bloodstains.

involves taking two pictures on one image exposure. Using a camera and flash (with manual firing capability), calculate the appropriate flash exposure for the camera to stain distance and stop down two f-stops from that exposure rating on the camera. For instance, if f-8 is recommended as the proper flash exposure, stop the camera lens down to f-16. Spray the Luminol onto the suspected bloodstain and darken the room as completely as possible. Open the camera lens to the lowest f-stop setting (e.g. f-2.8) and set the exposure setting for "B" (bulb) on the camera. Expose the film for approximately 40–80 s (using ISO 400). While the shutter is still open on "B," close the f-stop setting down to f-16 and manually fire the flash unit, then release the shutter. This technique allows the glow from the Luminol reaction to record itself on the image and the flash allows the same frame to record the surrounding areas so the photograph will detail where the bloodstains were found. This technique requires the use of a tripod and a lockable shutter release cable (see Figure 9.22).

Close-up photographs of bloodstains will record the evidence most graphically. A diagram or sketch of the stains should also be made so that the individual stains can be identified.

Whenever possible, color should be used to photograph bloodstains. When shooting in black-and-white mode, use a blue or green filter for stains on a light background. To obtain contrast of stains on a dark background, use a red filter in black-and-white mode. Bloodstains photographed under ultraviolet

FIGURE 9.22
Bloodstains on shirt with characteristic Luminol glow taken by fill-flash technique.

light will appear black even after the fabric has been washed, leaving only a trace of the stain. Using a higher than normal ISO speed (400 or higher) will help ensure a shorter exposure time.

BULLETS, CARTRIDGES, AND SHELLS

In any crime involving firearms, a thorough search is made at the crime scene for bullets, cartridges, and shells. If found, a firearms identification expert may be able to determine if a bullet or casing was fired from a particular firearm. A comparison microscope is used for examining a questioned bullet or casing and comparing rifling markings and ejector markings with a test bullet or casing fired from the suspect weapon.

Comparison photographs should be made with a comparison microscope in the same fashion as microphotography. Comparison photographs can also be made in a small department using macrophotography, but this requires a great deal of patience and hard work (Figure 9.23).

PARTICLES AND OTHER SMALL SPECIMENS

Small quantities of clue material such as glass fragments, paint flakes, soil particles, fibers, and other substances are often carried unknowingly to and from

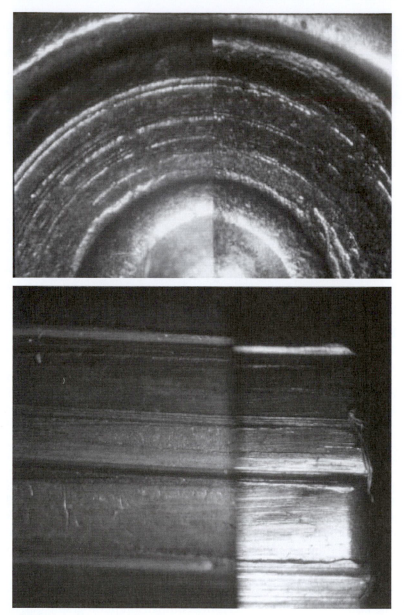

FIGURE 9.23
Comparison microscope photos of bottom of shell casing (top) and bullets (bottom).

the scene by the perpetrator. Their location on the suspect's clothing and at the crime scene should be documented carefully by close-up photographs for comparison purposes. Where such traces are minute, the evidence will be invisible in the overall crime scene photographs; hence, considerable care should be exercised to obtain a sharp close-up photograph that will clearly reveal the appearance of the substance in its original position. The location of the close-up can be indicated on the overall view by an overlay.

Identifying a hit-and-run vehicle can be accomplished by matching paint fragments. A paint fragment found at the scene of an accident may correspond with an area of a suspected vehicle from which paint is missing.

If the case warrants it, clothing should be photographed with infrared and ultraviolet illumination or the ALS, to bring out any marks that are invisible to the human eye.

PHOTOGRAPHING AT THE IDENTIFICATION BUREAU

The identification photography performed at the crime scene to show the appearance of small objects of evidence can usually be supplemented or improved upon by photographs taken at the identification bureau or the police laboratory. Here, under the carefully controlled conditions of the laboratory, the photographer can arrange the object so as to present the most informative view to the camera.

Photography will also be required for recording the appearance of evidence delivered to the laboratory or identification bureau by a police officer for special processing. Because the analysis, physical testing, or processing of evidence frequently results in a change of appearance or a decrease in quantity, a record of the original condition of the article or substances submitted should be made in anticipation of any questions that might be raised in court concerning the identity or nature of the evidence. A standard lighting and photographic arrangement can usually be used for this type of photograph. However, some materials may require experimentation with lighting to obtain the best results.

Every piece of clothing brought into the laboratory should be photographed on the body before undressing, then photographed individually. Be sure to include a data sheet in each photograph.

PHOTOGRAPHS MADE WITH THE ALTERNATE LIGHT SOURCE

Obtaining good photographs of evidence illuminated by an ALS can also challenge the photographer. One might think of the ALS as being just another source of illumination such as an electronic flash. However, the illuminating light source for the photograph is the object that luminesces or the chemical that fluoresces, not the ALS light. Digital cameras are especially well suited for photographing objects under ALS illumination since immediate exposure results can be obtained and corrections can be made to exposure settings. Goggles are often used by crime scene investigation personnel to help visualize fluorescence when using an ALS. Remember that the camera lens also needs the same barrier filtration to record images.

PHOTOGRAPHIC TECHNIQUES

Several methods can be used to photograph small objects in the laboratory. If the purpose of the picture is simply that of identification, the objective of the photographer should be an image that is sharp in all details, free from confusing shadows, and large enough to show all important details of the article of evidence.

If the object is small, make a natural or life-sized photograph. Larger objects and groups of small objects should be arranged symmetrically and photographed so that the image almost fills the frame.

Focus on a midpoint in the field and stop down the lens opening until both ends of the object are in acceptable focus. For groups of objects, focus on the central object and stop down the lens opening until the objects at the borders are in sharp focus. If an aperture smaller than f-22 is necessary for good focus, increase the lens-to-object distance. The smaller image size should give the required depth of field. Include a ruler and data sheet in all evidence photographs of this type.

Often, the aim in small-object photography is to show texture and give an impression of depth of field in a surface by means of contrasting shadow. This may be achieved by using grazing, oblique light with a black background or using focus stacking or both. The lighting arrangement is deceptively simple; actually, the success of the photograph depends on a careful balance between the distances of the illumination and reflector from the subject.

DARKFIELD ILLUMINATION PHOTOGRAPHS

Some objects of evidential value are transparent or "colorless." Darkfield illumination is a technique whereby transparent objects may be photographed showing detail and contrast. A light source is placed behind or underneath the object and directed through it at a 45°angle (see Figure 9.24). This makes the object appear bright against a dark background. Darkfield illumination is useful for glass, plastic, clear fingerprint lifters, etc.

BACKLIGHT ILLUMINATION PHOTOGRAPHS

A lighting setup similar to darkfield illumination is background illumination. Background illumination works well with small opaque objects. An object is placed on a transparent surface against a white (or other color) background.

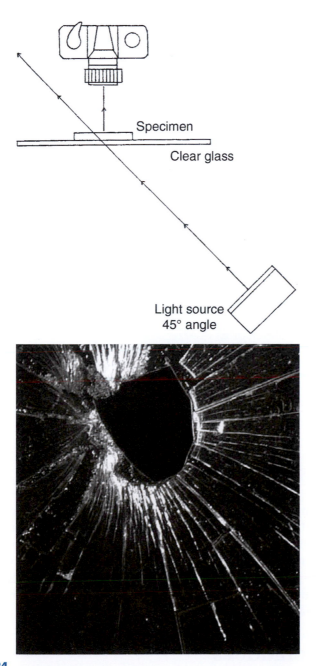

Specimen

Clear glass

Light source
45° angle

FIGURE 9.24
Diagram showing darkfield illumination setup (top) and photo of bullet hole in glass taken by the darkfield illumination technique (bottom).

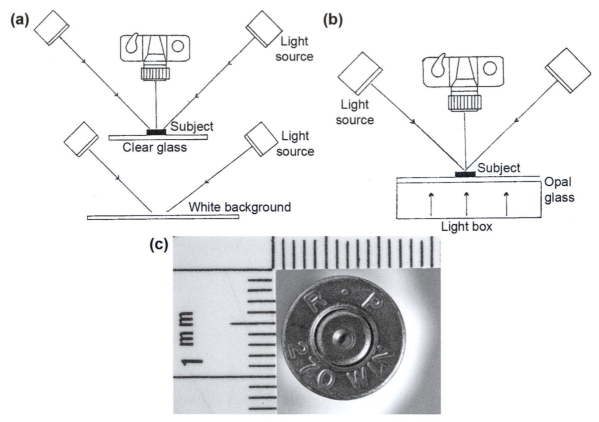

FIGURE 9.25
Diagrams showing backlight illumination setups. Illustration (a) depicts a four light setup and illustration, (b) depicts the use of a light box. Both methods produce excellent results. Photo (c) shows a cartridge photographed with backlight illumination.

The object on the transparent surface is raised several inches from the background. The background is illuminated with two or four light sources. The object is illuminated from above with an additional two or four light sources. The background illumination must be about four times as intense as the object illumination (see Figure 9.25). Exposures are made, disregarding the background illumination, by using a spot meter or by turning off the background illumination and taking a light-meter reading.

COPY TECHNIQUES

Macrophotography requires a suitable camera, close-up lens, or close-up lens attachments (extension rings, bellows, etc.), a camera mounting system

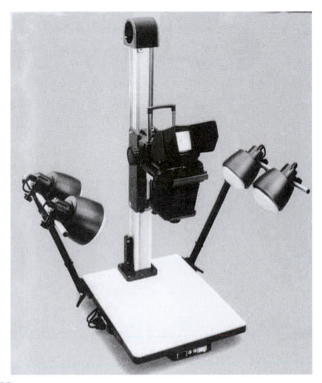

FIGURE 9.26
Polaroid's MP-4 copy camera. Note the position of the copy lights.

capable of holding the camera securely, and copy lights. Although there are copy cameras and systems designed exclusively for this type of photography, any digital SLR cameras may be used. A camera mounting system for copy work can be purchased separately. Photoflood lights, tungsten lamps, or LED lamps may be used for illumination.

The most common lighting arrangement for copy work is to have two or four lamps on both sides of the object to be photographed, directed onto the object at a 45° angle (see Figure 9.26).

Photographing glossy objects may introduce reflections. Reflections and glare may be reduced by using a polarizing filter or spray matte finish (such as Calm), available at most art supply houses. Another method is to take a flat, black piece of cardboard with a hole just large enough for the camera lens to protrude and use it as a light shield in front of the camera. This technique also works well when photographing latent prints on mirrors or chrome surfaces (see Chapter 11).

Ultraviolet and Infrared Imaging

CONTENTS

ABSTRACT

The police photographer may need to photograph items of evidence using specialized lighting techniques, such as ultraviolet (UV) and infrared (IR). Many items of physical evidence may only be visualized using wavelengths outside the visible spectrum. UV and IR photography may be used to visualize body fluids, fingerprints, hair and fiber, gunpowder residues, ink discrimination in questioned documents, to see through paint pigments for traces of blood, bruising and injuries, tattoos on decomposed bodies, and so on. Taking photographs with UV and IR lighting requires special equipment, cameras, and filters. Exposure settings and focusing are also different with UV and IR photography compared to regular visible spectrum photography.

KEY TERMS

Alternate light source (ALS)
Barrier filter
Black light
Excitation
Exciter filter
Fluorescence
Full spectrum
Infrared radiation
Long-wave ultraviolet
Luminescence
Night vision
Phosphorescence
Radiation
Short-wave ultraviolet
Transmitting filter

ULTRAVIOLET AND FLUORESCENCE PHOTOGRAPHY

Ultraviolet (UV) photography has been considered fluorescence photography, but although it is a common technique to use UV radiation to produce fluorescence, this is not the only radiation that can be used for this purpose. Also, because it is possible to completely photograph an object by UV radiation with no fluorescence produced, the reason for the division is further justified. If an object is photographed by UV radiation reflected from it or transmitted through it (as in microscopy), the technique should be called UV. In the latter case, involving a microscope, the technique is sometimes referred to as UV micrography. If certain radiations (including UV) are used to excite fluorescence in an object, the recording of the resultant fluorescence is called fluorescence photography.

UV Photography

The main purpose of UV photography is to obtain information about an object or material that cannot be obtained by other photographic methods. Obviously, if differentiation between two substances is produced in photography with visible light or infrared (IR) radiation, there is little need to resort to UV photography. If the first two methods fail, however, there is always the possibility that the third might succeed. In many cases, it is worth a try.

Ultraviolet photography is usually performed by using reflected radiation, and it depends upon the premise that two (or more) elements of an object will reflect or absorb UV radiation differently. Techniques in visible and IR photography operate on essentially the same principle, except, of course, that, in most visible-light photography, the elements of an object may show color contrast.

Some materials absorb UV radiation, whereas others reflect radiation. Some have partial absorption and partial reflection. These effects can be recorded photographically by using UV radiation.

UV Radiation

Ultraviolet radiation cannot be seen by the naked eye and is often termed "invisible," as are other electromagnetic radiations except those in the short visible range. UV wavelengths range from 200–400 nm and are usually divided into three types: long-wave (320–400 nm); medium-wave (280–320 nm); and short-wave (200–280 nm). Many digital camera image sensors are sensitive to some wavelengths of UV radiation. However, many camera lenses have UV blocking coatings. These limit the lens from being easily used in UV photography. Lenses vary with these coatings and test shots should be made to determine how much of a UV blocking coat is on the lens. If UV photography will be used frequently, it would be a good idea to purchase a quartz or silicon lens, which does not block UV light (these tend to be very expensive).

UV Radiation Sources
Sunlight

Sunlight is probably the most common source of UV radiation. Although the long waves and some middle waves of UV radiation pass rather freely through the atmosphere, the short waves are attenuated by scattering and by absorption because of moisture and gases in the atmosphere. A sufficient amount of long-wave UV radiation is usually present, and bright sunlight could be used to illuminate large areas with UV radiation, particularly on a dry day. For UV photography using sunlight, a filter is placed over the camera lens. This filter should transmit long-wave UV radiation freely and should absorb all visible light. The filter should be closely fitted to the camera lens so that no visible light enters the lens. This filter is commonly known as a Wratten 18A filter. These filters are made of special quartz glass and tend to be expensive.

Fluorescent Tubes

Fluorescent tubes are often used in the photographic laboratory to provide visual illumination over a large area. Special tubes of this type can be used to provide UV radiation for photography. UV radiation is produced in these tubes by a discharge of electricity through a carrier gas, such as argon. The gas ionizes enough to cause a glow, and develops enough heat to cause mercury in the tube to vaporize. As the mercury vaporizes, it is ionized by the electrical discharge and gives off visible light (mostly green and blue), but it also emits UV light, both long wave and short wave. Because long-wave UV light is wanted for most UV photography, this tube is coated on the inside with a phosphor that absorbs short-wave and emits long-wave UV radiation. The glass of the tube usually contains a chemical salt that acts as a filter. It is opaque to most visible light but freely transmits the long-wave UV radiation. Tubes of this type are often called "black light" tubes because they appear visually black (Figure 10.1). These tubes can be obtained in several lengths, up to 48 inches long. They can

FIGURE 10.1
Typical ultraviolet lamp.

be used to illuminate large areas with UV light. These tubes can be operated in standard fluorescent light fixtures, with the standard starter coil and ballast. Tubes of this type are called "low pressure" mercury vapor lamps.

Mercury Vapor Lamps

Mercury vapor lamps of "high pressure" consist of small, tubular, quartz envelopes in which mercury vapor is produced under a pressure of several atmospheres. These lamps require high electrical current for operation and have a considerable output of long-wave UV radiation. They also emit some middle-wave and short-wave UV radiation. They are of particular advantage in illuminating small areas with high UV brightness. Special mercury vapor lamps of this type with high wattage are of particular interest in both UV photomicrography and UV spectrography. These mercury vapor lamps produce extremely bright spectral lines in both the UV and the visible range. Special transformers are usually required for operation, and a warm-up period of several minutes is necessary for greatest brightness.

Arc Lamps

Arc lamps are also used to produce very intense UV radiation, either medium wave or long wave. The cored carbon arc is probably the best-known lamp of this type. An arc is produced by passing electricity as a large spark across two electrodes of carbon in close proximity. Because the carbon is consumed in the process, a mechanical means is used to maintain a constant separation between the electrodes. In a similar manner, electrodes of cadmium can be used to produce an extremely bright line at 275 mµ. The Xenon arc is enclosed in a small glass tube that contains metal electrons in a high-pressure atmosphere of Xenon gas. Although this arc lamp emits some long-wave UV radiation, its primary use is in visual-light photography and photomicrography. A continuous spectrum is produced in the UV, visible, and IR spectral ranges.

Electronic Flash Lamps

Electronic flash lamps vary considerably in UV output, depending to some extent on the type of gas contained in the tubes, the reflector color, and the plastic used in the flash lens. A tube containing a high percentage of krypton or argon emits more blue and long-wave UV radiation than one in which Xenon predominates. Most electronic flash lamps, however, emit some long-wave UV radiation and can be used in reflected UV photography. Some of the lamps in which the tube and envelope are composed of quartz emit some shorter wavelengths of UV radiation.

Illumination for Reflective UV Photography

Restating, there are many sources that emit UV radiation. The selection of a source for UV photography depends primarily upon factors such as availability, cost, convenience, object size, and source emission. Sunlight, of course, is the most readily available; it costs nothing, and provides a broad source of illumination. On the other hand, the intensity of UV radiation available from sunlight is quite variable because of changes in light conditions and by attenuation of UV radiation by scatter and absorption in the atmosphere. A bright, cloudless, dry day is best.

To control illumination conditions more satisfactorily, UV photography is usually performed indoors. The most readily available source of UV radiation is the "black light" fluorescent tube (see Figure 10.1). Tubes of this type can be obtained from all major electrical supply firms (General Electric, Sylvania, Westinghouse, etc.). These tubes can be fitted to, and used in, regular fluorescent light fixtures. They can be obtained in a variety of lengths to suit the size of the object to be illuminated and are reasonably priced. Because the glass for each tube contains a visibly opaque filter element, it is usually necessary to illuminate the subject temporarily with an auxiliary light source (such as a tungsten flood lamp). Long tubes of this type are excellent for UV illumination of large areas, such as the photography of large documents.

Mercury vapor lamps of the "high pressure" type are usually small and are most suitable for illuminating small objects in close-up photography, photomicrography, and spectrography.

Carbon arc lamps are not generally suitable for UV photography. They can be erratic and inconvenient. Also, they provide no advantage over previously mentioned light sources. They can be used for specific purposes, however, in photomicrography by transmitted or reflected light, and in spectrography. The Xenon arc can be used for long-wave UV photography by filtering the visible emission.

Electronic flash lamps provide a broad source of visual illumination, with some UV emission. The efficiency of UV illumination is limited, however, by the type of gas contained in the tubes, the reflector color, and the plastic used in the flash lens. If there is enough UV radiation emitted from an electronic flash, it will permit instantaneous exposures with a hand-held camera, provided that the subject distance is not too great.

Filters

Regardless of the source of illumination used, a filter must be placed over the camera lens. This filter should have a high transmittance of UV radiation, and should not transmit any visible light. The goal of UV photography is exposure by UV radiation. UV transmitting filters are usually made of quartz glass in which coloring agents are contained to control transmittance. Most types of glass will transmit some long-wave UV radiation, but will absorb all medium-wave and short-wave UV radiation. This is not a disadvantage in general UV photography, because lenses used in cameras are made of optical glass, whose transmittance is also limited to long-wave UV radiation. Gelatin filters are unsuitable for this type of photography. The gelatin itself will often fluoresce.

Kodak Wratten Filter no. 18A is a glass filter with a high percentage transmittance of long-wave UV radiation, particularly the 365-mμ line of the mercury spectrum. It is available in both 2-inch and 3-inch squares, and as a threaded lens filter. It can be obtained through photographic supply dealers. This filter, or its equivalent, is highly recommended (nearly mandatory) for long-wave UV photography.

A square no. 18A filter can be attached to a camera lens by means of a Kodak Gelatin Filter Frame Holder and a suitable adapter ring. Threaded UV-transmitting filters can also be obtained from other filter manufacturers. It is suggested, however, that filter transmittance curves be obtained and examined for efficiency of both UV transmittance and visible light absorption. Filters used for this purpose should have no visible light transmittance. Because the no. 18A filter is essentially opaque, the use of the removable square filters is more convenient when focusing the camera (Figure 10.2).

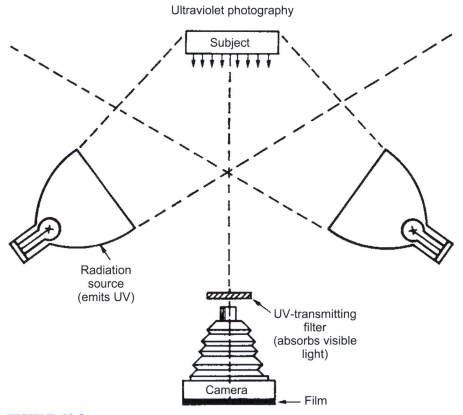

FIGURE. 10.2

Typical setup for reflected ultraviolet (UV) photography. The no. 18A UV transmitting filter may also be placed over the light source rather than the camera lens.

ISO Rating

The ISO rating is determined for visible light, and it does not readily apply to UV radiation. An arbitrary UV ISO speed can be determined by making test exposures. Most of the camera meters do not operate well in the UV region.

Specially designed meters can be obtained for making a reading of UV intensity by doing an internet search. One model is called the Blak-Ray UV intensity meter, and is a hand-held device for measuring the intensity of emission from UV sources and the radiation incident on a surface from a source. Visible light has no effect on the meter. Two sensors are available, one for long-wave UV radiation and another for short-wave UV radiation. Meter readings are in microwatts-per-square centimeter, which can be correlated to exposure time in UV photography. The meter requires no batteries, electrical supply, or other source of power. However, these meters are very costly and the belief is that one can get adequate exposures by doing testing and bracketing of exposures.

In general, exposure time will be considerably longer than if visible light were used (for one aperture setting). A test series could therefore be made at a small focal (f)/number, with variations in exposure time over a wide range, starting with a short exposure time and increasing by a factor of 2. An approximate series could be 1/10, 1/5, 1/2, 1, 2, 4, and 8 s, etc. If all exposures are too long, then overexposure will result, and shorter periods are indicated. Conversely, if all exposures are too short, underexposure results and longer periods are necessary. Once a reasonable exposure period is determined for a given set of conditions, exposures for different conditions can probably be estimated. A shorter test series can be applied. Of course, if a different higher or lower ISO is used, another test exposure series must be made.

Focus

Although a camera lens is specified as having a definite focal length, this characteristic pertains to visible light only. When IR radiation is used to form an image, the focal length of the lens is, generally, slightly longer than specified; when UV radiation is used, it is generally shorter. An image in sharp focus, visually may be quite blurry in a photograph taken by UV radiation. For UV photography, a good technique is to achieve focus visually and then to stop down the lens aperture to obtain greater depth of field. The amount of aperture decrease is a function of normal focal length. Lenses of short focal length inherently have more depth of field, and will require less aperture decrease than those of long focal length. A lens-aperture decrease of at least two stops below wide-open will usually suffice. Test exposures at various apertures, however, will definitely establish the largest f-stop number aperture for sharp focus in reflected-UV photography.

Exposure

The methods by which exposure can be determined in reflected-UV photography include using an exposure meter, making test exposures, or establishing a guide number when flash lamps are used.

Most conventional exposure meters have some small sensitivity to UV radiation. The incident-light type of meter is the most convenient for this work. If the cell can be covered with a Kodak Wratten Filter no. 18A (or equivalent) so as to exclude all visible light, the meter may give an indication of UV intensity. The intensity will vary, of course, as the distance from radiation source to subject is varied. The source should be positioned so that the entire area to be photographed is well illuminated. If a mercury vapor lamp is used, no filter is necessary in front of the lamp, and the visible light emitted will ascertain efficiency of illumination. If the lamp contains an UV transmitting filter that cannot be removed, the coverage and evenness of illumination probably must be determined by exposure tests alone.

Flash

The determination of exposure with flash lamps is simplified, because a guide number can be determined from one test exposure series. The duration of a flash is fairly constant, so a fixed shutter speed (example: 1/60 or 1/125 s) can be used for the series. All exposures in the series should be made at the same lamp-to-subject distance. The test series should include exposures at all available lens-aperture settings.

Here is an example of a test series: a digital camera with an f/2.8 lens is used to make a test series with an ISO setting of 400. With the shutter set at 1/60 s, exposures are made at f/2.8, f/4.0, f/5.6, f/8, f/11, f/16, and f/22. A Kodak Wratten Filter no. 18A is placed in front of the lens. The subject in front of the camera is 6 feet away. On viewing the images made, the frame showing good exposure is determined. In this case, assume the exposure at f/4 appears best. Because a flash guide number is equal to the subject distance multiplied by the lens-aperture number, 6 (the distance) is multiplied by 4 (the f/number), and a guide number of 24 results. This figure can be used for future exposure determination when the same camera, ISO, and flash are used. For instance, if the distance were changed to 4 feet, the new f/number would be 6; if the distance were 2 feet, the new f/number would be 12, etc. With this technique, a flash guide number can be determined for any combination of ISO and flash.

Fluorescence Photography
Luminescence

When certain materials (solids, liquids, or gases) are subjected to short-wave electromagnetic radiation, they will emit another type of radiation of longer wavelength very often in the visible spectrum. The exciting radiation may be X-rays, gamma rays, electrons, UV radiation, or even some visible wavelengths. This phenomenon of induced light emission is called luminescence, of which there are two distinct types. These types are known as fluorescence and phosphorescence.

Fluorescence

If the luminescence ceases within a very short time (8–10 s) after the exciting radiation is removed, the phenomenon is called fluorescence. Although fluorescence is commonly produced by excitation with UV light, other radiations can be used in some applications. Blue light, for example, stimulates green fluorescence in some compounds.

There are many thousands of materials that exhibit the phenomenon of fluorescence, and fluorescence photography has numerous applications because it provides information that cannot be obtained by other photographic methods.

Just the fact that a substance will fluoresce is an important characteristic. The particular radiation that excites fluorescence and the specific position of that fluorescence in the visible spectrum can be clues to the identity of a substance. Also, contrast between the elements of a material can often be produced by fluorescence, even if all appear similar in visible light.

Phosphorescence

Although fluorescence ceases almost immediately after the exciting radiation is removed, there are some substances that continue to luminescence for a long time, even hours, after removal of the exciting stimulus. This phenomenon is called phosphorescence and is produced in compounds called phosphors. Phosphorescence, like fluorescence, is stimulated by many radiations, but in fewer substances. The image on a television screen, for example, is produced by phosphorescence.

IR Luminescence

Although most luminescence appears in the visible spectrum and is excited by either UV or the short, visible wavelengths of blue, it is also possible to excite luminescence in the IR range by irradiation of certain materials with blue-green light. The phenomenon is referred to as luminescence, instead of fluorescence or phosphorescence, because it is not known whether the effect ceases immediately after the exciting stimulus is removed. Infrared luminescence photography will be discussed in more detail later in this chapter.

Excitation Sources

The most common radiations used to excite fluorescence are the long UV wavelengths, and many of the radiation sources used for UV photography in geologic work can also be used for fluorescence photography. Some shorter visible wavelengths are occasionally used to produce fluorescence, either at longer visible wavelengths or in the IR.

Although it is possible to use sunlight as a source of UV or visual light to produce fluorescence, it is not a practical procedure. Artificial radiation sources are preferable because they are constant and consistent, easily procurable, and convenient to use.

Mercury Vapor Lamps

All mercury vapor lamps, both high-pressure and low-pressure, have application in fluorescence photography. The selection of a lamp depends to a great extent on the application. If the subject is large, then a source is needed that can illuminate a large area with the desired radiation. If a small object is to be irradiated, then a small, intensely bright source will be advantageous. All mercury vapor lamps, however, emit long-wave UV radiation, and if the tube is made of quartz, then the shorter waves of UV may also be emitted.

Electronic Flash

Most electronic flash lamps are suitable for UV photography because they emit long-wave UV radiation to some degree. They can also be used for recording fluorescence excited by UV radiation in close-up applications, such as photographing fingerprints dusted with fluorescent powder. A flash-tube with high intensity output should be obtained for this purpose. One of the difficulties encountered in using electronic flash is that resulting fluorescence is not visible during the short flash interval. A continuous UV source is often necessary for preliminary inspection to ascertain the presence of the fluorescence.

Visual Light Sources

As stated, fluorescence can be excited in certain materials by irradiation with blue or blue-violet light, and it occurs at a longer wavelength in the visible spectrum, often green or yellow-green. A light source that has a high intensity with continuous emission in the blue region of the spectrum is needed for this application. The Xenon arc is probably the most suitable light source, although electronic flash might also be used. Carbon arc lamps also emit light of high intensity, but they can be quite erratic unless a mechanical (or electrical) means of maintaining electrodes in a constant position is available.

There are several light sources that can be used for producing IR luminescence. This phenomenon is exhibited in some materials by stimulation with blue-green light. Although it is possible that IR luminescence may also be stimulated by irradiation with specific wavelengths of blue or green, it is suggested that a source that has continuous emission in the blue and green spectral regions be

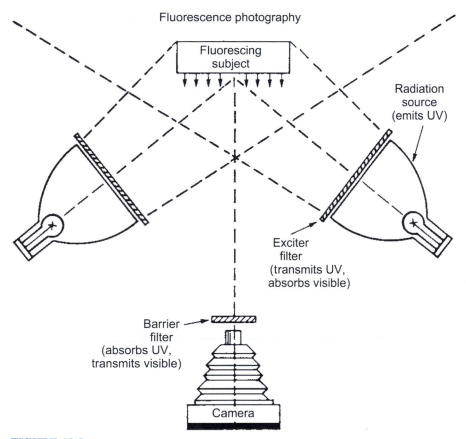

FIGURE 10.3

Typical setup for fluorescence photography using ultraviolet (UV). The exciter filter is a no. 18A UV transmitting filter and the barrier filter is a no. 12 filter.

obtained. High-wattage tungsten lamps, the Xenon arc, or even ordinary fluorescent lamps can be used for this purpose. More notable are lasers, and light emitting diode arrays that can be found in many forensic light (ALS) sources (Figure 10.3).

PHOTOGRAPHIC TECHNIQUE

When fluorescence is stimulated with either UV or visible wavelengths, there are several factors that must be considered for efficient photography. The subject must be illuminated with the exciting stimulus, and this is accomplished by selecting a suitable source that emits the necessary radiation. A filter is used with the source to screen out other radiations and to transmit the exciting radiation. Another filter, usually placed between the subject and the camera, absorbs any exciting radiation and transmits the fluorescence. The fluorescence can then be recorded by a suitable digital or film camera.

Illumination

One of the main factors influencing the brightness of fluorescence is the intensity of the exciting radiation. Fluorescence brightness is generally of very low order compared with the image brightness in other types of photography. It is important, therefore, that the radiation source be as close to the subject as possible, while furnishing even illumination over the area to be photographed.

The size of the subject must be considered when selecting an appropriate source of illumination. When a large subject is to be photographed, the source should cover a large area with as bright an illumination as possible. Long fluorescent tubes (low-pressure mercury vapor lamps) are suitable. High-pressure mercury arcs are also useful, but they are small sources. If they are used to illuminate a large area, there may be a sacrifice in fluorescence brightness, resulting in extremely long exposure times. If the long tubes are selected, two or more (in suitable reflectors) can be placed on each side of the subject to provide a considerable quantity of exciting radiation. If the subject is large and flat, such as a large document, the tubes should be placed so that the incident illumination angle is less than 45°. Make sure, however, that no direct light from the source is "seen" by the camera. The lamp reflectors can be placed so that this does not occur. Again, many of the various forensic light sources (ALS) can produce the same results.

High-pressure mercury vapor lamps are excellent for illuminating small objects or small areas. One lamp, however, is usually inadequate, because illumination is then provided for one side only. At least two lamps should be used, one on each side of the subject, especially when the subject is three-dimensional.

Electronic flash lamps are especially useful when living subjects that exhibit fluorescence are to be photographed, because instantaneous exposures are possible. Although one lamp may be sufficient, two lamps (one on each side of the subject) will provide twice as much light and will allow smaller lens apertures (for increased depth of field) to be used.

The illumination of the subject should consist only of the radiations needed to excite fluorescence. All ambient illumination (room lights) and all other illumination from the source must be excluded from the subject. Fluorescence photography is often accomplished in either a darkened room or in a light-tight enclosure.

Exciter and Barrier Filters

At least two distinct types of filters are used in a fluorescence photography system. The first, called an exciter filter (example: Wratten no. 18A), is placed between the radiation source and the subject. It transmits the radiation to excite fluorescence. The second, a barrier filter (Wratten no. 12), is placed in front of the camera lens (or somewhere behind the objective lens in a microscope), to remove any exciting radiation and to transmit the fluorescence.

The exciting filter is used with the radiation source and its purpose is to transmit the exciting radiation efficiently and absorb all, or almost all, of the other radiations emitted from the source. When UV radiation is used to excite fluorescence, the exciter filter should pass a high percentage of the UV light radiated from the source. If visible blue or blue-green light is used to excite fluorescence, then the exciter filter for this purpose should transmit these radiations freely and absorb all others.

Fluorescence brightness, as previously stated, is usually of low intensity, and if light other than the exciting radiations are incident on the subject, they may mask the fluorescence. Therefore, this should be done in a dark, or nearly dark, environment.

The exciter filter in front of the light source transmits the radiation necessary to excite fluorescence. Not all of this radiation is absorbed, however, and some reflected exciting radiation will be reflected from or transmitted through the subject. If this exciting radiation is not removed, it will be recorded in the image. Because it is usually of higher brightness than the fluorescence, it will cause more exposure than the fluorescence. Therefore, a filter must be used in front of the camera lens in order to prevent the reflected exciting radiation from causing exposure. This filter acts as a barrier to the exciting radiation, and is therefore known as a barrier filter. An efficient barrier filter absorbs all radiation transmitted by the exciter filter and transmits only the wavelengths of light evident as fluorescence. If UV radiation is used to excite fluorescence, then the barrier filter must absorb UV radiation. If the exciter filter passes both UV and some short visual blue radiation, then the barrier must absorb both UV and blue radiation. For UV fluorescence photography, a no. 18A filter is used as the exciter filter and a Wratten no. 2A or 2E or similar can be used as a barrier filter for color imaging. A deep yellow filter (example: Wratten no. 12) can be used as a barrier filter in monochrome (black and white) work.

Exposure Determination

Because of the very low brightness of fluorescence, the most practical method of gaining exposure is by test. In a manual camera, operational mode, bracket exposures by making several exposures, increasing time at a fixed lens aperture by a factor of 2 in successive steps over a wide range can be done. Lens apertures could also be varied using a fixed time, but this technique would cause a variation in depth of field that might not be desirable. Once an exposure time and aperture has been determined, however, the lens aperture can be changed to achieve the appropriate depth of field. As in all other photographs, if lens aperture is changed, the exposure time must be changed in inverse proportion.

An alternative to the manual mode might be to use the camera in the aperture priority setting and achieve bracketing by using the exposure value control on the camera.

When a constant light source is used, such as a mercury arc lamp, the exposure time will be several seconds or even minutes if the fluorescence is extremely low in brightness. Extremely long exposures result when large subjects are to be photographed and illumination is spread over a large area. Extremely long exposures can also result when an image size is greater than the object size, as in photomacrography. However, by using the in-camera meter and having the camera operating in aperture priority mode (with the proper lighting and filters), one should gain a starting point for exposure compensation and fine tuning the exposure.

When electronic flash is to be used (as in close-up fluorescence photography), an experimental guide number can be determined for a specific subject, flash unit, and film. However, if the subject is changed, the guide number may, or may not, apply. This is because fluorescent brightness may change. In this case, exposures should be bracketed. Exposure time will be constant with flash, so changing the lens aperture and/or ISO setting is the only practical means of varying exposure.

No matter how exposure is determined, it is a good idea to make a record of all exposure conditions for future reference. These conditions include the subject, the radiation source, the exciter filter, the barrier filter, the position of the source, the film, the exposure time, lens aperture, and other details pertinent to fluorescence photography.

Focus

When fluorescence occurs in the visible spectrum, there is no problem involved in obtaining correct focus. Recording IR luminescence, however, involves an invisible image, and the lens focal length is longer for IR than for visible light. The use of a small lens aperture is a practical means of obtaining correct focus. Usually, the image is focused with visible light; a focus shift to the IR focus point (if the lens has one) is made and the lens aperture is decreased to at least two stops below the wide-open position. Then the IR-transmitting filter is placed in front of the lens and the exposure is made. The exact lens aperture would be determined by the depth of the field necessary to record a satisfactory image as well as any lens aberrations (donut) that may be encountered.

Applications

Because there are many thousands of substances that exhibit fluorescence when excited by specific radiations, it is reasonable to expect that there are many photographic applications in which this phenomenon is of particular interest. As with any type of photography, the photography of fluorescence is practiced to supply information that cannot be obtained by other means. The fact that a substance does fluoresce differentiates it from one that does not. When two substances fluoresce they may differ in fluorescence color, or their fluorescence may occur in distinctly different portions of the spectrum; visible or invisible. Most fluorescence occurs in the visible spectrum with long-wave UV excitation. Fluorescence can also occur, however, in long-wave UV (or in the visible spectrum) with short-wave UV excitation. It can also occur in the long-wave visible region with blue light excitation. Finally, some materials, as stated, produce IR luminescence when excited by blue-green light.

QUESTIONED DOCUMENTS

An outstanding application of fluorescence photography is in the field of questioned documents. When other photographic methods fail to reveal suspected alterations in, or additions to, a document (check, letter, will, etc.), it is always possible that a fluorescence technique will provide fruitful results. Different inks may show a difference in visible fluorescence. The effects of bleaching or erasing can also often be detected by this means. Most papers on which documents are written or printed contain cellulose fibers. These fibers often fluoresce brightly when the paper is illuminated with UV radiation in a darkened room. Erasures will alter this fluorescence and the effect can be recorded and enhanced. If inks have been bleached (e.g., with an "ink eradicator") the bleaching material still on the paper may show a fluorescent color. If it does, the effect can be recorded on either black-and-white or color imagery (see Figure 10.4).

Because visible fluorescence may be produced by excitation with either long-wave or short-wave UV radiation, photographs should be made using each method.

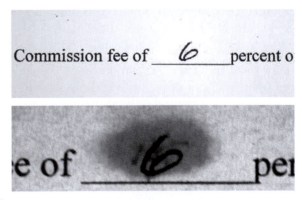

FIGURE 10.4
Altered contrast showing the original commission fee as 15% under ultraviolet radiation.

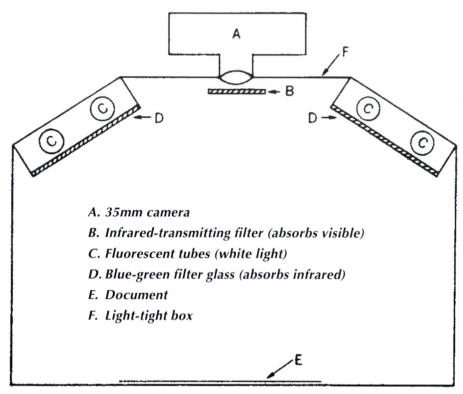

A. 35mm camera
B. Infrared-transmitting filter (absorbs visible)
C. Fluorescent tubes (white light)
D. Blue-green filter glass (absorbs infrared)
E. Document
F. Light-tight box

FIGURE 10.5
Suggested technique for photographing infrared (IR) luminescence in questioned documents.

To produce fluorescence by short-wave UV radiation, a radiation source that emits this wavelength is needed. A high-pressure mercury arc in a quartz envelope emits several spectral lines of UV radiation, including the short-wave UV at 254 mμ. A filter that passes only short radiations must be placed in front of the source to provide only the necessary excitation. Narrow-band "interference filters" can be used for this purpose and are available from several firms.

Different inks may show different "IR luminescence" when irradiated with visible blue-green light. This can prove invaluable in detecting alterations in documents. The following is a method of illuminating a document in a light-tight box with blue-green light (provided by fluorescent tubes) and photographing the resultant IR luminescence (see Figure 10.5). A box of this type can be constructed of wood (or other material) to accommodate average-sized documents, such as checks and letters. Because the camera is reasonably close, special close-up lenses are usually necessary if a camera with an extendable bellows (or extension tubes) is not available. The box should be light tight, so that no ambient light containing IR radiation is incident on the surface of the

FIGURE 10.6
Altered check under normal illumination (a) and infrared (IR) luminescence (b).

document. A Kodak Wratten Filter no. 87 (and others in the spectral region), which transmit IR radiation but absorb visible light, are suggested for the front of the camera lens. Focus is accomplished first, however, with the blue-green light. The lens opening is decreased to a small aperture to assure good focus in the IR. The blue-green filter in front of the lamps can be Corning Glass no. 9780, available from the Corning Glass Works (Corning, NY). A long, narrow size is suggested for use in front of the fluorescent tubes. Information about available sizes and prices can be obtained from Corning. An IR sensitive digital camera would be used (Figure 10.6).

The exposure box just described can also be adapted for regular close-up photography of visible fluorescence in documents or other objects. "Black light" fluorescent tubes, which emit UV radiation, can be used in place of the white light tubes. The blue-green IR barrier filters would be removed and the IR-transmitting filter on the camera lens can be replaced by a barrier-type filter to absorb the UV radiation reflected from the subject. Fluorescence photographs can be made either in color or monochrome.

The same equipment could also be used to photograph documents by reflected UV radiation. In that case, the "black light" tubes remain in place and a Kodak

Wratten Filter no. 18A would then be used in front of the camera lens to transmit only UV radiation.

The size of the box is governed by the length of tubes to be used and the sizes of documents or other subjects to be photographed.

FINGERPRINTS

Photographing fingerprints with visible light is a well-known, long-established procedure. Latent fingerprints on a dark surface are dusted with a light or white powder; those on a light surface, with a dark or black powder. In this way, a high-contrast effect is produced that can be photographed as a monochrome rendition. As long as the surface is smooth and uniform in color or density, the fingerprint should photograph well. If a surface is multicolored or of alternate light and dark areas, however, neither a light nor a dark powder will give satisfactory contrast. Visualization of an entire fingerprint may be difficult. In this case, the area containing a latent print can be dusted with a powder that will fluoresce brightly when irradiated with long-wave UV radiation in a darkened room. The background will usually appear very dark, with little or no fluorescence, so that the fingerprint stands out, and excellent contrast is achieved (Figure 10.7).

A suggested technique for photographing such fingerprints is to use a single-lens reflex-type camera focused on the area suspected of containing a fingerprint (Figure 10.8). It must be placed perpendicular to the plane of the print. A

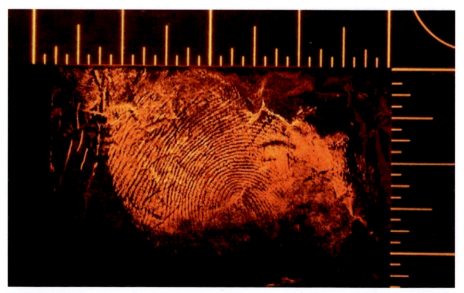

FIGURE 10.7
Fluorescent fingerprints.

suitable electronic flash unit would be attached to the camera with a long synchronizing cord. It should provide enough UV intensity to produce very bright fluorescence. The flash unit is placed at one side and is directed at the area to be photographed. A Kodak Wratten Filter no. 18A (or equivalent) can be taped in place on the front of the flash in order to provide only UV radiation, the exciting stimulus. This will also prevent all visible light from reaching the subject. There are various powders made for this purpose that fluoresce various colors. A barrier filter must be placed in front of the camera lens to prevent reflected UV radiation from exposing the film. A Kodak Wratten Filter no. 2A is suggested for this purpose. Focus and composition can be accomplished in room light, which is extinguished for the fluorescence exposure. The camera should

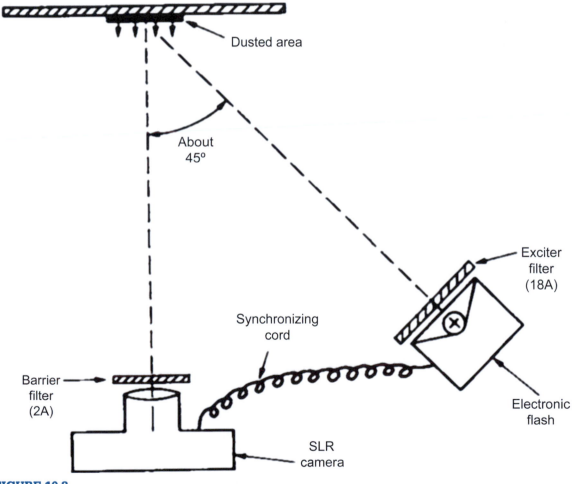

FIGURE 10.8
Flash technique for fingerprints.

be placed on a small tripod, or bench clamp, because exposures are made in a darkened room and this would hold the camera position. Exposure time is fixed at the flash duration, so it is usually necessary to vary test exposures by changing lens apertures and flash distance. The actual lens aperture used will depend upon the brightness of the source and its proximity to the subject. An exciting source of relatively low intensity would necessarily have to be very close to the subject. However, it could produce a fluorescent brightness high enough (from the instantaneous flash) to cause adequate fluorescent exposure.

If an electronic flash lamp is not available, the dusted area can be illuminated with long-wave UV radiation from any source that emits this radiation. In any case, the exciting source should be placed very close to the area to be photographed in order to produce the highest fluorescent brightness and the camera would naturally be placed on a steadying device, such as a tripod.

INJURIES

Dermatologists have long used a photographic technique, known as reflective ultraviolet photography (RUP), during examinations of patients to detect skin cancers and fungi growth. It is also useful in documenting pattern injuries that may have faded or disappeared visually. Pattern injuries are injuries that have a recognizable pattern or shape that can be identified, such as bite marks, bruising, abrasions, scratches, cigarette burns, and whip or belt marks.

Victims of sexual assault may delay reporting the crime to police. During the delay, evidence of physical injury may heal, or visually disappear, creating problems documenting the injuries sustained. Child abuse victims may be too young to be credible witnesses and documenting injuries they may have sustained is a valuable source of evidence. Often, injuries that need to be documented are faded or healed to the point that normal photography will fail to capture the necessary details of the injuries. RUP has been used to document pattern injuries up to 9 months after they have visibly healed (Aaron, 1991).

The basic principle of the reflective UV photographic technique is that only UV light rays that have been reflected from the surface of the skin are recorded on film. A Kodak no. 18A UV transmission filter is used over the light source (such as an electronic flash) in a darkened room, or over the camera lens with normal light conditions. The no. 18A filter is visually opaque and transmits only long wave UV rays between 300 and 400 nm.

Exposure and focusing using the RUP technique must be performed manually. Automatic focusing lenses must be switched to manual mode and focusing must be performed prior to placing the filter over the lens if normal light sources are used. Exposure should be bracketed because the metering system of the camera will not differentiate UV illumination. Exposures should be made by as many as five stops to insure a good exposure. One of the keys to

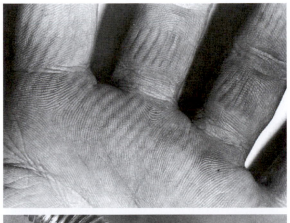

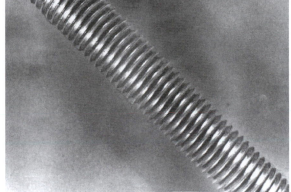

FIGURE 10.9

Photograph of an assault perpetrator's hand using a reflective ultraviolet (UV) technique. The perpetrator's hand was first sprayed with trace metal detection solution then photographed using an electronic flash fitted with a UV filter. The thread marks correspond to the threaded three-quarter inch, 3 foot long bar the perpetrator used in the assault.

successful RUP photographs is to use sufficient illumination. If the no. 18A filter is placed over the lens of the camera, two electronic flashes may make better exposures than one. Place the camera on a tripod and position the subject about 12–14 inches from the camera lens. If the subject is living, advise them to keep their movements to a minimum so that a series of photographs, with and without the filter, can be made in the same position. Take a normal photograph with scale included and then take the UV photograph, again with scale included. Two electronic flashes may be used, one attached to the camera and one with a slave attachment. Hold the slaved flash close to the injured area.

If the no. 18A filter is placed over the illuminating source (i.e., flash), the flash should be handheld, using the off-camera flash technique, and close to the injured area. The room lights should be turned off allowing only the flashed UV light to reach the camera lens (Figure 10.9).

FORENSIC LIGHT SOURCES OR ALTERNATE LIGHT SOURCES

ALSs are single portable lighting units that are capable of providing light from UV to IR. There are a variety of manufacturers of alternate light source units. Most have a fine-tuning device that allows it to be tuned to any peak wavelength in the visible region (400–700 nm). In addition, the UV (300–400 nm) range may be selected and an IR range (700–1100 nm) is optional. The resulting illuminated subject may be videotaped or still imaged. Barrier filter goggles must be worn to visualize fluorescence and to drop out the excitation source. Goggles also protect the eyes from the intense light source. Camera filters must be used when photographing fluorescent evidence. These range from the yellow (Wratten no. 15), the orange (Wratten no. 21 or 22), to the red (Wratten no. 29).

ALSs can be used to examine and detect various forms of physical evidence including (but not limited to):

- Biological substances, such as blood, semen, saliva, urine and bone;
- Bruises;
- Bite marks;
- Fibers;
- Oils and lubricants;
- Gunshot residues;
- Fingerprints;
- Document forgeries.

The most common setting used on a tunable wavelength source is the crime scene search (CSS) mode on an SPEX instrument otherwise referred to as a broad-band excitation wavelength setting. This setting encompasses a range of wavelengths spanning from near-UV, violet, blue, and green light. The CSS setting is adequate for scanning of the crime scene to identify many forms of evidence, including fluorescent physiological stains and fibers. Fluorescence occurs when light is sufficiently energetic to promote electrons from the molecules of a substance into an excited state. As these electrons return to their normal state, energy is released in the form of light that is of a wavelength longer than the excitation wavelength. This phenomenon is referred to as stokes-shift and the light that is emitted by the electrons is called fluorescence (Figures 10.10–10.12).

Many of the substances listed above will fluoresce under light from an ALS although the excitation wavelengths will vary. Bloodstains, however, may differ from other body fluids and materials in that blood absorbs light. A CSS setting may be adequate when searching for blood. Searches performed with UV and 415–455 nm light may be more helpful when dilute blood is suspected. Because blood absorbs light, bloodstains, of either whole blood or dilute, may appear as dark spots under the above lighting conditions when coupled with an orange barrier filter (Figure 10.13).

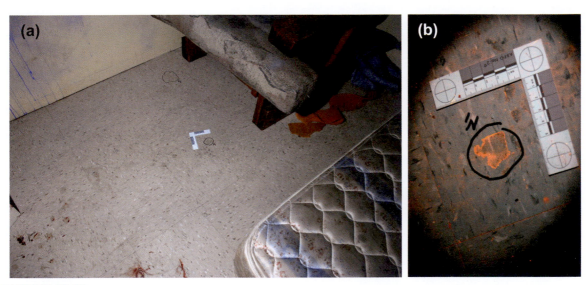

FIGURE 10.10

Scanning the scene with an alternate light source using broadband excitation wavelengths such as the crime scene search (CSS) setting of an SPEX light source can be a quick and effective way of identifying several forms of physical evidence. In the above example, the scene of a rape/homicide was examined with an alternate light source (ALS) set to CSS, visualized as an orange barrier filter. A few fluorescent stains were identified not far from where the deceased was found, which were documented with both midrange (a) and close-up photography (b). The fluorescent stain was identified as semen belonging to a suspect in the case.

Physical injuries, such as bruises, can also be imaged in a manner similar to bloodstains. Because a bruise represents damage to tissue and blood vessels beneath the surface of the skin, light in the 420 nm range can be used to show contrast between damaged skin and non-damaged skin. This occurs because blood exhibits its peak light absorption at 420 nm and light in the 420 nm range can sufficiently penetrate into tissue to image it. Furthermore, whereas non-damaged skin can produce a uniform reflectance of light from the ALS, damaged skin where blood and melanin has collected in the tissues will absorb light from the ALS and can appear as darkened areas in the photograph (Figure 10.14).

For the purposes of photography, when using an ALS it is important to understand which barrier filters correspond to the wavelength of light being used. Barrier filters serve to block light that is emitted from the instrument while transmitting light from fluorescent materials into the camera. Filtration is necessary to create contrast, visualize, and photograph evidence that is fluorescing. It should be noted that manufacturer supplied goggles, which are used to visualize fluorescing materials, do not necessarily correspond to photographic filters of the same or similar color. A proper photographic barrier filter will prevent light contamination from the instrument in the photograph. A quick test that may be performed to determine if the photographic filter will adequately block light from the ALS is to simply place the filter over the light guide of

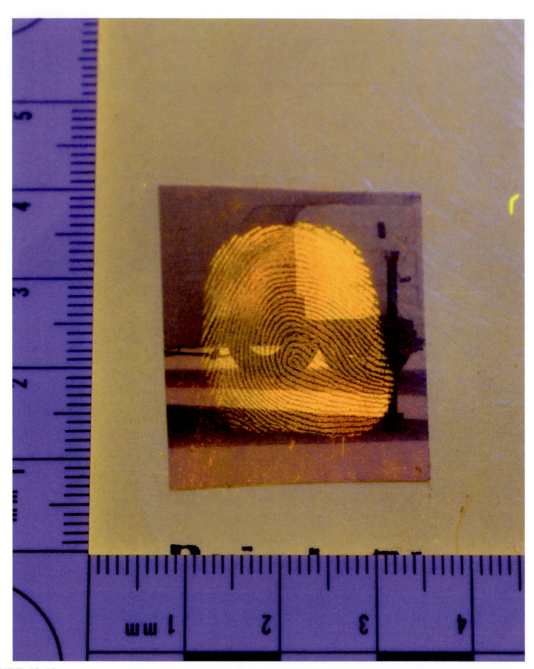

FIGURE 10.11

In the above figure, a fingerprint was developed with the use of a fluorescent powder. Fluorescent powders and dyes are commonly used to aid in the visualization of pattern evidence through fluorescence. In the above figure, because the print is on a portion of a photograph, the fluorescence reduces the convoluting effects of the background rendering the ridge detail clear.

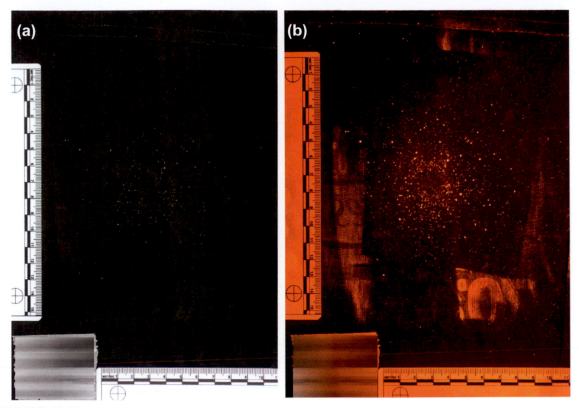

FIGURE 10.12

Gunshot residue may be difficult to visualize with the naked eye especially on dark clothing (a), however, fluorescence of the particulate may be induced when illuminated at a wavelength of 450 nm from an alternate light source (ALS) and visualized/photographed with an orange barrier filter (b).

the ALS. If light is transmitted through the filter, the filter will not be suitable for photographic documentation. If a filter that allows light from the ALS to leak into the camera is used, the resulting image will exhibit reduced contrast between any fluorescent stains and the background.

The following ALS wavelengths and camera filter combinations can be used (Table 10.1):

Table 10.1 ALS Wavelength and Camera Filter Combinations

ALS Wavelength Used	Recommended Barrier Filter
300–400 nm	UV transmitting, clear or yellow filter
410–450 nm	Yellow filter
455–520 nm	Orange filter
530–700 nm	Red filter
700–1200 nm	IR filter

ALS, alternate light source; IR, infrared; UV, ultraviolet.

FIGURE 10.13

In the above figure, a swatch of white linen was stained with blood diluted to 10^{-2}, 10^{-3}, and 10^{-4} and illuminated with light at 420 nm. The swatch was photographed with a yellow barrier filter. The quenching effect of blood can be noted on the right of the swatch in the row where blood is the least diluted (10^{-2}).

Photographing findings made through the use of an ALS is a relatively straightforward process with digital camera equipment once an understanding is gained regarding the wavelength of light that is used on the ALS and the filtration that is required. However, there are other photographic considerations. Because photography is being performed using narrow wavelengths of light, the automatic focusing capabilities often cannot be used. Documenting evidence under wavelength-specific lighting will typically require manual focusing with careful consideration for depth of field in the image. Additionally, working with narrow wavelengths of light means that exposure times will be much longer than usual. The use of a tripod or copy stand is often necessary under these conditions. The ISO of the camera may be increased in order to shorten the exposure time of the photograph as long as the artifacts are not introduced from the use of high ISO settings.

The following equipment is recommended for UV photography:

- Digital single-lens reflex (DSLR) camera;
- Wide-angle zoom lens;
- Normal or macro lens;

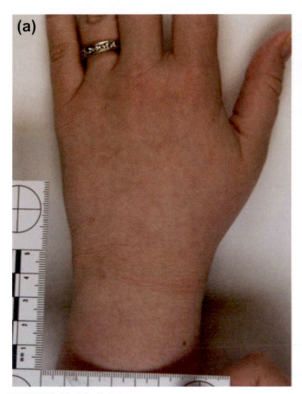

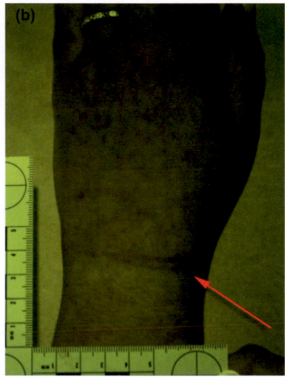

FIGURE 10.14

In the above images, an individual's wrists were bound with zip ties causing some minor bruising of the skin. In the flash photograph of the injury (a), redness of the skin can be seen on the medial side of the wrist. The same area under 420 nm light photographed with a yellow barrier filter shows bruising in the same area (b).

- Copy stand or tripod;
- Shutter release cables;
- Alternate/forensic light source;
- Barrier filters (UV, orange, yellow, red).

Depending on the type of evidence being photographed, wide-angle lenses or normal lenses can be used. If the evidence is an enhancement of an impression that may be compared to another object (such as fingerprints or footwear impression treated with fluorescent dyes), a normal or macro lens should be used for examination quality photograph.

The camera can be set to aperture priority exposure mode for these types of photographs. With this setting, the photographer can control the depth of field in the image while allowing the camera to determine the exposure time required for the given wavelength of light detected by the camera. In some cases, exposure bracketing may be needed in order to capture a properly exposed photograph.

Baldwin (1997) has suggested four rules for photographing fluorescent images using ALSs, including laser light:

1. Know the limitations of the camera being used.
2. Maintain a constant distance of the light source to the object for consecutive exposures.
3. Locate a starting point by a camera meter reading or a separate hand-held light meter.
4. Bracket exposures by at least two stops (Figures 10.15–10.18).

UV REFLECTANCE PHOTOGRAPHY

While UV fluorescence typically occurs in the visible spectrum, UV reflectance photography occurs only in the non-visible portion of the UV spectrum. UV reflectance imaging is used to record a substrate's response to UV light, where absorption of UV light is seen as darkened areas in the image and reflectance appears as white or bright areas in the image. This form of photography

FIGURE 10.15
The Rofin Polilight.

FIGURE 10.16
The Mini-CrimeScope alternate light source (ALS).

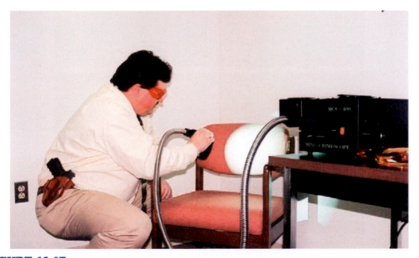

FIGURE 10.17
Officer demonstrating use of the Mini-CrimeScope alternate light source (ALS) unit.

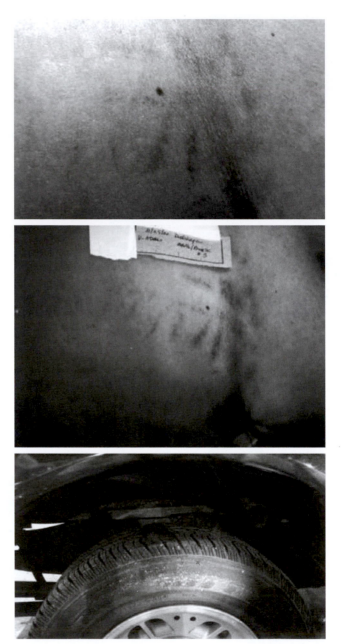

FIGURE 10.18
A hit-and-run fatality. Bruising injuries shown in the first photograph and enhanced using the alternate light source (ALS) ultraviolet (UV) wavelengths in the second photo. The third photo shows the tire that produced the injuries.

requires the use of a filter that blocks the visible portion of the electromagnetic spectrum and allows light only in the non-visible UV portion to pass. The filter typically used for this form of imaging is the Kodak no. 18A filter, or its equivalent, which has a band pass of 310–400 nm.

Because of the sensitivity of silicon-based sensors, UV reflectance best documents the response of a substrate to UV light between 300 and 400 nm in a full spectrum camera with a proper UV lens. Conventional lenses usually have optical coatings that limit the amount of UV light transmitted by the lens. These lenses may still be used; however, imaging will likely be limited to the near UV region (350–400 nm) and not short-wave UV.

Although light in the near UV region can be very energetic, it has little penetration into a substrate and therefore has specific uses. UV reflectance can therefore be used to see differences in the composition of a substrate (UV absorbing vs UV reflecting materials) and differences in the topography of substrate. Evidence, such as bite marks, fingerprints, and impressions in dust, can be imaged using the UV reflectance technique.

IR PHOTOGRAPHY

IR photography has found many applications in the field of criminalistics. These applications include the detection and deciphering of erasures and forgeries; deciphering of charred documents or those that have become illegible as the result of age or abuse; differentiation between inks and pigments that are visually identical, but represent different compounds; detection of gunshot powder burns (see Figure 10.19), stains, and irregularities in cloth; examination of cloth, fibers, and hair that are dyed too dark to be easy to study by visible radiation; study of fingerprints; examination of the contents of sealed envelopes; detection of certain kinds of secret writing; determination of carbon monoxide impregnation of victims of gas poisoning; and photography in the dark, especially in the surveillance or apprehension of a burglar.

IR photography deals with the near IR region of the spectrum which is generally considered to be from 700–900 nm. The human eye is sensitive to near-IR wavelengths up to 700–720 nm. In the past, this was done with IR film. Because of decreasing demand, IR film is no longer being made or is difficult to obtain. However, some digital cameras can be used for IR work. These cameras generally will not be sensitive to IR wavelengths beyond 1000 nm unless it is a specialty camera. There are, however, special imaging devices that can record images in the far-IR thermal range but these are mainly used by the military and firefighter personnel. For instance, thermal radiation emitted by human bodies in room temperature lies in the far-IR wavelength region of about 3000 nm, far beyond the reach of digital cameras and commercial IR films.

FIGURE 10.19

The top photograph shows the visual appearance of a gunshot hole and the infrared (IR) image below shows more detail of the powder burn traces.

CAMERAS

Most digital cameras have an internal IR cut filter (called a hot mirror) built into the body covering the charge coupled device (CCD) or complementary metal oxide semiconductor (CMOS) sensor. This "hot mirror" filter prevents some IR light from being recorded. However, some IR light is passed and, depending upon the make and model of the camera, it may be used effectively with IR photography. The most useful digital equipment for IR photography is a single-lens reflex camera with an automatic diaphragm. It is well-suited to hand-held operations. Also, when visually opaque IR-transmitting filters are placed over the lights instead of over the lens, the camera can be used for hand-held IR photography, if the exposure shutter speed will allow it. But when such filters have to be placed over the lens, a camera with a viewfinder may be useful for focusing, because one cannot see through the lens.

If the camera has an automatic through-the-lens exposure meter, the meter should be turned off when an opaque filter is used. Some work, especially outdoor work, can be done with a visible red filter and with the meter in operation. The camera should be set for a high ISO speed rating. However, a red filter will affect the spectral response of the meter and may indicate an incorrect exposure for automatic operation. Test shooting will determine the best exposure settings.

Earlier digital cameras were much more sensitive to IR than newer cameras and even current production models vary widely in their ability to record IR images. Some of the best older digital cameras for IR photography were the Olympus C-2020Z; the Nikon CoolPix 950 and the Minolta Dimage 7 (D7). Fuji also had limited productions of their professional S-series and IS Pro cameras that were designed to be sensitive to both IR and UV wavelengths. Although these cameras are not in current production they may be obtained used through camera stores and on the internet. A good way of checking a digital camera for suitability with IR photography is to hold a television remote control unit in front of the camera lens and push one of the remote's buttons. If a white light is seen in the camera electronic viewfinder or display, the camera is capable of IR photography. SONY currently produces a video camcorder with a "nightshot" capability that makes it an excellent choice for IR photography. This feature is also found on some of their still image cameras. The "nightshot" mode is a switch on the camera that moves the "hot mirror" away from the sensor and simultaneously turns on a built in lamp with an IR transmitting filter. There are specialty companies that will modify digital cameras and remove the "hot mirror" to increase IR sensitivity. One example is MaxMax (www.maxmax.com). There are also web sites that give instructions on how to accomplish the same thing at home. Either of these choices would certainly void the warranty on a camera (Figure 10.20).

LENSES

Unless a lens has been especially achromatized for IR photography, there will be a difference between the IR focus position and the visual-focus position. Usually, this difference causes no serious problems for the photographer, but

FIGURE 10.20
The Fuji IS Pro infrared (IR) and ultraviolet (UV) camera.

it should be investigated. Good lenses have a red or white dot or mark (or in some cases) a letter "R" on the focusing scale to indicate an average correction for IR photography (see Figure 10.21).

In the field of document copying, a high-quality lens should be used because fine detail is often needed.

FOCUSING

Focusing for an IR image is often difficult. An IR image, even when focused correctly, will not be as sharp as a normal image because aberrations in the camera lens have been corrected for normal, visible photography. Many IR images (particularly those of biological specimens) are formed from details that are not on the visible surface of the subject. Also, many images will have a translucent, scattering medium interposed between their outlines and the lens. Thus, a misty appearance may result from the most carefully focused image.

When focusing for a normal, visible image, it is customary to use manual focusing to shift back and forth across the sharp-focus position. For a correct IR focus, this action should be stopped just when the image of the subject goes slightly out of focus and the lens-to-image distance is being increased. For simpler focusing, sharp detail in the subject should be sought. Absent this, a ruler or some other marker can be placed in the scene to facilitate focusing, and then it is removed from the photograph. Some digital cameras can correctly focus on IR images using the camera's autofocus mode. However, this is not always

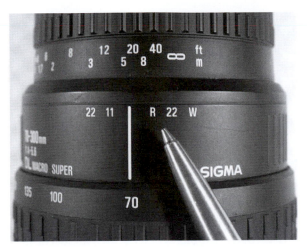

FIGURE 10.21

A Sigma lens with the letter "R" on the focusing ring indicating the focus adjustment for infrared (IR) photographs.

true. The autofocus capability may also vary with the type of filters that are used. It is recommended to make a series of test shots to determine what the capability of the particular camera is on focusing for IR images.

For most subjects, the lens must be stopped down to at least f/11 so that sufficient depth of field will be provided. This procedure also helps to offset the difference between visual and IR focus. Occasionally, when small apertures are used, one may find a circular density pattern (a donut) in the image. This pattern generally will disappear when a wider aperture is used. This means you will have less depth of field, but no pattern. The solution may be to use a different lens.

IR CONTRAST IMAGING

IR photography involves imaging in the region of the electromagnetic spectrum that is beyond 700 nm. Recall, the visible region of the electromagnetic spectrum, lies between 400 and 700 nm, therefore, imaging in the IR region is not perceived by the human eye. The sensor of a digital camera, however, can record a material's response to IR light, as the sensitivity of the sensor can range between 300 and 100 nm. IR imaging with full spectrum DSLR cameras will therefore occur between 700 nm and approximately 1000 nm.

The goal of IR imaging, like imaging in UV, is to establish contrast between some analyte and the substrate on which it resides. Whether IR imaging can be used to show contrast in evidentiary material relies primarily on the physical properties of the material being photographed. Some materials, such as vaporous lead, are strong absorbers of IR light and will appear dark against

IR reflective substrates. When a substrate reflects IR light it can appear white. Other materials, such as blood, can absorb some IR light because of its composition; lipids, heme, and other proteins in blood will absorb IR light. But whether blood can be seen in an IR photograph may depend on the material the blood is on. If blood is on a highly IR reflective surface, it may appear transparent. However, on some fabrics, blood will appear as dark stains. An IR photograph or IR contrast imaging therefore depicts the absorptive and reflective properties of the subject being photographed.

IR CLOSE-UP PHOTOGRAPHY

Cameras with non-extendable lenses can be used conveniently for photographing small specimens if the various close-up attachments and supplementary lenses are used. When supplementary lenses are used, it is not necessary to compensate in the exposure for close-up work because the effective f/value remains unchanged. However, for best definition, the lens should be stopped down to f/11 or f/16. Again, the previous "donut" caution may apply.

LIGHTING

Most lights used in photography generally have high emission in the IR region of the spectrum. IR emission is closely related to heat radiation; thus, heat from a lamp indicates that IR emissions are present. It is even possible to feel a surge of heat from an electronic flash unit. Therefore, only rarely must the photographer use special lighting for IR photography.

Visible light intensity need not be greater for IR photography than for normal photography. Photographic exposure-meter readings for various setups with photoflood and similar lamps can be directly related. However, the fundamental exposure must be based on exposure tests in order to obtain images of a desired quality.

It is wise to check the evenness of the spot of illumination from any lamp because variations will usually be exaggerated by IR techniques. This can be done by photographing the spot of light itself on a sheet of cardboard or on a wall. Also, shadows from indistinct images of filaments or dirty condensers in spotlights should be guarded against.

To image physical evidence using IR light, an adequate controllable light source rich in IR light is required. Flash units operate via electrical discharges that are passed through sealed bulbs containing Xenon gas. Xenon flash lamps, in addition to emitting visible light, also have a strong relative output of IR light making them good controllable sources of IR light. Likewise, ALSs that operate with Xenon arc lamps will provide IR light. Some alternate light sources, such as the SPEX CS-16, have dedicated IR light-emitting ports with a dedicated light guide that can be used to illuminate a subject with wavelength-specific IR light. By contrast, common fluorescent bulbs, which also operate by the discharge of electrical currents through a gas sealed tube, are not good sources of IR light.

Light bulbs, tungsten lamps, and floodlights operate by heating a filament to incandescence. In addition to emitting visible light, these sources are also rich in IR light and can be used in a controlled manner in both the laboratory and CSS. These sources have the advantage of being inexpensive and are easy to obtain.

Electronic Flash Lamps

Electronic flash units have many advantages in the photography of living subjects. Their benefits of coolness and short exposure time are extendable to IR photography. The amount of IR radiation emitted in a given electronic flashtube may be comparable, exposure-wise, to the intensities in copy stand setups with tungsten photo lamps. Another advantage of these units is that they are more readily obtainable with compact reflectors than with tungsten flood equipment.

Electronic flash illumination is best for indoor IR color photography. It is worthwhile to make every effort to utilize electronic flash illumination in this technique. Not only can simpler filtering be achieved, but the advantages of coolness and quick exposure times can also be gained.

However, photoflood and quartz halogen lamps may be used when circumstances require them. These may require special filtering, as discussed in the section on filters. In some cases, it may be necessary to use heat-absorbing glass in order not to have heat damage to the subject. Low-voltage lamps have a higher proportion of IR radiation than high voltage units and generally do not have as much damaging heat generated.

FILTERS

Because CCD/CMOS sensors are somewhat sensitive to the blue region of the spectrum, as well as to part of the red and to the near-IR region, filters are needed for IR photography. Filters vary in the visible light cutoff point and, depending upon the photographic situation, the choice of which filter to use must be considered.

It should be noted here that some other filter manufacturers make filters equivalent to the Wratten filters written of in this publication. Wratten filters, by Kodak, are a standard, even though Kodak may no longer manufacture them.

Several considerations govern the choice of filters. The following Kodak Wratten filters will absorb violet and blue doing black-and-white photography: no. 25 (A, red); no. 29 (F, dark red); no. 70 (very dark red); and no. 89B, 88A, 87, 87C, 87B, and 87A. The red transparent filters (no 25, no. 29, and no. 70) can be used when the camera must be hand-held, or when circumstances, like activity on the part of a live subject, make the addition of an opaque filter after focusing impractical. It should be noted again that critical focusing through the red filter is somewhat difficult.

The Kodak Wratten Filter no. 89B was designed for aerial photography. It produces records quite similar to the no. 25 filter. However, it affords additional penetration of haze with only a slight increase in exposure time.

In the past, most Kodak Wratten filters were available in unmounted 2, 3, 4, and 5-inch gelatin squares. The commonly used ones could be obtained mounted between optical glass in the first three sizes. Used ones may still be found. Gelatin filters are particularly useful when photographic techniques are being determined. Once a standard procedure is established, it may be more convenient to have threaded filters to fit the lenses that are available for the particular camera in use. As previously stated, there are a number of filter manufacturers that produce IR filters (i.e., Hoya, Tiffen, Peca, and Schott). However, filter manufacturers differ in the way they identify certain filters. For instance, the Kodak Wratten no. 89B is the same as Schott's RG695 and Hoya's R72.

The choice of what filter to use is largely a matter of experimentation. Because each filter blocks and transmits certain wavelengths, the results can be varied depending on what is being photographed. For instance, certain dyes in clothing and writing inks will react differently under various IR wavelengths. Gunshot powder residue is generally best photographed with a Wratten no. 87 or 87C filter, but this can vary depending upon what type of fabric the residue is on and the residue itself. It is highly recommended that a complete set of IR filters be obtained and used (Tables 10.2 and 10.3).

IR FILTERS

In order to image in IR with full spectrum cameras, visible light needs to be filtered from the camera. Visible light can contaminate IR photographs, essentially eliminating the ability to see contrast in an image. Light filtration for IR imaging in full spectrum cameras is achieved with over-the-lens IR filters. These filters function to block visible and UV light from the camera, allowing IR light to pass.

Filters, in general, serve to block certain wavelengths of light while allowing the transmission of other wavelengths. IR filters are a type of filter commonly referred to as long-pass filters. These filters will block wavelengths of light up to about 700 nm where light will start to be transmitted through the filter. The peak light transmission in these filters will occur in the IR region. Because visible light is not transmitted through these filters, they are visibly opaque

Table 10.2 Kodak Wratten Filter Transmissions for Black and White Infrared Photography

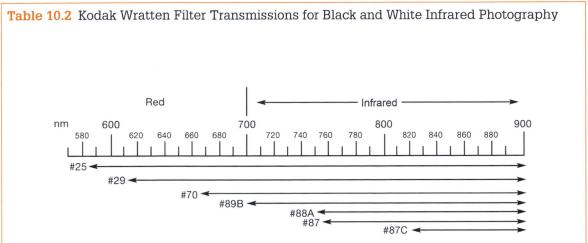

Table 10.3 Filter Equivalents by Manufacturer

Kodak Wratten	Schott	Hoya	Tiffen	BþW	Wavelength
No. 25	OG590	25A	25	090	580–600 nm
No. 29	RG630	–	29	091	600–620 nm
No. 70	RG665	–	–	–	640–680 nm
No. 89B	RG695	R72	–	092	680–720 nm
No. 88A	RG715	–	–	–	720–750 nm
No. 87	RG780	–	87	–	740–795 nm
No. 87C	RG830	–	–	093	790–850 nm
No. 87B	RG850	RM90	–	–	820–930 nm
No. 87A	RG1000	RM100	–	094	880–1050 nm

and appear predominantly black. With the use of these filters, the optical view-finder of the camera cannot be used to compose and focus on the subject. In order to perform this, the photographer must use live view, a feature for which the image can be previewed on the liquid-crystal display (LCD) screen on the back of the camera. Alternatively, the subject can be composed and focused prior to placing the IR filter over the camera. A drawback to this method is that the subject that appears in focus in visible light may not be properly focused when imaged in IR. The IR focus shift in this case can be corrected by either using a higher f-stop, which increases the depth of field, or using IR focusing marks that may be present on the lens.

There are several manufacturers of IR filters, including Kodak, Hoya, Tiffen, B + W and Peca, to name a few. Sadly, they do not share a uniform terminology with regard to IR filters, which can lead to confusion. For example, a common all purpose IR filter is a Kodak Wratten no. 89B filter. The equivalent filter for Peca filters is called 914, B + W is 092, and Hoya is R72. What is common to these filters is that they have a cut-on wavelength of approximately 720 nm. The term cut-on is used to denote the wavelength of light where transmission through the filter is 50%. This specification is commonly used to describe the performance of a filter and can be used in place of non-uniform nomenclature.

In terms of the Kodak Wratten numbers, as the filter numbers decrease, from 89B to 87A, the cut-on wavelength progresses deeper into the IR region. Depending on the effects desired in the IR image, a certain cut-on wavelength can be selected. For example, if there is evidence on a fabric that bears a complex pattern composed of various dyes, the degree to which the pattern made by the dyes appears in the photograph can be controlled by imaging progressively deeper into the IR region. In the case of the 89B filter, where 5% of the light transmitted is in the deep red spectrum (695 nm), some of the dye that reflects red light may show a pattern in the image. If an 87B filter is used, it has a 5% transmittance wavelength of 795 nm, where no visible red light is transmitted; the pattern may be completely eliminated from the image. The photographer can gauge the degree to which red light can be captured in the photograph by using 5% transmittance value for IR filters.

IR PHOTOGRAPHY

Camera Equipment

As mentioned previously, IR imaging requires that the camera sensor be stripped of its internal filter, the hot-filter. This filter essentially blocks IR and UV light from the sensor, allowing the camera to image light primarily in the visible spectrum. Removal of the sensor can be performed via aftermarket services, which can modify the camera to either a dedicated IR camera (where an IR filter over the sensor can be used) or a full spectrum camera. A dedicated IR camera may have to be calibrated with a specific lens in order to compensate for focus shift typically encountered with IR imaging. Because cameras are manufactured with the intent of imaging in the visible spectrum, the internal components and optics are positioned and manufactured so that visible light will come to focus on the sensor. IR light, which consists of wavelengths longer than visible light, will focus past the camera sensor when using a setup intended for recording visible light. The result will be images that are out of focus. To correct this on dedicated IR cameras, the sensor must be repositioned within the body of the camera so that IR light will properly focus on the sensor. This calibration must be performed with a specific lens. This option limits the photographer to one IR transmitting filter and one lens that can be used for IR imaging.

In the case of full spectrum cameras, the internal filter is removed from in front of the sensor and replaced with quartz glass. This essentially makes the camera sensitive to light across the IR, visible, and UV spectrum. As mentioned, silicon based sensors can have sensitivity between approximately 300 and 1000 nm wavelengths of light, varying slightly between manufacturers.

WHITE BALANCE AND COLOR

As with conventional color photography, the white balance for a camera to be used with IR must be corrected. However, as opposed to establishing what is "white" under specific lighting conditions, the camera must be white balanced on an object that reflects IR light for a given filter and light source combination. This is achieved through the use of the camera's custom white balance. Artistic photographers who utilize IR photography may perform a custom white balance on grass or tree foliage under sunlit conditions as these subjects reflect IR light and therefore appear white in IR light. In the laboratory or crime scene conditions, any IR reflecting object, such as white ceramic floor or wall tiles, can be used for this purpose. If the automatic white balance setting on the camera is used, the camera will interpret the IR light as predominantly red and the resulting photographs will appear as an oversaturated red image with little contrast.

It should be noted that, although the hot-filter of the camera is removed, the Bayer color array filter remains over the camera sensor. Because this filter does not block IR light, the camera is interpreting IR light and assigning color values to pixels based on both the Bayer filter array and Bayer interpolation algorithms that are used to construct full color images, even though IR light is not composed of any visible color. For this reason, color IR images are often referred to as "false color" images. The colors represented in IR photographs are not the actual colors of the subject they are simply the camera's color interpretation of light it is detecting that is actually devoid of any color. Because IR images are a function of reflection and absorption of IR light, these images are often converted to gray scale in post-processing.

RECOMMENDED EXPOSURE SETTINGS

When imaging with IR, it is best to affix the camera to a tripod or copy stand for stability and set it to manual exposure mode for complete control over the exposure parameters. The subject can be initially framed and focused without the IR filter. The ISO of the camera should be set to a low number (ISO 100) and the subject should be illuminated with a light source rich in

IR. Even if a flash is being used, when imaging with a full-spectrum camera that uses an over-the-lens filter, an incandescent source should be used to preview the image in IR. Furthermore, the position of the light source, whether an incandescent source or flash, should be considered. Placing the light source at a 45° angle will minimize specular reflections, whereas an oblique angle can enhance any patterns or emphasize textured features of the subject. With the desired IR filter placed over the lens, the exposure can be metered and adjusted manually. A small aperture setting (high f-number) is typically used as this may help overcome any artifacts resulting from IR focus shift. The camera's live view can then be turned on to visualize the effects of the IR filter being used, determine whether the evidence is responding to IR light, or to further compose the image and make additional focus corrections. The exposure should be bracketed in order to obtain a good exposure. If the images appear excessively bright, shutter speed or aperture adjustments can be made, additionally, the distance between the light source and subject may be increased.

REFLECTED IR

The reflected IR photographic technique has been widely used in numerous applications, often in conjunction with other nondestructive methods of examination, such as UV photography and radiography. One of the categories that has a broad application in forensic science is in the investigation of questioned, illegible, censored, deteriorated, or forged documents. This method is valuable when inks and pigments that appear to have the same color can be differentiated photographically. Other uses are examination of paints, wood, and vegetable materials, textiles, and gunshot powder residues.

There are numerous filters available for IR photography. Each one transmits a different portion of the IR spectrum. Because of this fact, one should use each filter on a given subject. If you do not do this, you may not obtain details needed to make an informed statement about the subject qualities of the evidence.

IR LUMINESCENCE

One IR photography technique discussed earlier is to use cyan-wavelength-induced IR fluorescence (usually called IR luminescence). With this technique, the subject is illuminated with a blue/green light and the luminescence is produced in the IR region. The visually unseen luminescence is then recorded on an IR sensitive digital camera. The blue/green excitation filter can be a Corning 9788 (or a Schott BG-38 available from most scientific supply houses) and is fitted onto the light source. This blue/green filter stimulates radiation at about 480 nm and the IR emission occurs at about 800 nm. The barrier (IR transmission only) filters used on the lens should be each of the filters in the set at hand. These filters are placed in front of the lens. Exposure is made in a darkened room with only the blue/green excitation lamp for illumination. If a Corning 9788 or Schott BG-38 filter is not available, an alternate light source, such as the Mini-CrimeScope, Omniprint, or Lumilite, may be used by tuning the wavelength to 440–460 nm. Exposure will be long, even several seconds in some cases, because of the faint luminescence of some materials. It is imperative that the camera be placed on a copy stand or tripod and a cable release attached to the camera in order to eliminate camera motion.

APPLICATIONS

IR photography can be used to document many types of physical evidence, including but not limited to:

- Gunshot residue;
- Bloodstained items;
- Fingerprint evidence (powders);
- Tattoos on decomposed tissue;
- Questioned documents.

It is important to note that not all evidentiary materials benefit from IR contrast imaging. Some materials, such as leathers, synthetic fabrics, and other fabrics containing certain dyes, can absorb IR light and therefore may not produce contrast on IR absorbing analytes, such as blood or gunshot reside. The photographer must, unfortunately, preview the subject under IR lighting while varying IR filters to see how the subject responds under IR imaging conditions (Figures 10.22 and 10.23).

IR IMAGING OF GUNSHOT RESIDUE

Patterns and distributions of gunshot residue may be difficult to visualize on clothing that is dark in color or clothing that has a complex pattern composed of different dyes. By imaging these items in the IR spectrum, it is often possible to lighten the background or diminish, if not altogether remove, complex patterns that obscure discharge residues from a firearm. The analysis of discharge residue can be beneficial in an investigation. A criminalist can use this information coupled with test fires made from the same firearm to make a muzzle to target distance determination at the time that the firearm was discharged. Because vaporous lead and propellant materials absorb IR, they will appear dark in IR photographs. When these patterns are photographed in IR their distribution can be readily visualized. Additionally, bullet wipe consisting of lead and lubricants may also be seen

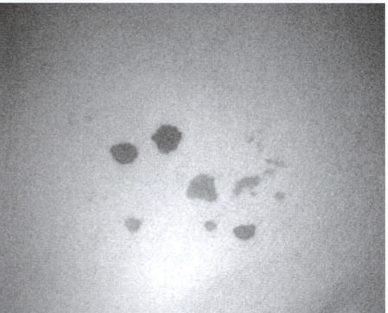

FIGURE 10.22

Black fabric with blood spatters. First shot under normal lighting conditions, second shot taken with infrared using a SONY "Nightshot" equipped digital camera with a Kodak Wratten no. 87C filter over the lens.

FIGURE 10.23

Blood deposited on dark fabric may be difficult to visualize and therefore may benefit from infrared (IR) contrast imaging. In the above figure, blood was deposited on dark cotton fabric and allowed to dry. The fabric was photographed with conventional flash photography (a), which failed to show the presence of blood on the fabric. When imaged in IR (b), the fabric, which reflects IR, is lightened in the image and the blood, which absorbs IR, appears as dark spots in the image. The IR photograph in (b) is a false color IR image.

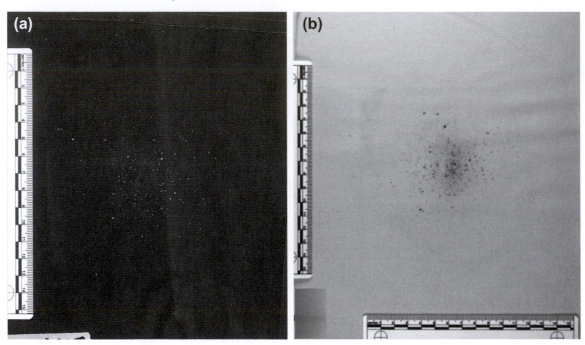

FIGURE 10.24

The above figure illustrates how IR imaging can be used to visualize gunshot residue (GSR) in dark colored fabrics. (a) Shows a flash photograph of clothing with GSR on it. (b) Was photographed using a FIJI S3Pro equipped with a 60 mm lens and a no. 89B filter, illuminated with a tungsten light source. The clothing, which reflects IR, is lightened in the image, whereas the lead deposits absorb and appear dark. Bullet wipe and vaporous lead can also be seen in the IR photograph.

on the side of the garment through which a firearm projectile entered. In cases in which gunshot residue is obscured from clothing because of an intervening object, or the firearm is at a distance from the subject such that discharge residues are not deposited on the garment, the entrance side of the projectile on clothing can still be determined and documented with IR photographs (Figure 10.24).

IR IMAGING OF TATTOOS ON DECOMPOSED TISSUE

In missing person's cases, medico-legal investigations, and mass-fatality incidents, tattoos may be used in family assistance centers to make quick preliminary identifications of deceased individuals compared to other means. Tattoos are typically injected into the skin with the use of a machined needle. Some of the pigments that are used in tattoo inks will readily absorb IR and can appear dark in IR images. Skin by contrast reflects IR and will typically appear white regardless of the subject's skin color and condition. These

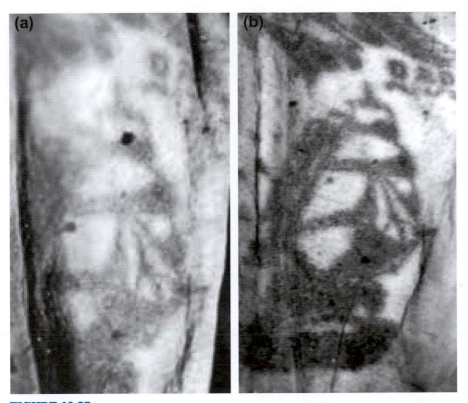

FIGURE 10.25

Tattoos on decomposed body. Under normal lighting, the tattoos are barely discernible (a) but are brought out in more detail using reflective infrared photography (b).

circumstances make IR photography the ideal method for documenting this form of evidence (Figures 10.25 and 10.26).

IR IMAGING OF QUESTIONED DOCUMENTS

The most important application of reflected IR and IR luminescence photography is the deciphering of indistinct writing and ink differentiation in questioned document examinations. The text may have been made illegible by charring, deterioration as a result of age or the accumulation of dirt, obliteration by application of ink by a censor, invisible inks, deliberate chemical bleaching, or mechanical erasure and subsequent overwriting.

Inks, pigments, and other materials that appear identical to the eye are frequently rendered quite different by an IR photograph. If an ink transparent to IR radiation is applied over one opaque to it, the underlying ink will show up in an IR photograph (see Figure 10.27). Destructive ink tests, such as thin

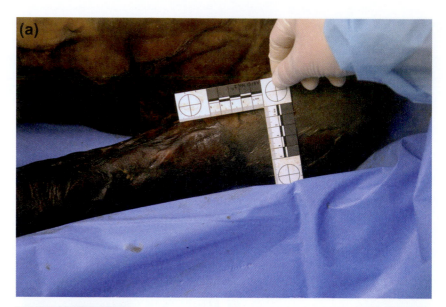

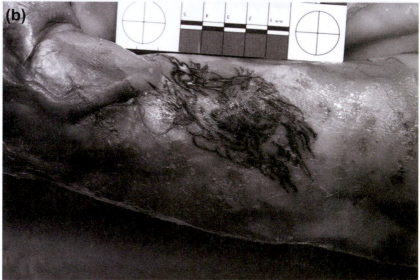

FIGURE 10.26

In the above figure, the mummified body of an unidentified deceased individual was examined by a medical examiner. During the external examination, tattoos were noted on the deceased and were imaged with flash photography (a) to be used in the identification process. Because flash photography could not reveal any discernible detail of the tattoos, infrared (IR) photography was used to drop the discoloration of the decomposed tissue, which reflects IR light. The tattoo pigments, which absorb IR light, become visible in the IR spectrum (b). The above IR photograph was taken with a Fuji S3Pro using a 60 mm lens and a no. 89B filter. A Nikon SB-800 flash unit was used as an IR light source.

layer chromatography may be examined using IR reflected and luminescence photography as well. The original inks used in writing documents that have become blackened may be revealed by reflective IR photography, although success will depend on the condition of the paper. Writing that has been mechanically erased may be revealed in an IR photograph by virtue of the traces of carbon or other pigments left embedded in paper fibers. Chemically bleached writing is often deciphered by IR photography. The reaction of the bleach with the ink absorbs more IR radiation than the surrounding paper. Documents that have become wet, charred by fire, and those blackened by age, dirt, or stains can sometimes be deciphered in an IR print. The investigation of papers surviving willful attempts to burn them and of forged documents is very important. Sometimes, wear will obliterate writing so that it can no longer be seen with the naked eye or photographed with visible light. Yet, traces may remain that can be picked up by IR photography (Figures 10.28 and 10.29).

DIGITAL FULL SPECTRUM PHOTOGRAPHY

Digital camera sensors are natively sensitive to light spanning the near-UV to the near-IR spectrum of light. Light in the near-UV and IR spectrum, however, is purposefully filtered out from commercially available cameras because this light often leads to unappealing photographs that lack color accuracy. Because UV and IR light can oversaturate the camera sensor with electromagnetic radiation that the camera will interpret as an excess of red and blue light, the resulting image will display an excess of red and blue hues. The internal filter that blocks UV/IR light is often referred to as a "hot mirror" or "hot-filter" and is typically positioned directly in front of the camera sensor. The "hot mirror" functions to block light in the UV/IR region allowing light primarily within the visible region of the electromagnetic spectrum (~400–1000 nm) to be recorded by the camera sensor. This allows the resulting photograph to exhibit a color accuracy that is more commensurate with human color perception. However, to utilize UV/IR wavelengths of light to document physical evidence requires the removal of the hot mirror. Cameras that have the hot filter removed are often referred to as "full-spectrum" cameras.

SPECIALIZED FULL SPECTRUM CAMERAS

Fuji was the only manufacturer to market full-spectrum DSLR cameras to the law enforcement community, entirely dedicated to UV/IR imaging; however, these cameras, the Fuji S3Pro and IS Pro, were discontinued. As a result, several aftermarket full-spectrum conversion services developed to meet the demands of both artistic and forensic photographers alike for cameras that could record UV/IR light. A quick internet search should yield several companies that will perform these services.

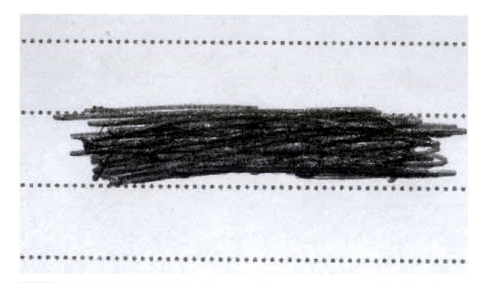

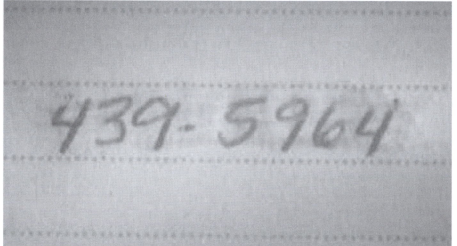

FIGURE 10.27
Infrared photograph with Kodak Wratten Filter no. 87 used to decipher obliterated writing and to render it as shown in the lower photograph.

Because full-spectrum conversion requires the dismantling of the camera in order to expose the internal sensor and remove the hot mirror, professional aftermarket services are recommended. Keep in mind that aftermarket conversion will likely result in a void of warranty and any repair agreements from the camera manufacturer. Furthermore, full-spectrum conversion requires that the hot mirror is replaced with either glass or an IR transmitting filter. The position of this filter within the camera must be precise. The position of the sensor must also not be affected. If these components are not properly placed within the

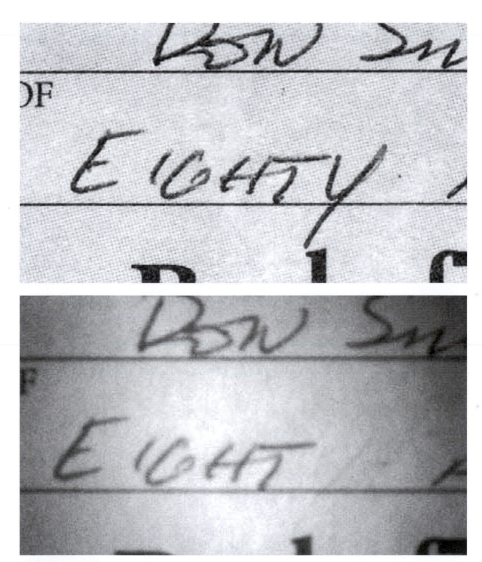

FIGURE 10.28
Check for $80 (top) when photographed with infrared method (bottom) shows that the "Y" was added later.

body of the camera, the camera will not be able to achieve proper focus. Careful research is recommended before submitting a camera to an aftermarket conversion service.

If the hot filter of a camera is replaced by clear glass, the camera will be considered "full-spectrum" capable, meaning that the camera should be able to record light spanning the UV visible and IR regions (~300–1000 nm). These cameras will often require the use of over-the-lens filtration, which will afford

FIGURE 10.29
The same check (top) photographed with infrared (bottom).

the photographer ample flexibility in the selection of light wavelengths that will enter the camera. In the case of IR imaging, because IR transmitting filters will block visible light, the filters are visibly opaque. This means that the photographer will not be able to focus the camera through the optical viewfinder of the camera. For this reason, a camera that is selected for aftermarket conversion should have a live preview function (i.e., an image of the subject can be displayed on the LCD screen of the camera, similar to a point-and-shoot camera). Alternatively, if no live preview is available, the image can be composed and focused prior to the placement of the IR filter.

Another option is to replace the hot-filter with an IR transmitting filter. Because this filter will be placed directly over the sensor, the image path through the optical viewfinder is not blocked and it can be used to compose and focus the camera. It should be understood that because IR light is of a longer wavelength than visible light and UV, there is usually a focus shift associated with IR imaging. Although the optics of a camera are designed so that visible light focuses directly on the sensor, IR light will actually focus beyond the sensor. This can be corrected in several ways. If the camera has live preview, the lens can simply be focused manually so that the image appears sharp. Some older lenses may even come with IR focus adjustment marks that are directly on the lens. The f-stop of the camera may also be increased so that there is adequate depth of field in the image that may cover the range of the focus shift. In the case of a camera where the hot filter was replaced by an IR transmitting filter, the sensor can also be repositioned within the camera to compensate for IR focus shift. In this case, the position of the sensor is calibrated with the use of a fixed focal length lens. Unfortunately, this often means that you will be limited to the lens with which the camera focus was calibrated. The use of different fixed focus length lenses or wide-angle zoom lenses can therefore result in out-of-focus images.

REFERENCES

Aaron, J. M. (November 1991). Reflective ultraviolet photography sheds new light on pattern injury. *Law and Order*, 38, 213–218.

Baldwin, H. B. (1997). *Photographic techniques for the laser or alternate light source.* http://homepage. interacess.com/~hbaldwin/.

CHAPTER 11

Identification and Surveillance Photography

ABSTRACT

One of the oldest uses of police photography is identification photography. The use of mug shots is, perhaps, the earliest known use of photography in police work. Capturing an accurate image of an individual that may later be used for identification purposes in photographic lineups or as a means to locate suspects may be challenging. Simple changes to exposure, lighting, and angle may distort an individual's true physical demeanor. In addition to mug shots, identification photography deals with fingerprint photography. The ability to capture a readable photographic image of a latent fingerprint at the crime scene requires knowledge and skill. Specialized equipment such as macro lenses and/or close-up filters may be required, along with the effective use of light and illumination techniques. Surveillance is also a challenging task in which the photographer may find themselves attempting to photograph individuals covertly, in darkness, and at long distances.

KEY TERMS

Fingerprint camera
Filmless photography
Mug shots
Latent prints
Cyanoacrylate fuming
Overt photography
Covert photography
Clandestine photography
Night vision photography
ARGUS

INTRODUCTION

Photography has played a large part in the importance of fingerprints in police work. Were it not for photography, it would be impossible to bring fingerprints found at the scene of a crime into a courtroom and present them to a jury. There are times when fingerprints are not visible to the naked eye, but by using powders, chemicals, or alternative light sources on the latent prints, the images of the ridges can be brought out and photographed. These can be enlarged to a size that makes the print easily viewed by a jury. The known fingerprint can be placed alongside the unknown fingerprint and a point (or minutiae) fingerprint comparison made of the two prints, along with notation of their individual characteristics (see Figures 11.1 and 11.2). Photographing fingerprint impressions found at the scene of a crime is a rather difficult chore that demands an immense knowledge of photography in order to do a good job.

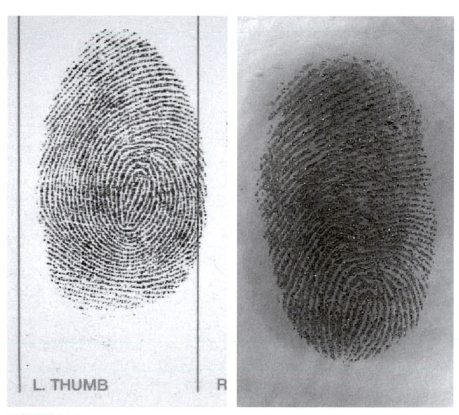

FIGURE 11.1
Single print, known (left) and unknown (right). The unknown print has been taken from the scene of the crime.

The importance of identifying individuals in police work is obvious; identification photographs—like fingerprints—are one of the best means. Using photographs to preserve the personal appearance of an individual at a given time is necessary. The advantage of police "mug shots" is their unflattering realism, and the ease and economy with which they can be produced.

An identification photograph should be an accurate likeness of the subject, from which he can be recognized by witnesses or police officers. The photographer should strive to reproduce every freckle, mole, scar, or other blemish that might aid in identifying the subject. Close-ups of head and shoulders with a generally flat front lighting will accomplish this.

Identification photos are placed on file, together with the prisoner's record and other useful data, such as height, weight, age, and a description of significant characteristics. Files of such photographs are extremely valuable in investigating crimes involving unknown perpetrators observed by witnesses. The witness

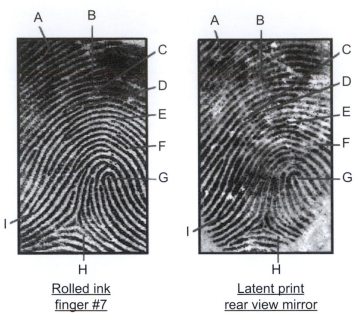

Rolled ink
finger #7

Latent print
rear view mirror

FIGURE 11.2
Comparison exhibit using digital technology. The inked and latent print were digitally photographed and compared using a computer with Adobe Photoshop software and printed using a Kodak XL8600PS printer. *Courtesy Free Radical Enterprises.*

is asked to visit police headquarters and is shown a number of photographs of criminals selected on the basis of the descriptions of observers. The witness is asked to examine the pictures at leisure and to select any that resemble the perpetrator of the crime. To aid in searching the files, special classifications of photographs are set up. For example, the file may be arranged according to the crime, such as burglary, forgery, robbery, and so forth. In crimes such as burglary, an additional classification may be made, according to the modus operandi (method of operation) of the criminal. Thus, under burglary, the use of a pass key, climbing through transoms or skylights, using an electric drill on safes, and many other criminal techniques can be used to classify the photograph.

Another use of identification photographs is circulation to other police departments. Some of the larger police departments provide their officers with photographic files of "wanted" criminals. Such pictures enable investigators to become familiar with the facial characteristics of known criminals and can lead to arrests that otherwise might never be made. The mug shot itself is hardly sufficient proof of identity, but it is proof that may be taken into consideration when accompanied by other evidence, such as fingerprints.

EQUIPMENT FOR FINGERPRINT PHOTOGRAPHY

Fingerprint technicians traditionally used specially built fingerprint cameras for their normal fingerprint work (Figure 11.3). Traditional fingerprint cameras were equipped with an anastigmat lens set for 1:1 reproduction, and with an extension in the front of the lens equal to the distance between the optical center of the lens and the film. The camera opened in the middle, where inside there were usually eight batteries, along with lights built into the front so that the camera could be placed directly over the surface that bears the fingerprints. Because the lens-to-subject distance was set, the camera did not need to be focused. The film size of these fingerprint cameras was usually 2 × 3 inches but most of the more recent fingerprint cameras used Polaroid backs. While the film size and Polaroid print size is a good workable size for one or two prints, usually four or five prints are found on an object. It is always best to try and get as many fingerprints as possible in a 1:1 reproduction ratio on the same sheet of film. That is why many fingerprint technicians preferred the old 4 × 5 fingerprint cameras. Although there are several companies that still manufacture specially built fingerprint cameras (i.e., Sirchie Finger Print Laboratories, Inc.), most fingerprint and crime scene technicians use digital SLR cameras equipped with a macro lens and/or close-up filters.

FIGURE 11.3
The Sirchie EV-CAM fingerprint camera with Polaroid film back.

FILMS AND FILTERS

Whatever technique is used, whether it is powder, chemicals, lasers, or alternate light sources, to develop a latent fingerprint, nothing will lead to success as much as the proper photographic exhibit of the evidence. In the courtroom, an exhibit of a fingerprint photograph is one form of law enforcement photograph in which black-and-white photographs are as useful as color photographs. In evaluating a fingerprint case, an unknown print will be compared to an inked fingerprint taken from the suspect under ideal conditions.

For courtroom exhibits, fingerprints taken from colored objects should depict a black fingerprint on a solid white background. The judge and jury will have an easier time concentrating on the pattern of the fingerprint itself on a solid white background.

Most of the time, fingerprints will be found on colored objects, and this will usually require the use of filters when photographing in black and white mode. Filters are not needed when photographing impressions on white surfaces such as bathroom fixtures, or on gray or black surfaces such as gun barrels. However, filters are required when using alternative light sources and/or fluorescent powders (see Chapter 10 for a more in-depth discussion of these techniques).

The fingerprint photographer must know how to use filters with black and white photography to control lightness or darkness of colored surfaces upon which fingerprints are found. Ordinarily the photographer can, by using filters, make a colored background photograph either dark or light at will. The decision as to how a given colored surface should be made to photograph will depend upon the tone of the fingerprint. If the fingerprint will photograph light gray or white, the surface upon which it appears must be made to photograph as black as possible (Figure 11.4). Conversely, if the fingerprint will photograph dark gray or black, the background must be made to photograph as white as possible. A yellow filter is good for bringing out the definition of the print. A medium yellow filter needs as much exposure as a weak yellow-green filter. But the deep yellow filter gives a more effective picture of this same exposure. When using filters, the exposure must be trebled. Any time a filter is added, the exposure will have to be increased. An SLR camera with through-the-lens metering is a near necessity for this. The filter process may also be accomplished on computer software such as Adobe Photoshop. However, most high-end digital cameras allow a monochrome setting that will produce black and white images. Once in this mode, the digital camera can use filters like a black and white film camera. It is much easier to use filters on the camera rather than attempt to make filtration adjustments on the computer. It will also lessen the likelihood of objections being raised in court over photograph manipulation if the computer is used for such enhancements.

When photographing black fingerprints on colored objects in black and white mode, the photographer must make the colored background appear as light as

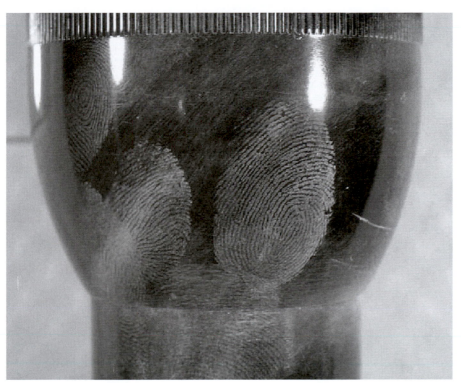

FIGURE 11.4
White fingerprint on black background.

possible in order to provide the greatest possible contrast with the black finger-print. To photograph a black fingerprint on a colored background, a filter that has the same color as the background is appropriate. A filter that transmits the color of the object and absorbs other colors will usually solve the problem (see Chapter 5).

Because of the way light strikes it or because it has been developed with white powder, a fingerprint may appear white. This is especially true with cyanoacrylate (Super Glue) fumed fingerprints. To photograph these on a colored surface, a fil-ter should be used that will absorb the color reflected by the object while allow-ing light of other wavelengths through to expose the image. The student should take a good set of fingerprints from an individual, and photograph them first with no filter, then photograph the print one time each with a yellow, red, blue, green, and orange filter. The letter of the filter used should be put in to identify the filter type in the finished print. This is the best way to learn how to use filters.

For photographing fingerprints found on multicolored objects, any fil-ter used will eliminate certain colors but will emphasize other colors in the background. It is best to eliminate all the colors in order to produce a plain background that will contrast well with the prints. With multicolored

(a) 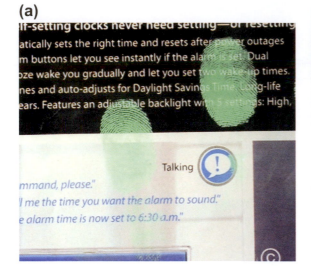 **(b)**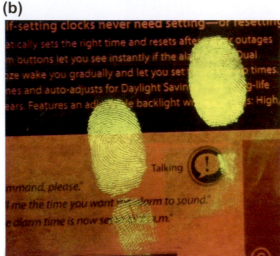

FIGURE 11.5
Multicolored magazine page with prints dusted with fluorescent powder and photographed with ultraviolet illumination.

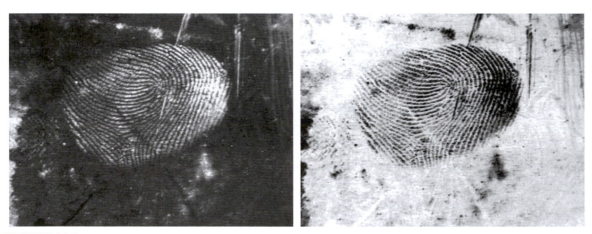

FIGURE 11.6
Fingerprints illuminated with an alternate light source and digitally photographed. Same fingerprints with "reversed" color using Adobe Photoshop to show black ridge detail. *Photos courtesy of Hayden Baldwin.*

backgrounds, it may become necessary to resort to ultraviolet photography to photograph fingerprints. Results obtained from these methods are very unpredictable, however. Ultraviolet photography is discussed in detail in Chapter 10 (Figure 11.5(a), (b)).

Another method used in photographing light-colored latent fingerprints on dark or multicolored backgrounds is to reverse the colors in Photoshop. This technique is particularly useful with cyanoacrylate-developed fingerprints (Figure 11.6).

EXPOSURE FOR FINGERPRINT PHOTOGRAPHY

It is difficult to name a particular exposure for any shot, because no one knows what the particular circumstances are at the time a certain job has to be done. A person in this field has to do a great amount of experimenting with the camera, filters, computer, and other tools of the trade. By experimenting with filters in combination with different situations, and keeping a record of everything performed along with the results obtained, one can figure out just what the camera and filters will do for a particular job.

When fingerprint photographers used the old box fingerprint camera, exposure results could be predicted by past experience because the lamps were always in the same position and distance from the photographic subject. This was an advantage of the fingerprint camera, consistent results. However, when batteries began to weaken, the internal illuminating bulbs would dim, causing inconsistent results. Using a 35 mm SLR or a digital SLR camera simplifies the tediousness of exposure determination greatly, especially when using a macro lens. The camera's internal light meter system will correct for use of filters and, if flash is necessary, the same techniques as close-up photography may be used (review Chapter 9). Additionally, the use of digital cameras and imaging are particularly well-suited for fingerprint photography since compensation for errors in exposure can be made on the spot.

FINGERPRINTS FOUND ON WOOD

Many times fingerprints will be found on wood surfaces, such as a kitchen or dining room table, dresser, or bed, or on other pieces of wooden furniture. There are primarily four kinds of wood used to make household furniture: oak, walnut, mahogany, and cherry. One of the biggest problems confronting the fingerprint technician is whether to use black or white powder. The answer depends on whether it is best to make the stained wood appear light in order to contrast with a black fingerprint or whether it should appear dark in order to contrast with a white fingerprint.

It is best to develop fingerprints on dark stained woods with white powder and to photograph them in black and white mode and a blue filter. However, if a court exhibit must be made that will show the ridges as black lines on a white background, it is necessary to reverse the image colors on the computer. Fingerprints on light oak should be developed with black powder and photographed in black and white mode through a red filter.

FINGERPRINTS FOUND ON GLASS

Visible fingerprints found on glass should always be photographed before applying powder to them. Latent fingerprints found on sheet or plate glass can sometimes be photographed without the use of developing powders, by oblique lighting from behind the glass, and against a black background. Here again the ridges will show up as white lines against a black background unless the court exhibit is printed from a reversed color image.

Glass bottles and tumblers will often yield fingerprints. Even though the print consists only of colorless perspiratory secretions, it may be photographed successfully without the use of powders by filling the bottle or tumbler with a dark liquid, such as grape juice, and photographing with oblique lighting. The photo lamp must be adjusted with great care because the convexity of the bottle or tumbler will cause disturbing reflections when the lamp is in certain positions. A polarizing filter may help reduce reflection. With a dark impression, the bottle or tumbler should be filled with a white liquid, such as milk, before it is photographed.

Fingerprints that are found on a mirror can be photographed if great care is given to focusing and lighting. The major problem encountered in photographing prints on mirrors is a strong secondary image on the second surface of the mirror. This secondary image will create a blurred appearance on the photograph. A piece of black or white cardboard with a hole cut to allow just the photograph of the fingerprint image may help reduce glare as well as the secondary image. Also, use a larger aperture opening to throw the secondary image out of focus. Using magnetic fingerprint powder may also help with mirrors. The magnetic powder tends to "smear" the glass surrounding the latent image, which reduces glare. Another technique is to use a piece of white cardboard with a hole cut about the size of a dime. The lens is placed up to the hole opposite the mirror and the photograph is taken through the hole. In this way, a straight-on shot can be made minimizing the secondary image. If it is possible to do so, the job can be made easier by scraping the silver off the back of the mirror (Figure 11.7(a), (b)).

FINGERPRINTS FOUND ON PAPER AND PLASTIC

Fingerprints found on paper and plastic should be treated with powders, fumes, or liquid reagents to bring them out so that they are clear enough to be photographed. Latent fingerprints from iodine-fumed and ninhydrin-treated papers may be brought out for better contrast by using filters. Cyanoacrylate (Super Glue) fuming leaves white crystalline latent prints, but can be darkened by using black magnetic powder. For ninhydrin-treated paper, try photographing in monochrome (black and white) mode with a green filter.

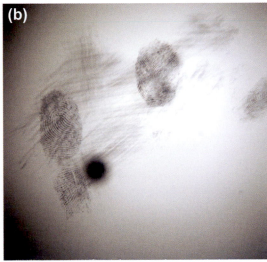

FIGURE 11.7

Photograph of fingerprints on a mirror surface. Straight-on photographs will show the camera and obliterate the prints (a). Using white cardboard with small hole for the lens to "see through" allows the fingerprints to be visualized (b).

PHOTOGRAPHING LIFTED FINGERPRINTS

Many fingerprint technicians find the lifting process so easy that they have a tendency to lift prints when it is not necessary. Rarely should fingerprints be lifted when they can be photographed successfully while still on the original surface. Fingerprints have the highest value as evidence while they remain on the objects on which they are found. It is true that latent fingerprints may disappear in some instances, but fingerprints developed with powders probably will last indefinitely, especially if protected with a plastic cover. Large items, such as furniture, may not be movable or storable until needed in court. Photographs should be taken of latent prints on these objects before they are lifted. Great care should be taken when lifting fingerprints. Accidents do happen, and it is possible that the act of lifting a print will destroy some ridge detail, especially if bubbles or wrinkles appear in the lifting tape. For this reason, the photographer should follow the golden rule of crime scene investigation and photograph before the print is lifted from the object.

ENLARGING FINGERPRINT PHOTOGRAPHS FOR TRIAL

A fingerprint photographer must have the case well prepared to present before a judge and jury. In testifying to comparisons between fingerprints, the expert witness should utilize some graphic representation of the facts presented, such as enlarged photographs. For this purpose, enlarged photographs from corresponding fingers may be mounted side by side. The degree of enlargement is not important, as long as both photographs are enlarged to the same degree, and the ridges of both prints are distinguishable. Generally, enlargements of five to six times the natural size are best. Smaller enlargements are difficult to see more than a few feet away, while larger ones lose some of their contrast between ridges and background. A white border of at least 1 inch should be left for numbering purposes. An enlargement to about 22 × 30 inches should be made to serve as a demonstration exhibit to the court, and 11 × 14-inch exhibits for each member of the jury. Court exhibits may be used from a digital projector to allow the expert witness to point out the comparison details. Even if projected images are used in court, it is a good idea to prepare hard-copy exhibits for the jurors and judge to hold while the expert is testifying.

The corresponding ridge formations in the two prints should then be similarly numbered and marked with straight lines drawn from the characteristic to a numbered point in the margin. Care should be taken that lines are drawn to the characteristic to be noted, not short of it or beyond it (Figure 11.8).

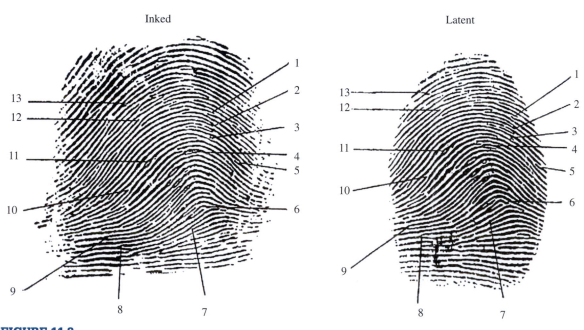

FIGURE 11.8
Enlarged comparison of fingerprint properly prepared for court exhibit.

When the degree of enlargement is greater (25–30 diameters), a circle should be drawn around the characteristic and a line should be drawn from the circles to the number in the margin. In such cases the ridges will be much larger than the illustrating lines.

Because the enlarged photographs appear in black and white, it is preferable to use an ink other than black or white to line the chart. The ink used should be translucent, so that it will be possible to see the details of the ridges underneath it.

A cleaner, neater, and more pleasing appearance is obtained if the numbers are evenly spaced and made to follow a sequence, such as by placing them in a clockwise or counterclockwise order. Some states do not permit numbering on these exhibits. A clear sheet of plastic placed over the exhibit and then numbered will avoid this problem.

In addition, there are several computer software programs available for digital photographs that can produce court exhibits quickly and easily. However, if enlargements are necessary, caution should be taken to avoid pixelating the image (see Chapter 2). Exhibits may be presented using a color monitor and computer with programs such as PowerPoint. Using a color monitor avoids the problem of pixelating enlarged images.

THE IDENTIFICATION PHOTOGRAPHER

Many police departments in cities with populations of more than 15,000 possess an "Identification Bureau" or at least a skilled photographer assigned to perform identification work. However, because the importance of photography in law enforcement is well recognized, many smaller towns are now training selected police officers to do photographic work. It will often be found that the identification photographer in a small community is required to deal with a greater variety of tasks than is his counterpart in the large city. The latter will tend toward specialization in one particular branch of identification work. For example, in a city with a population of one million, several police photographers may be occupied exclusively with "mug" shots, while others will perform only "on-the-scene" photographic tasks.

The typical responsibilities of an identification unit with respect to photography are the following:

1. Photographing prisoners charged with serious crimes.
2. Photographing deceased person in homicide cases (see Figure 11.9).
3. Photographing the scenes of serious crimes, fires, and accidents.
4. Dusting and photographing fingerprints.

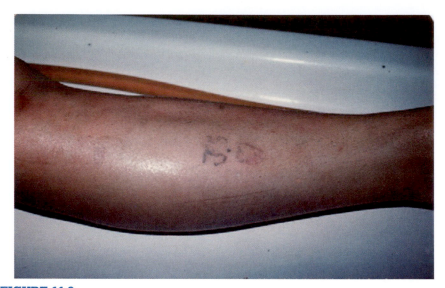

FIGURE 11.9
Tattoos and other identifying marks on deceased persons should be photographed.

5. Reproducing checks, documents, and other evidential papers by photographic methods.
6. Copying and reproducing photographs.
7. Reproducing official records and notices.

IDENTIFICATION PHOTOGRAPHS

There are three basic ways of shooting identification photographs: (1) the front and side views; (2) the front, and two three-quarter face views; and, (3) the front, side, and standing views. Color should be used to accurately capture skin tones, hair color, and eye color.

1. The front and side views. Many police departments photograph their prisoners with a front view and a profile (or side) view (Figure 11.10). The front view permits ready recognition of the individual, but the side view is also necessary for certain identification characteristics. Persons are so often viewed from the front that it is quite possible, at first sight, not to recognize someone when a profile photograph is shown. The public can generally recognize front-view photographs much more readily than they can profile-view photographs.
2. The front and two three-quarter face views. This type of identification photograph has proven to be quite satisfactory. Many times identification can be made more easily from the three-quarter face view when the front and side method fails.

FIGURE 11.10
Typical "mug-shot" showing front and side view.

3. The front, side, and standing views. This may be preferred because the standing view can be most helpful in identifying a suspect.

LIGHTING

In identification work, it is particularly important to be consistent in performing all of the photographic procedures. Changing the lighting arrangements, for example, can produce markedly different facial contours and skin tone. Hence, a standard lighting arrangement should be selected and strictly adhered to in all photographs. In this way, lighting, image size, and exposure can be fixed for standard poses. The operation can easily be one of routine procedure in exposing and storing the images.

The flat lighting provided by two No. 1 photoflood lamps with diffusers will be satisfactory for this work. They should be placed close enough to the subject to permit the use of a fast shutter speed, but not so close as to become oppressive because of heat and glare. Preferably, two electronic flash units can be used in place of photoflood lights. The flash units are placed at 45° angles to the subject and diffused by using diffusers over the flash or by bouncing the flash against an "umbrella" designed for portrait photography.

CAMERAS

There have been numerous identification and mug shot cameras available for years. The old 4 × 5 Speed Graphic had a split-back adapter to allow front and side views to be taken on one sheet of 4 × 5 film. The Deardorff identification camera allowed three poses to be taken on one sheet of 4 × 5 film or with a 4 × 5 Polaroid film back. The three poses included front, side, and standing views. Polaroid has produced the 4 × 5 identification camera, a four-lens camera capable of producing four identical images on one 4 × 5 sheet of film or Polaroid film. Most police departments use a standard digital SLR system to take advantage of the low cost and adaptability to the department's other photographic equipment.

DIGITAL IDENTIFICATION PHOTOGRAPHY

This is one area where digital imaging has a distinct advantage over normal film (analog) photography. Digital cameras allow for images to be taken and stored on digital or electronic media. This, alone, is a distinct advantage over traditional film photography. Since mug shots are, most likely, the largest single part of a police department's photographic file, the ability to store large numbers of digitally produced images on electronic media is a definite space saver. Any digital camera capable of producing 5 megapixel or better resolution can be used for mug shots, although if enlargements need to be made the resolution should be higher. There are several software programs available that allow for storing and retrieving digital images. The RiMS mug shot and digital imaging software program allows mug shots to be taken, filed, and linked to other files. RiMS can produce electronic "mug books" viewable on a computer screen and transmittable over phone systems (i.e., internet and smart phones). Hard copies can be readily produced by using a good-quality color printer capable of printing photo-quality digital images. In addition, the RiMS software allows for quick photo lineups by searching its database of mug shots on file for similar characteristics of suspects (race, sex, age, etc.). The photographic lineup produces six images with the key subject randomly placed on the screen. Software such as RiMS can also file crime scene photographs, traffic accident photographs, or any digital image associated with a particular case.

SURVEILLANCE PHOTOGRAPHY

Police surveillance photography has been around for as long as cameras have been available for general use. Police use of photographic surveillance is for the purpose of creating a deterrence from criminal activity, recognizing and/or monitoring potential threats to public safety, and gathering evidence during criminal investigations. The use of police surveillance may be overt (out in the open) or covert (hidden from view). Overt surveillance is an attempt to prevent criminal activity by displaying a visible presence of a camera to the public view. Covert surveillance is an attempt to gather evidence associated with criminal activity or to gather intelligence related to criminal activity and usually targets a specific person, group of persons, and/or location. The use of photographic surveillance by law enforcement and the intelligence community has received recent criticism and public concern due to the rise in technology and intelligence gathering devices widely available to the government. While new laws may emerge from the use of high-technology surveillance, the courts have generally held that no warrant is needed for police photographic surveillance as long as the subject under surveillance has no reasonable expectation of privacy (in a public place). However, as always, when in doubt, get a warrant.

OVERT PHOTOGRAPHY

The use of overt photography assumes that the presence of a camera will deter someone from engaging in criminal activity. Retail establishments have long used photographic video surveillance in stores and parking areas to help deter criminal offenses. Because of the deterrence effect of the camera presence, many businesses use "dummy" cameras equipped with flashing red lights mounted in conspicuous locations. Patrons of these establishments may not recognize the camera as being fake and conduct their behavior as if they were being monitored. Using this same deterrence philosophy, many cities across the United States have installed video surveillance cameras in high-crime areas in an attempt to dissuade criminal activity.

The use of video surveillance in cities has received mixed results. According to a recent study by the Urban Institute (LaVigne, Lowry, Markman, & Dwyer, 2011), some camera surveillance worked well at reducing criminal activity in some neighborhoods while other camera systems failed to impact criminal activity. The study was performed in Baltimore, Chicago, and Washington, D.C. and examined the methods used by the police to set up and monitor camera surveillance systems within those cities. The study found that success of camera surveillance was dependent on how well the camera was being monitored by police. In areas where police sporadically or never monitored the camera in real time, there was no effect on criminal activity. However, where police were active in real-time monitoring, crime was reduced significantly. Apparently, the public became quickly aware of which cameras were being actively monitored and which ones were not. Where cameras were being actively monitored in real time, a police officer could be dispatched and arrive at the scene quickly during the commission of a criminal offense. There was some success with cameras that were not monitored in real time. These cameras did record offenses that became useful later in court or in investigating the criminal activity. However, the issue of image quality was also a concern. In many cases, unmonitored cameras captured only a portion of the criminal activity and/or was of a quality that identification of perpetrators became problematic (Figures 11.11 and 11.12).

Police agencies in the United States have recently began using camera-equipped drone aircraft to monitor activities from an aerial location. Aerial surveillance is not new as it has been used for years looking for drug locations and searching for fugitives. However, drone use is on the rise, and the technology available has produced great strides in the ability of police to observe behavior and recognize fugitives from an aerial platform. The ARGUS-IS camera system is able to be mounted on a helicopter or a drone and has a 1.8 gigapixel resolution digital camera. ARGUS (which stands for Autonomous Real-Time Ground Ubiquitous Surveillance Imaging System) is capable of infrared photography, of facial recognition, and even has a microphone that can capture personal conversations. It can capture digital images of a 25 square mile area from 20,000 feet altitude and record high-resolution images of objects as small as 6 inches on the ground. Another aerial surveillance drone is the Hummingbird, which looks like the bird, is the same size as a hummingbird, and weighs less than one AA battery. It can fly up to a window and take photographs or video images without being noticed.

FIGURE 11.11
Nest of surveillance cameras on pole.

FIGURE 11.12

A nightclub in Seattle burned due to arson in 2014 and police released this image of a "person of interest" captured on the nightclub's video surveillance camera.

COVERT (CLANDESTINE) PHOTOGRAPHY

Police typically use covert or clandestine photography to gather intelligence on criminal activity (organized crime figures, drug dealers, suspected terrorists) and to gather evidence for procuring search and arrest warrants. A common use of covert photography is recording the activities around a suspected drug dealing location to obtain a search warrant. Unlike overt photography, it is imperative that the persons under surveillance are not made aware of the presence of the camera. Because of this, the camera must be concealed or in a location that it is not readily recognizable. The use of telephoto lenses is usually a necessity. Also, low light situations and weather conditions may require additional equipment, such as night vision, to capture usable images.

The main purpose of covert photography is to gather photographic information without being observed in doing so. There are many techniques to hiding cameras or disguising them, and many of these methods involve the use of miniature cameras. Unless the photographer is conducting an undercover operation and wearing or carrying a disguised camera, most police covert photography involves shooting from a distance. As such, any professional-grade DSLR camera is suitable so long as it has the capability of different lenses. Many times the camera may be secluded inside a vehicle, shooting through a window or windshield. Or, from inside a building through a window. The camera may require a telephoto lens to capture the subject with sufficient detail from a distance. For most covert photographic situations, a 400–600-mm telephoto lens is suitable. Many of these lenses are available as zoom lenses that may range from 100 to 600 mm. And, many are available as mirror lenses where the lens barrel is considerably shorter than a long, nonmirrored telephoto lens. This is particularly useful when shooting images from cramped locations such as inside a car (Figure 11.13(a) and (b)).

When using a telephoto lens it is necessary to keep the camera stabilized during shooting. Higher magnification means keeping the camera steady to prevent blurring. The use of a tripod or some other mounting device is necessary when using high-magnification lenses. Supporting the camera on the dash or window sill of a car may help when photographing from a vehicle. Also, the use of a polarizing filter may be necessary to reduce glare when shooting through windshields or glass windows. If the surveillance must be conducted from a longer distance requiring higher magnification, the photographer may consider using a telescope or spotting scope as a lens for the camera. Adapters for DSLR cameras may be purchased through most telescope supply houses that will enable the camera to be mounted to a high-magnification telescope or firing-range spotting scope. These, of course, will require the use of a tripod to stabilize the image. A remote control may also be useful for manually selecting shutter speeds and aperture settings with the camera mounted on a long lens or telescope. The remote control is also useful for reducing camera shake during exposure at such high magnifications (Figure 11.14).

Siljander and Juusola (2012) recommend that the surveillance photographer:

1. Know your camera well enough to operate it in the dark.
2. Take steps to darken any reflective or bright components of your camera and gear.
3. Become familiar with how the camera functions under various day and night conditions with emphasis on working with available light and telephoto lenses.

(a) **(b)**

FIGURE 11.13
A typical 500-mm mirror lens (a) and 500-mm-long (nonmirrored) lens (b).

FIGURE 11.14
A high-powered telescope with camera mounted (a) and a spotting scope with camera mounted (b).

4. Become a student of physical surveillance by learning about effective concealment, avoiding detection, selecting an appropriate vantage point, "escape" routes, covert techniques, awareness of your surroundings, weatherproofing when needed, learning about your subject (habits, background, known hangouts, schedule, usual attire, etc.).

PHOTOGRAPHING IN DARKNESS WITH INFRARED

The capability of making infrared photographs "in the dark" is extremely pertinent to the area of surveillance in law enforcement, because evidence can be gathered without the knowledge of those committing the offense.

It is relatively simple to rig infrared photoflash setups to make still photographs in the dark. Human subjects can be photographed without being aware of it. This is of special value in apprehending burglars at safes, cash drawers, etc.

For still photographic traps, cameras usually must be preset and flash-fired by circuits triggered with infrared detectors. It is necessary for the photographer to know where the subject is going to be. No lens filter is needed.

A piece of plastic equivalent to Kodak Wratten Filter No. 87 or 87C can be purchased in a size large enough to cover the front of the flash unit. Because optical quality is not required for this light-source filter, the plastic filter can be used. A housing, or even a rubber band, can be devised to hold this filter on the flash unit. Guide numbers are easily determined by the user with a simple trial exposure series. Most of the portable low-voltage units (around 500 V) yield guide numbers in the 200–300 range depending on the camera and filter used as well as the ISO setting used on the camera.

Most individuals can detect a slight red glow through a No. 87 filter with scotopic vision when they happen to be looking directly at the source during an exposure. Bouncing the radiation off a low ceiling, a reflector, or a wall is often helpful when a subject might see the telltale glow as photographs are made in the dark. Alternatively, a darker No. 87C filter may be considered. Large and custom-cut plastic infrared filters may be obtained from Serial Port Engineering, Co. (serialporteng.com).

NIGHT-VISION DEVICES

Surveillance is often performed under adverse lighting conditions or in complete darkness. When there is insufficient ambient light for observed suspects to be identified, a light amplification device may be employed. Using night vision, the ability to focus properly and see what is happening becomes problematic.

Using infrared in surveillance has the same disadvantage as using night-vision devices. That is, the photographer may not be able to distinguish those under surveillance and focusing becomes a problem. Infrared image converters may be used to convert infrared radiation to a visible image. An infrared image converter is a device similar to an image intensifier, but it extends the response to the infrared wavelength. The converter then converts infrared images into visible green images. The green image may be photographed with a digital camera or may be video recorded. As with any other infrared recording, the scene requires sufficient amounts of infrared illumination. If the use of infrared illuminators (filtered flashes or lamps) is not feasible, a passive thermal infrared video camera may be used. These cameras detect wavelengths of infrared light that are emitted from warm objects, such as human beings, vehicles, etc. Thermal images appear white while cold objects appear black. Thermal imaging does not visually have the image quality to identify individuals under surveillance; therefore, a thermal imaging device is used primarily to locate the presence of individuals in dark areas as well as identifying recently used automobiles.

Electrophysics Corporation (Astroscope) and FJW Optical Systems both offer several models of night-vision devices, thermal imaging devices, and infrared viewers that can be attached to cameras. The night vision module is usually attached to the body of the camera and the lens attached to the module. The hand-held infrared viewers are excellent for in-the-lab use (i.e., questioned documents) or in the field. Also, MaxMax Optical Systems (maxmax.com) offers a number of digital still and video cameras specially modified for infrared photography (Figures 11.15–11.17).

FIGURE 11.15

The Astroscope night-vision device mounted on a digital SLR camera.

FIGURE 11.16

FJW Industries Find-R-Scope handheld infrared viewer.

FIGURE 11.17
Infrared view camera capturing an auto burglar at work.

REFERENCES

LaVigne, N. G., Lowry, S. S., Markman, J. A., & Dwyer, A. M. (2011). *Evaluation of the use of public surveillance cameras for crime control and prevention – a summary.* Washington, D.C.: Urban Institute.

Siljander, R. P., & Juusola, L. W. (2012). *Clandestine photography: Basic to advanced daytime and nighttime manual surveillance photography techniques for military special operations forces, law enforcement, intelligence agencies and investigators.* Springfield, IL: Charles C. Thomas Publishers.

The Digital Darkroom

CONTENTS

ABSTRACT

With film photography, the photographer needed to know not only how to take proper photographs but how to develop them in a photographic darkroom. With today's digital cameras, the police photographer is required to know how to "develop" pictures using computer software to produce an image that will be useful in court. The computer has largely replaced the traditional darkroom as a means of enhancing photographs through contrast, filtration, color separations, and so on. This chapter covers the use of Photoshop and other software programs useful to the police photographer in creating accurate details of evidence and scenes that will help not only criminal investigators but also aid the judge and jury in understanding the facts of a case. This chapter also covers the use of digital scanners and printers.

KEY TERMS

Bracketing
Dots per inch (DPI)
High dynamic range (HDR)
JPEG
Posterization
RAW
Resolution
Scanners
TIFF

DIGITAL IMAGING EQUIPMENT

Scanners

Scanners are nothing more than stationary digital cameras. Instead of having the two-dimensional square or rectangular CCD/CMOS image sensor found in digital cameras, scanners have a singular row of light-sensitive sensors mounted on a bar. This bar passes over the document to be scanned and records the image one line or row at a time. There are several types of scanners. The most common are the flatbed scanner, the sheet fed scanner, and the film scanner.

Flatbed scanners can, commonly, accommodate documents up to 8.5 × 11 inches. Some flatbed scanners are capable of scanning 8.5 × 14 inches and some have attachments to scan 35 mm slides and negatives. Flatbed scanners have a moving image sensor bar that moves across the item being scanned. Sheet fed scanners, on the other hand, pull documents to be scanned across the image sensor bar. Film scanners are specifically designed to scan negatives and slides and, generally, have more resolution than flatbed scanners equipped with slide/negative attachments.

Scanners are rated by resolution, color depth, and dynamic range. It is important to select a scanner based on its true optical resolution. This is the resolution that captures detail in the scanned image without adding to or subtracting details from the image. Some scanners will state the true optical resolution as 600 × 1200 or 1200 × 2400 dpi. The first number is the highest optical resolution and the second number is the resolution for the scanning head. Therefore, use the first number to determine the true optical resolution. Color depth is measured in bits per pixel. The higher the number, the more colors and densities the scanner can distinguish. Most flatbed scanners have between 32 and 48 bits per pixel and are capable of distinguishing billions of colors. Dynamic range is the measure of how well the scanner can record levels of brightness and darkness on the item being scanned. The dynamic range measurement scale is generally between 0 (white) and 4 (black). The higher the dynamic range, the more sensitive the scanner is to changes in light intensity. Most high-end scanners describe dynamic range in terms of Dmin and Dmax. If a scanner has a Dmin of 0.4 and a Dmax of 3.2, these numbers are subtracted to find the dynamic range of the scanner ($3.2 - 0.4 = 2.8$).

Scanners have a range of dots per inch (dpi) resolution that can scan items. The range can be from 25 to as much as 9600 dpi and more. As one might think, the higher the resolution, the greater the size of the computer file that stores the image. It is necessary to determine the use of the final printed output when scanning. If one only needed photographs to be displayed on a television, or computer monitor, then scans of 75–200 dpi would suffice. However, if enlarged printed copies of the scanned image are required, the image should be scanned based on the printer's dpi capability. This is usually 300 dpi for inkjet printers. If one were scanning an image that needed to be enlarged and printed later, the following formula can be used:

$$\text{Scanner Resolution} = \text{printer dpi} \times (\text{intended image width/original image width})$$

If a 4×6 original photograph needed to be enlarged to 8×10 for example, the scanning resolution should be:

$$300 \text{ dpi} \times (8/4) = 600 \text{ dpi scanner resolution}$$

As a result, the image of the 4×6 original would need to be scanned at 600 dpi in order to enlarge it to an 8×10 print on a 300 dpi printer. This is in order to avoid pixelating the image, when printing.

When 35 mm slides and/or negatives are to be scanned, they are best scanned on a film scanner. Generally, they have much higher resolution than flatbed scanners. If a police department wished to archive traditional film images and store and print photographs on the computer and printer, a film scanner is, truly, a necessity.

As stated, scanned images with higher resolutions will also result in large memory files to store the images. To determine how large a file will be for a scanned image, the following formula can be used:

$$\text{File Size} = (\text{resolution} \times \text{horizontal size}) \times (\text{resolution} \times \text{vertical size}) \times \text{scan mode.}$$

So, if a 4×6 image is scanned at 300 dpi, the file size would be:

$$(300 \times 6) \times (300 \times 4) \times (300) = 6 \text{ megabytes of memory.}$$

FIGURE 12.1
Epson flatbed scanner.

The same image scanned at 600 dpi would require over 51 megabytes of memory required to store the image. In addition, the file sizes are also determined by the file type of the image (i.e., JPEG, TIFF, etc.) discussed later in this chapter (Figures 12.1 and 12.2).

PRINTERS

Even low-end digital cameras and cell phone cameras can produce acceptable images on a computer or television screen. However, if hard-copy prints are needed, a quality color printer will be required. As a rule, this has traditionally been the most disappointing area of digital photography. Printers have not been able to keep up with the increased image quality improvements of digital cameras. Although a few printers can boast of photograph quality prints, most printers are not capable of producing photographs of the same quality as regular photographic film processing.

There are three basic types of printers commonly used to produce digital photographs: laser, inkjet, and dye-sublimation. Laser printers, like photocopy machines, use toner powder to come into contact with electrostatic charged paper. Laser printers are fast and economical. However, laser printers often perform poorly in accurately reproducing color photographs. Generally, a color print from a color laser printer tends to look dull and flat. Plus, most laser printers are only capable of producing 8 × 10 or smaller photographic prints. Inkjet printers are more commonly used with digital photographs, particularly with consumers. They work by spraying microscopic dots of ink onto the paper. Inkjet

FIGURE 12.2
The Nikon 35 mm film scanner (top) and the Minolta Dimage film scanner.

technology has improved greatly over the past few years and many inkjet printers can produce near photograph quality prints. Print time, however, might be rather slow. Dye-sublimation printers are, by far, superior in quality to laser printers and many inkjet printers. Dye-sublimation printers use colored dye films to permeate the paper and produce continuous tone images (with no readily apparent dots). The disadvantages of dye-sublimation printers are they are expensive, especially those that can produce 8 × 10 size prints, and they do not generally print text as well as the others. If a police department only needed prints of 5 × 7 or smaller, then a dye-sublimation printer might be a good choice. However, enlargements of photographs are often needed for courtroom presentation. Ink-jet printers are capable of producing large prints (11 × 14, 16 × 20, and larger) with near photograph quality results. It can be said that inkjet printers are less expensive than dye-sublimation printers and that they can produce excellent text reproduction as well. As a result, for all around general purpose police photographs, an inkjet printer capable of producing larger than 8 × 10 prints would be a good choice.

Printer resolution is measured in dpi. Color laser printers are usually rated at 600 or 1200 dpi. Inkjet printers vary but most, generally, are between 200 and 300 dpi. However, the printer manufacturers may advertise print quality of much higher values (2880 dpi for example). This tends to be misleading for the consumer in that these higher dpi numbers only reflect the accuracy of the mechanical system of the printer, not true pixels per inch (ppi). In other words, a 2880 dpi printer's print may look little different than those from a 1440 dpi printer even though one might think that it has a higher resolution. One should read the specifications of a printer to determine the actual pixel resolution.

Large police departments that routinely use digital imaging may use a hybrid printing system. These systems generally use a combination of fast digital film scanning, silver halide paper with laser exposure, and chemical development. The result is an image that is virtually indistinguishable from a true traditional photographic print made from a negative. These types of machines produce high-volume output at a reasonable cost, although, initially, they seem very expensive (Figures 12.3 and 12.4).

(a)

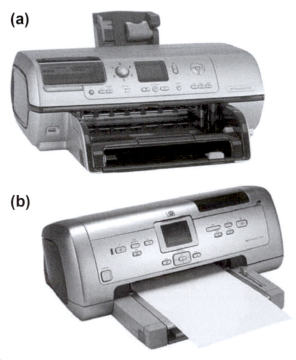

(b)

FIGURE 12.3
Hewlett Packard inkjet printer.

FIGURE 12.4

Thermal dye sub printers: Kodak 6800 (left) and the Fuji 4500 (right).

It is important to remember that a printer's dpi (or ppi points) resolution output is directly related to the size of the print that is required. If a 4 × 6 size print is needed and produced on a 200 dpi printer, the camera resolution needed would be about one megapixel to create a photograph quality print. This can be determined from yet another formula:

$$\text{Camera Resolution Required} = (\text{output size vertical} \times 200) \times (\text{output size horizontal} \times 200).$$

With our example: $(4 \times 200) \times (6 \times 200) = 960{,}000$ or rounded off to 1 megapixel. Printed at 300 dpi, the same 4 × 6 image would require a 2.2 megapixel digital camera.

IMAGE DEVELOPMENT AND PHOTOSHOP

Once photographs are taken in a case, the digital images should be transferred from the electronic recording medium to a server that is regularly backed up for archiving. These images may also be transferred to a CD or DVD for storage in the case file. The photographs should be reviewed by the photographer and examined for clarity, content, accuracy, and problem images. Occasionally, photographs are taken that may require enhancements to improve the visual appearance or an image may need to be developed in order to extract additional detail from the image. Some of the typical enhancements may include brightness adjustments, contrast adjustments, color corrections, and image sharpening.

With the advent of the digital platform, traditional darkroom based film development methods have been replaced with software-based methods that are capable of executing many of the same techniques previously utilized in the darkroom. The software most commonly used in digital image development is Adobe Systems Photoshop software. Adjustments made to images in a software environment are often referred to as post-processing.

There has been much concern in the past over the manipulation of digital images related to legal investigations, namely the potential for the doctoring of photographs whereby objects may be added or deleted from the photographs. This concept is not novel and was routinely performed with film images in order to generate some special effect or "trick photography." However, the ability to introduce special effects in images has become very generic and no longer occurs at the hand of a skilled darkroom image developer. Many of these concerns can fortunately be bypassed in the court of law when a proper chain of photographic evidence is demonstrated and the steps taken to develop an image are well documented. That being stated, there are several factors to keep in mind when developing images:

- Original images should not be developed, rather, a separate working image should be generated and saved as a separate image file. Developed images should be presented as a final image when the development process has ended.
- The steps taken to develop an image should be accurately recorded on notes and/or worksheets. An independent examiner should be able to reproduce the developed image from notes/worksheets.
- History logging should be activated in Photoshop. This will store the steps taken to develop an image directly to the metadata of the image file.

IMAGE DEVELOPMENT

A criminalist or investigator that has identified and photographed evidence at the crime scene or laboratory may have taken the photograph for the purpose of some specific intended use. For example, if a fingerprint was developed, an examination quality photograph may have been taken to use the fingerprint in a comparison to a known set of prints. Likewise, a footwear impression in blood may have been photographed at the scene for the purpose of comparing the footwear pattern to a known shoe. Whether sufficient detail and contrast was captured in the photograph taken at the scene may be a function of available lighting, available resources, and equipment, such as enhancement reagents, development powder, and alternate light sources. In many cases, photographs of enhancements made at the scene require additional post-processing to maximize the details present in the image to render it suitable for comparison. Additionally, photographs of evidence documented for the purposes of comparison may need resizing and scaling in preparation for a comparison to a known object. Therefore, when preparing for image development some intended or desired outcome must be anticipated by the image developer. This mindset is important to narrow down the myriad of possibilities that exist for image development. Some factors in the image that may be corrected in post-processing should be considered:

- Exposure corrections. Is the image underexposed? Are there details present in the shadows or underexposed areas of the photograph that can be developed?
- White balancing. Does the color accuracy of the photograph need to be corrected? Is color necessary? Would black and white conversions increase the contrast in the image?
- Contrast enhancements. Can the detail in the photograph be maximized using contrast enhancement tools in the software?
- Size adjustments. Does the scale of the photograph need to be corrected or scaled to the size of another photograph for a comparison?

DIGITAL IMAGES, FILE FORMATS AND METADATA

The file type of the image may limit the degree to which images can be developed in Photoshop. JPEG formats, as previously mentioned, can display artifacts as a result of the compression/decompression process these files undergo. RAW and TIFF images are preferred because, in addition to being uncompressed or using lossless compression, these file types also typically store more data about the scene being photographed.

Bit-depth or color-depth are terms that are used to describe the number of data points that are used to define the color of a single pixel. Because computer language utilizes a binary system, values for each bit can be defined as either "1" or "0." The number of colors displayed per color channel can be calculated by the expression 2^x, where x = the bit depth used by the file format. The JPEG format stores eight-bits per color channel and therefore can contain 2^8 colors, or 256 colors per channel. Because images are constructed via Bayer filtration, which is based on three color channels (red, green, and blue (RGB)), JPEG images can display 256^3 colors or 16,777,216 colors. Images that display 16 million colors are referred to as true color images, which is slightly more colors than can be perceived by the human eye. By contrast, TIFF files are capable of capturing 16 bits of color data per channel, which works out to approximately 281 trillion colors. RAW files can store 12 or 14 bits per color channel. Clearly, TIFF and RAW files use significantly more data to define the value of pixels, more than can be perceived by the human eye and more than can be displayed on a computer screen at any given moment. The use of Adobe Photoshop allows the photographer to develop an image with the use of all data present in the image. This can be used to adjust the hue, color, and intensity of the scene, or to develop details that may be present in darkened portions of the photograph. Image data that are not readily displayed by the software but can be displayed by adjusting the settings such as hue, contrast, or brightness is referred to as floating point data. The span of highlights and shadows that are capable of being displayed in the image is termed dynamic range.

In addition to bit-depth data, each image file also stores what is called metadata. Metadata contains information about the photograph that was taken and can contain information such as the file name, date and time the photograph was taken, the camera that produced the image, size of the image, file format and compression used, color depth of the file format, the camera exposure mode used, and exposure setting such as f-number and shutter speed. This data tag, which is stored with the image file, can also log any changes that were made to the file as well as the name and version of any software that was used to edit the file. Examining this file can help, not just in understanding the photographic conditions under which the image was captured, but can also be used to verify the integrity of the file. As previously mentioned, when working in Photoshop, history logging can be activated, which would store additional information in the metadata about functions and algorithms that were used to develop the photographs. These files can always be examined to determine what was previously done to a photograph. Some software packages that come with digital cameras can be used to read these details in the image and edit some of its contents. For example, the name of the photographer may be entered into the metadata as well as the location address where the photographs were taken and any other informational notes (Figure 12.5).

HISTOGRAMS AND LEVELS ADJUSTMENTS

Histograms are a graphical representation of the tonal range in an image. In addition to being present in Photoshop, histograms may also be displayed next to images on the camera's liquid crystal display. The left portion of the histogram represents the shadows in an image whereas the center represents the midtones. The right portion of the histogram represents highlights in the image. The peaks in the histogram represent the tonal range of the photograph. This data can be displayed as a combination of RGB values and may be displayed as separate histograms for each channel. In general, when the data are positioned predominantly in the center of the histogram the exposure is

FIGURE 12.5

The figure depicts the display of a metadata file from a digital photograph. Information, such as the date and time of the exposure, as well as camera and exposure setting, can be determined by examining this file. Also listed in this particular metadata file is a "creation software" line, indicating the file was opened and saved in Photoshop CS3. This information can be obtained from software packages that can read this data. The metadata displayed in the figure above was obtained by right clicking the image file and viewing the advanced properties tab on a computer running Windows XP.

balanced. If the histogram is shifted to the left or has shadows, this represents a preponderance of over exposures in the image. Likewise, a histogram that is shifted to the right would represent a preponderance of highlights or over-exposures in the image (Figures 12.6 and 12.7).

Adobe Photoshop allows one to balance an exposure, correct color, and reveal detail in shadows as well as adjust contrast with the use of the levels function.

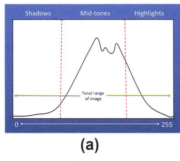 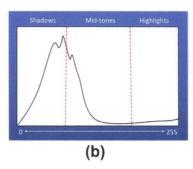 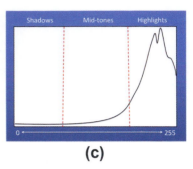

FIGURE 12.6

This illustrates the appearance of histograms and the locations where shadows, midtones, and highlights would be represented. Panel (a) represents how a balanced exposure would appear; the base of the graph represents the tonal range of the image. In panel (b) the data is shifted to the left indicating underexposures in the photograph. Panel (c) shows data shifted toward the highlights indicating overexposures in the photograph.

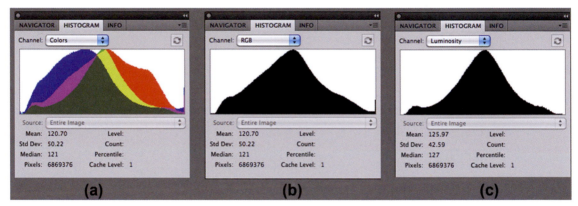

FIGURE 12.7

This illustrates the various ways in which image data can be represented in histograms. Panel (a) shows a histogram of individual color values. The blue channel on the left indicates that underexposed areas of the photograph are predominantly found in the channel whereas highlights are primarily in the red channel. In panel (b), the histogram illustrates the image data distribution of the combined red, green, and blue (RGB) values. Panel (c) is yet another histogram illustrating the overall luminosity of the photograph.

Once the image is imported into the software, the levels feature can be accessed with the following path:

Image > Adjustments > Levels…

The levels dialogue box appears as a histogram, where the individual color channels or a combined RGB histogram can be observed. Looking at the histogram, areas of the photograph that contain highlights can be identified and the tonal range of the image can be studied.

In the example provided, a photograph was submitted for development that was imaged with a film camera. The photograph was received as a slide film, which was

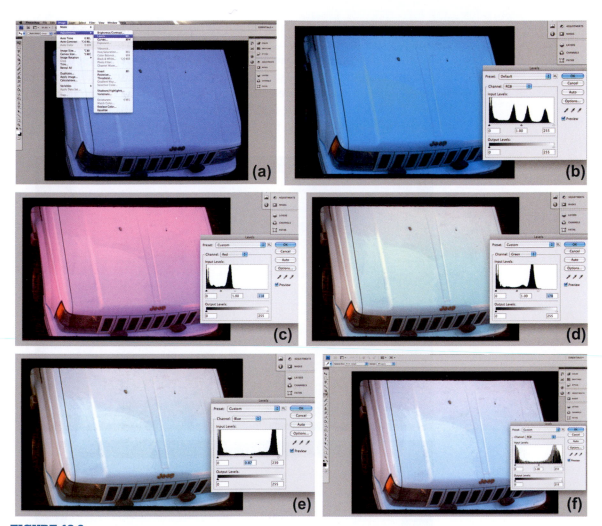

FIGURE 12.8

This figure illustrates the steps taken to make corrections to an image using the levels function in Photoshop. In panel (a), the image of the hood of a vehicle is seen displaying underexposures and incorrect white balance. The histogram for the image can be seen in panel (b). Panels (c–e) illustrate the steps taken to correct the histogram in each color channel. Panel (f) illustrates the final image and its histogram, which, when compared to the histogram in panel (b), shows a wider tonal range in the developed image.

digitized into a TIFF format with the use of a dedicated slide scanner. The digital image was imported into Adobe Photoshop. With the levels dialogue box open, the histogram for each color channel was examined. The original photograph was underexposed in addition to lacking the proper color balance. While looking at each color channel the histogram was corrected by sliding the highlights input level icon in the direction of the data. This, in essence, "stretches" the histogram so the tonal range is increased. An example of this can be seen in Figure 12.8(c), depicting the red channel histogram. The highlights tab is moved toward the data that are present on the underexposed end of the histogram, which corrects the exposure for that particular channel. The midtone tab could additionally be used to further develop unexposed areas in the photograph. By repeating this process for each color channel, the exposure and white balance was corrected in the image. The final corrected image was reexamined in RGB to see the overall effect of the changes. Once satisfied with the results, the levels adjustments to the photograph are applied by selecting "OK" in the dialogue box (Figure 12.9).

FIGURE 12.9
This illustrates before and after images of the car hood developed using levels in Photoshop.

CONTRAST ENHANCEMENTS USING CURVES

The curves function in Photoshop can also be used to achieve several effects in an image, including contrast enhancements and color corrections. The curves dialogue box can be found using the following path:

Image > Adjustments > Curves…

The curves dialogue box presents the user with a diagonal line superimposed upon an RGB histogram of the open image. The curve can be positioned in numerous ways, all of which will affect the color tone and contrast in the image. There are two typical curve configurations that are used, the s-curve and inverted s-curve. When the diagonal line in the curves dialogue box is positioned as an s-curve, such as illustrated in Figure 12.10(a), contrast is added to the highlights and shadows in the image. Conversely, an inverted s-curve (see Figure 12.10(b)) will add contrast to the midtones in the image.

Continuing with the example given in the above section on levels adjustments, the photograph of the car hood was developed using curves. The back story of the photographs of the car hood involves the investigation of a hit and run incident. The car, which struck a pedestrian, fled the scene of the incident.

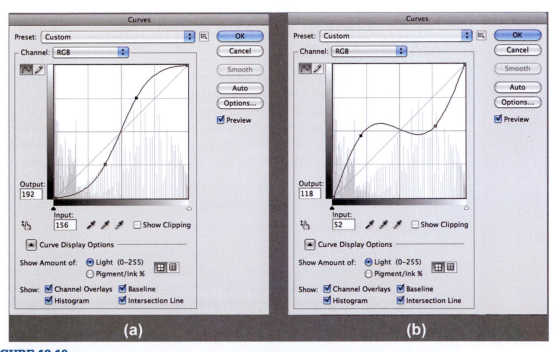

(a) **(b)**

FIGURE 12.10
The s-curve (a) and inverted s-curve (b).

According to witnesses, the victim was crossing the street when the car took a sharp turn from an intersecting road. The victim who was hit by the car tumbled over the hood and was projected from the side of the vehicle, breaking off the antenna from the car in the process. The car was found hours later and the driver was arrested. Although the car was being investigated, torn fibers from the victim's clothing were recovered from a broken section of the antenna that was still attached to the vehicle. During the recovery of fiber evidence, investigators noted a wipe pattern on the hood of the car, where dust and soot, which coated the hood of the car, was removed as the victim rolled across it. Efforts were made to document this pattern; however, it was a difficult photographic subject.

In order to develop the wipe pattern on the hood of the car, the image was corrected using levels. The corrected image was then further developed using the curves function. The curves dialogue box was opened using the above-mentioned path (Figure 12.11(a)). A variation of the s-curve was made by placing several anchors along the line (by clicking on the line) and then positioning the curve along the shape of the histogram seen in the background (see Figure 12.11(b)). The resulting image created color contrast of the car hood such that the wipe pattern is clearly seen in the image (Figure 12.12).

PHOTOSHOP BLACK AND WHITE USING CALCULATIONS

Converting photographs to gray scale or black and white is a simple way to establish contrast in an image. In Photoshop, there are several ways to convert an image to black and white, one of which is calculations. With the use of the calculations function, a black and white contrast image can be developed by blending color information from the photograph in various ways, including color overlays, dodging (lightening), burning (darkening), and subtracting color.

Prior to using the calculations function, the image should be viewed in each of its RGB color channels. This can be done by opening the image channels via:

Window > Channels

Selecting channels will open a palate where the image can be viewed under each of the RGB channels. The purpose of viewing the image is to gain an understanding of which color channel(s) provide the best contrast of relevant details in the photograph. Knowing which color channels provide the best contrast and detail can help when selecting the color channels that will be blended in calculations. In Figure 12.13, the curves developed image discussed in the previous section is examined under the different RGB channels. It was determined that the blue and green channels provided the most contrast in the image.

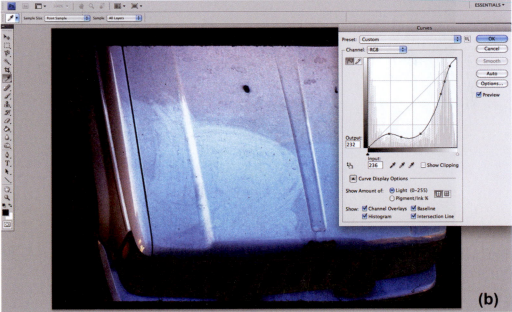

FIGURE 12.11

The image of a car hood involved in a hit and run incident bearing a wipe pattern resulting from the passage of the victim over the hood of the car. Attempts to photograph the pattern were not successful so the image was imported into Photoshop (a) in an effort to create contrast between the wipe pattern and the hood of the car. The wipe pattern was developed using a variation of the s-curve (b).

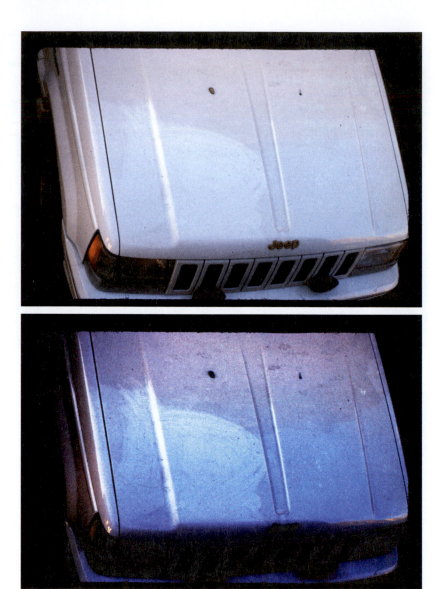

FIGURE 12.12
Before and after images of a car hood where contrast was established using curves in Photoshop. The curves post-processing technique established enough contrast in the image to enhance a faint wipe mark on the hood of the car.

The calculations dialogue box was then opened via:

Image > Calculations…

The source channels were set to blue and green. After observing the effects of several of the blending options, it was determined that an overlay of the

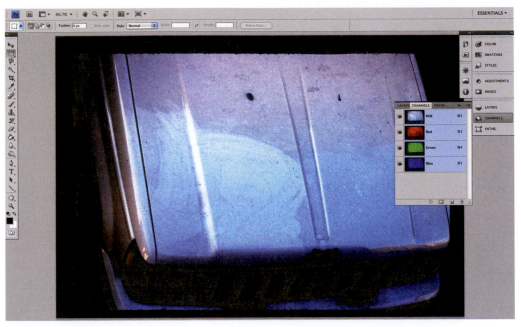

FIGURE 12.13

Prior to performing black and white conversions using Adobe Printshop calculations, the color channels should be viewed in order to understand which channels provide the most contrast in the image.

green channel and inversion of the blue channel provided excellent contrast. The process of determining which blending channel will produce the desired results can be a bit of trial and error. Several of the blending options should be experimented with, in addition to varying the color of the source channels. In addition to individual RGB channels, blending can be performed against the gray scale image. Blending combinations can be numerous in calculations and several should be tried (Figure 12.14).

Once the desired image is obtained, the calculation development steps can be applied to the image by selecting "OK" in the dialogue box. Revisiting the channels at this point will reveal the image created using calculation is stored in a new channel called the alpha channel. When using calculations, the source channels are layered virtually upon themselves. In the above example, the green channel was layered upon the blue channel. The alpha channel stores the methods by which the two layer's calculation sources interface; in this case, the two channels were blended using an overlay. Before the final image can be saved, it must be converted to gray scale. This is done via the following path:

Image > Mode > Grayscale

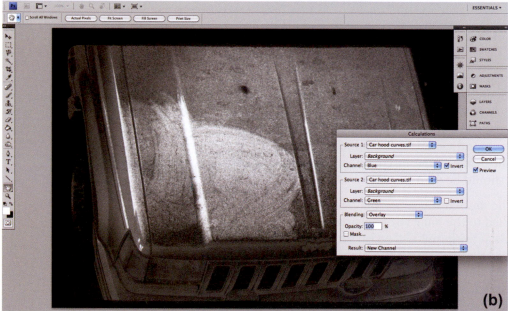

FIGURE 12.14

The image of the car hood was additionally developed using Photoshop calculation for a black and white conversion (a). From a review of the color channels, it was determined that the most amount of contrast could be seen in the green and blue channels. These channels were then selected for source 1 and 2 in the calculations dialogue box. By inverting the blue channel and using overlay blending, excellent contrast was obtained in the resulting black and white image.

FIGURE 12.15

The use of calculations creates a new channel called the alpha channel. This channel is a result of layer masks that are used to blend the two source channels selected in the calculations dialogue box. To save the image, it must be converted to grayscale in advance.

Once the image is converted to gray scale, the color channels and alpha channel will be converted to one gray channel. The image can then be saved as a TIFF file (Figure 12.15).

Although the above examples used photographs of a low contrast dust pattern on the hood of a car, the framework of these techniques can be applied to many different types of evidentiary photographs, such as images of fingerprints, footwear patterns, surveillance images, etc. in order to develop additional details that are contained, but not necessarily seen, in high-quality images (Figure 12.16).

DIGITAL COLOR CONTRAST IMAGING USING ADOBE BLACK AND WHITE

In color contrast photography, color filters are used to either darken or lighten colors in black and white photographs. A general rule, in black and white color contrast photography, a color filter will lighten anything in a black and white photograph that is the same color as the filter. Conversely, they will darken complementary colors. For example, a red filter will lighten red subjects when imaged in black and white. A red filter will also darken green and blue subjects

FIGURE 12.16

The starting image (top) and final developed image (bottom) of an enhancement, using levels, curves, and Photoshop calculations post-processing techniques.

in the photograph. Although this can be performed manually with the use of a physical filter over the lens of a camera, an alternative is carrying out black and white color contrast enhancements in Photoshop.

In the following example, attempts were made to image a fingerprint on a multicolored background that was developed with black fingerprint powder. The photograph was captured as a 12-bit RAW image and converted to TIFF format for post-processing. Once imported into Photoshop, the black and white adjustment mode was selected via the following path:

Image > Adjustments > Black & White…

Selecting this option displays the image in gray scale; however, the software will retain the color values for each pixel in the image. In this manner, color can be intensified or subtracted from the image with the effects of these adjustments displayed in black and white. This is very similar to how color contrast photography would occur. A black and white adjustments pallet will also be displayed alongside the image. This pallet allows one to vary the intensity or facilitate the removal of RGB and cyan, yellow, and magenta colors in the photograph. Presets for certain filtration effects can also be selected from the top of the palate, which allows the user to quickly view the effects of various color filtration options in the gray scale image (Figure 12.17).

The imported photograph depicts a black print across a dark blue and yellow background. The effects of a few preset options can be seen as they relate to the color contrast concept. For example, selecting a high contrast blue preset from the drop down menu lightens the blue background in the image revealing a section of the print, however, the yellow areas are darkened (Figure 12.18(a)). Similarly, applying a yellow preset lightens yellow but the blue background remains dark (Figure 12.18(b)). Use of the custom menu allows for the use of each color slider, giving the user maximum flexibility in the color contrast process. For the above image, the yellow and blue channels were lightened revealing the print. A close examination of the original image shows that the blue background contained areas of magenta colored ink. Lightening of the magenta channel created further contrast between the fingerprint and the blue background (Figure 12.18(c)). Once the desired result was obtained, "OK" was selected in the dialogue box, and the file was saved as a TIFF image (Figure 12.19).

BRACKETING PHOTOGRAPHS

The old photographer's axiom "expose for the shadows and develop for the highlights," refers to retaining details in both light and shadow areas of a photographic image. This was done by cutting the ISO setting of the film in half and increasing exposure by one f-stop or more, then developing the film at a 20–25% reduction of time in the developer. This can be done with digital images, not in a darkroom, but with computer software. Throughout this book, we have mentioned using bracketed exposures to capture the details of the subject area. Bracketing refers to making three or more images of the same subject with different exposure settings on the camera.

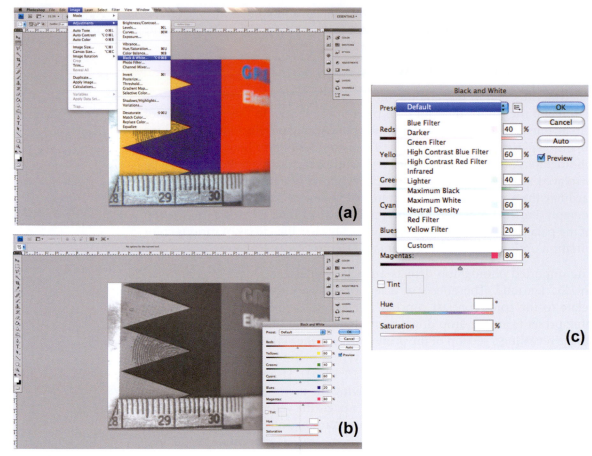

FIGURE 12.17

The photograph depicting a fingerprint on a multicolored surface was imported into Photoshop for development using Photoshop black and white (a). Photoshop black and white is very similar to color contrast photography (b). In the black and white dialogue box, many filter presets can be chosen that serve to intensify or drop patterns from a black and white image using color data (c).

Most digital single-lens reflex (DSLR) cameras can be used to bracket exposures, either manually or automatically. Many of the high-end DSLR cameras have an auto-bracket feature that can rapidly bracket a series of three or more exposures of the same subject at different exposure settings. Usually, the camera is set on aperture priority mode so the f-stop remains the same and each exposure image is taken at a different shutter speed. With cameras equipped with auto-bracketing, this is simple to do through the camera's menu. For example, with the Nikon D300, one would select Menu, choose Custom Setting E5, press the Fn button, and rotate the command dial to the number of bracketing sequence shots desired (up to nine). The shutter button is pressed once for each exposure increment. If the camera is not equipped with auto-bracketing but has a manual setting, the

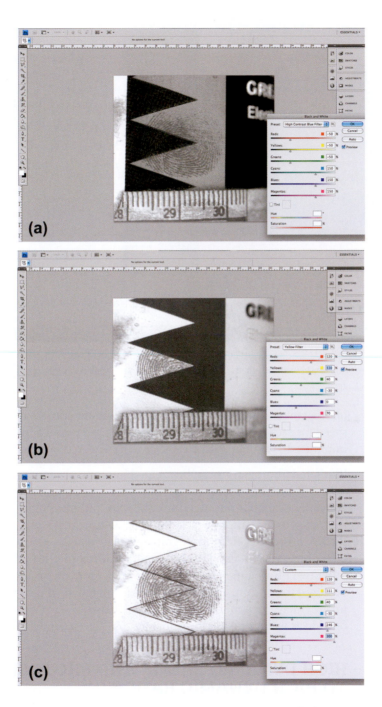

FIGURE 12.18

Adobe black and white option features numerous filter presets that are analogous to the use of color contrast photography. For example, selecting a blue filter preset lightens the blue background in the image and darkens yellow (a). Selecting a yellow filter preset will lighten the yellow portions of the image but darkens the blue background (b). Using the custom menu allows the user to lighten both the yellow and blue backgrounds, as well as lighten any additional colors that may reduce the contrast of the evidence (c).

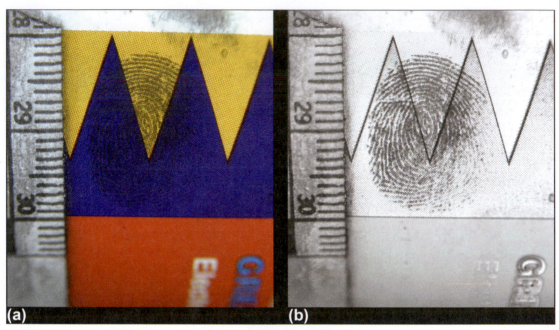

FIGURE 12.19
Before (a) and after (b) images of contrast enhancement of a fingerprint developed with black fingerprint powder on a multicolored surface using Photoshop black and white.

photographer simply sets the camera on aperture priority and changes the shutter speed for each shot. The camera should be on a tripod and movement should be minimized. A shutter release cable or remote would be useful in this instance.

Bracketed photographs can be merged into one photograph using Photoshop's merge feature or other photographic software program. Photomatix is a commercially available photographic software program that can quickly and easily merge two or more bracketed photographs into one image. Figure 12.20 shows three bracketed photographs taken inside a doorway during daylight. One photo was taken with the camera's normal light metered setting and the other two photographs were taken at one f-stop above and below. Photomatix was used to combine the three photos (panels a, b, and c in the figure) into one image (image in panel d in the figure). This allows for details to be seen on the outside as well as inside the doorway.

HIGH DYNAMIC RANGE AND PHOTOSHOP MERGE TO HIGH DYNAMIC RANGE

On occasion, a scene may be composed of darkened areas where little light illuminates the scene, juxtaposed with areas where adequate lighting exists. Subtle differences in the dynamic range of a scene may not be readily perceived with

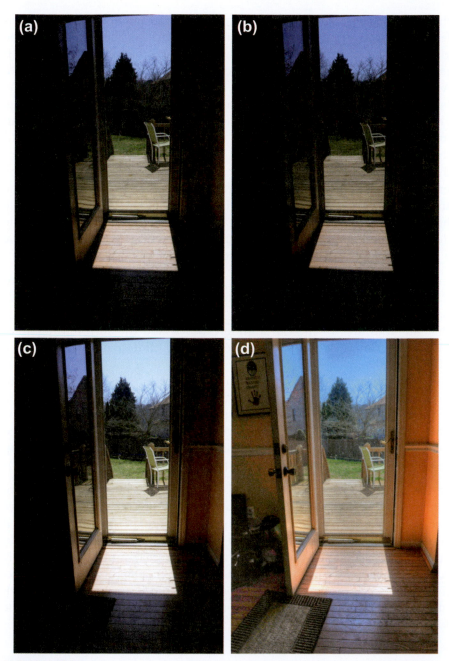

FIGURE 12.20

Bracketed photographs. Photographs in the panels (a, b, and c) were taken at different shutter speeds to emulate f-stop changes. The photograph in panel (d) was merged from (a, b, and c) with Photomatix software.

the human eye because the eye naturally adjusts to brightness and darkness levels with ease. A camera, however, can only record that same scene with one given exposure setting. Based on the area of the scene that is light metered with the camera, areas of over and underexposure will be present in the photograph. As previously mentioned, the dynamic range of an image refers to the extreme light and dark values that are present in the image for a given exposure setting. The dynamic range of a scene is sometimes expressed as a range of f-stops, an indication of the number of bracketed exposures needed to see detail in both the highlights and shadow of the scene. For example, if a scene is said to have a dynamic range of five f-stops, this indicates that five exposures may need to be bracketed in single f-stops to capture details within dark and bright areas of the scene being photographed. HDR imaging is a technique used where multiple bracketed exposures are merged to create one image file that displays visible detail from both the darkened and bright areas of the scene. These images have a broad tonal and brightness range that can be developed using Photoshop.

In the example provided (see Figure 12.21), a photograph into the front passenger area of a vehicle was taken to document a black knife on the front passenger floor. The dark and bright levels of the scene are extreme, such that the floor area of the car is underexposed and the surrounding areas outside the car are overexposed in the reference photograph. The reference photograph is the nominal exposure determined by the camera, which is based on the light metering mode and exposure settings used. In order to brighten the underexposed floor of the car, two exposures were captured that were brighter than the reference photographed. To capture the overexposed areas of the scene, the reference exposure setting was underexposed by two exposure values. The photographs were then merged in Photoshop to generate one HDR image.

In the above example, the bracketed photographs of the scene were captured using TIFF images, which included photographs taken two stops above and below the nominal exposure. When anticipating HDR photographs, it is important that the camera is set on a tripod and not moved when bracketing the exposure. Because merging a series of images to HDR essentially superimposes each image as layers in Photoshop, a slight shift in perspective of the scene in the bracketed exposures could result in a blurred HDR image. Once the images are in a computer, the HDR menu is found with the following path:

File > Automate > Merge to HDR…

Selecting merge to HDR (Figure 12.22(a)) launches a dialogue box that prompts the user to select the bracketed exposures that will be used to construct the HDR image (Figure 12.22(b)). It is helpful to copy these image files into a separate properly labeled folder in advance of HDR processing for easy

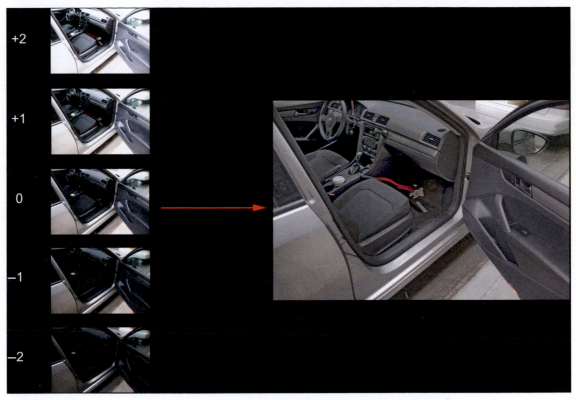

FIGURE 12.21

The images on the left are bracketed exposures needed to capture the full dynamic range of the scene. The reference photograph (adjacent to the zero) is the nominal exposure determined by the camera's internal light meter. Bracketed overexposures are then used to capture details on the darkened floor of the car to properly document a knife. These photographs can be merged to form one high dynamic range (HDR) exposure, depicted on the right of the arrow.

access. Once these files are selected, Photoshop will generate a preview of the merged result (Figure 12.22(c)). In this preview, the source images are displayed on the left of the screen. The individual files can be selected and deselected in order to view their effect on the merged HDR image. If there is an image that negatively impacts the HDR image, it can be deselected and it will not be used in the construction of the HDR image. On the right of the screen is also a histogram of the merged result where the white point of the image can be adjusted. Also, it should be noted that the merged result consists of 32-bits per color channel. Selecting "OK" finalizes the merge and any changes that are made to the white point of the image. Photoshop then generates a 32-bit HDR image of the merged result. The 32-bit HDR image file should be saved at this point.

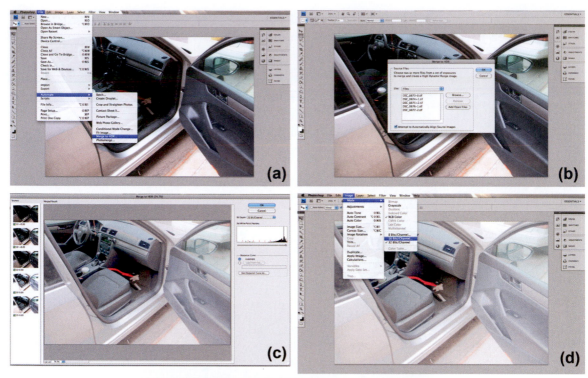

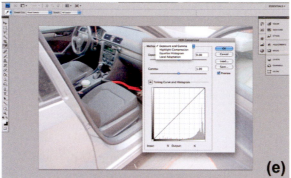

FIGURE 12.22

Converting a photograph to high dynamic range (HDR) allows the photographer to create an HDR image by merging bracketed exposures of the same scene into a single file. Figure 12.17(a–e) illustrates the steps that can be taken in Photoshop to generate a tone-mapped image from an HDR file. The final image (see Figure 12.16) was tone-mapped using the equalize histogram method.

The 32-bit HDR image itself is not a usable image and typically requires some additional development in Photoshop using a technique called tone-mapping. When an image is tone-mapped, the full dynamic range and bit depth data in the HDR file is used to make a final image that is perceptually similar to the dynamic range and luminance of the original scene. To achieve this in Photoshop, the

HDR image must be converted to a 16-bit image, which launches the HDR conversion menu (Figures 12.22(d)). This is executed via the following path:

Image > Mode > 16-bits/Channel…

The HDR conversion dialogue box allows the user to develop the image from four settings that can be selected from a drop down menu at the top of the dialogue box (see Figure 12.22(e)). These four settings are:

- Exposure and gamma;
- Highlight compression;
- Equalize histogram;
- Local adaptation.

The exposure/gamma, highlight compression, and equalize histogram options apply preset tone curves to the image that can be further adjusted by the user with the use of sliders in the dialogue box. Each preset allows the user to vary the brightness, midtones, and contrast in the image within the constraints of the preset tone curve. For example, exposure and gamma allows the user to vary the brightness and midtones of the image in a manner similar to level adjustments discussed above. The equalize histogram preset will, in essence, spread the histogram out in an effort to normalize the image. When the local adaptation dialogue box is used, a dialogue box similar to the curves function becomes available to the user at the bottom of the screen. The local adaptation dialogue box will display a diagonal curves line that is superimposed on a histogram of the HDR image. The curves lines can be adjusted to vary the contrast, brightness, and color tones of the image manually, affording the user significant control over the appearance of the final image. Once a satisfactory image is obtained, "OK" is selected in the HDR conversion dialogue box and the image is converted to a 16-bit image file. Conversion to 16-bit deletes the extraneous floating-point data from the image file that is not used to display the image. The image is therefore no longer considered HDR; however, because the image was tone-mapped, it is displaying the range tonal data obtained from the exposure bracketed source images. When done correctly, the image can potentially display a tonal range of approximately 10–14 stops, which is more than can be visualized in a photograph taken with a single exposure setting. The final tone-mapped image can be saved in as 16-bit TIFF format.

PHOTOSHOP SHADOWS/HIGHLIGHTS

Bracketing exposures for the purposes of generating HDR photographs are not considered the standard regimen in crime scene or evidence photography and requires proper planning. Also, bracketed exposures generally require the use of a tripod. For scenes that contain moving objects or where a tripod is impractical or simply not an option, a single exposure can be used. In the event where bracketed exposures are not obtained for HDR processing, information contained in shadows and overexposures can still be extracted from high-quality images with the use of Photoshop's shadows/highlights function. Photographs should be taken in RAW in order to properly access this function.

Continuing with the example used in the above section on HDR images, the same nominal exposure of the front passenger area of a vehicle is opened in Photoshop. The shadows/highlights menu can be accessed using the following path:

Image > Adjustments > Shadows/Highlights…

The shadows/highlights dialogue box allows the user to make corrections that affect the underexposed areas as well as overexposures independently. In the shadows menu, the shadow slider can be used to brighten the underexposed areas of the image. The tonal range slider allows the user to determine the range of midtones that are affected by the shadows adjustments. For example, if the tonal range slider is kept to the left, only the shadows are brightened and little of the normally exposed areas of the photograph are affected. As the tonal range slider is moved to the right, the midtones will become brightened as well. The radius slider can be used to further balance the transition between the lightened shadows and the rest of the photograph. Likewise, the highlights section in the dialogue box can be used to darken overexposures in the image, while the tonal range and radius slider can be used to balance the exposure. The use of shadow/highlights, like HDR tone-mapping, is somewhat trial and error and will typically require experimentation with all settings in the dialogue box until the desired outcome is obtained. In the above example, the shadows/highlights option is used to brighten the darkened areas of the front passenger floor, revealing the black knife (Figures 12.23 and 12.24).

The degree to which many of post-processing functions in Photoshop will produce usable results depends on several factors, including the file format being used, as this is directly related to the bit-depth of the image. As previously discussed, JPEG files can produce a maximum bit-depth of eight-bits per color channel, which translates to approximately 256 colors per red, green, and blue (RGB) color channels. When compared to 12–14-bit RAW images and 16-bit TIFF, which can record thousands of colors per-channel, it is clear that JPEG image files store far less color data. The following chart can be used to quickly see the differences in bit-depth as related to the number of colors recorded per color channel (RGB) and total range of colors that can be displayed by the image (Table 12.1).

One of the effects produced when post-processing using a JPEG file or other low bit-depth file format is called posterization. Posterization occurs when there is lack of bit-depth in an image, such that transitions from bright to darks areas in the photograph are not gradual. A posterized image will instead show abrupt transitions between light and dark areas of the photograph because there is simply not

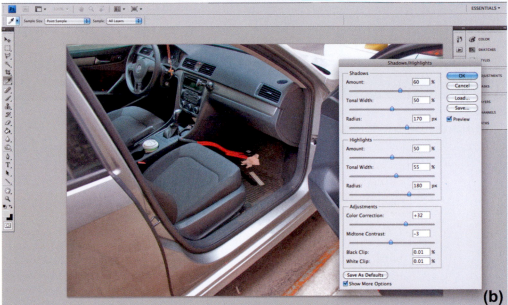

FIGURE 12.23

In the absence of bracketed exposures that may be used to construct a high dynamic range (HDR) image, the shadows/highlights menu in Photoshop (a) can be used to develop an image with an effect similar to a tone-mapped image made from an HDR file. Within the shadows/highlights menu (b) the underexposed areas in the image may be brightened so that objects in the darkened areas of the image become visible. Likewise, making adjustments in the highlights dialogue box can reveal objects in overexposed areas of the image.

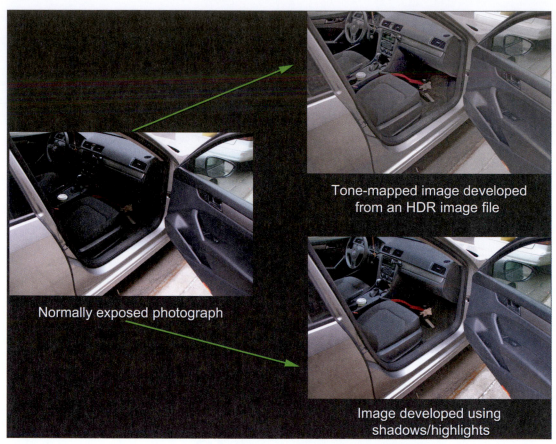

FIGURE 12.24

The same image developed using both high dynamic range (HDR) and the shadows/highlights methods.

Table 12.1 Differences in Bit-Depth

Bit-Depth	Colors Per Channel (2^x)	Total Number of Colors (x^3)
8-bit	256	16,777,216
12-bit	4096	68,719,476,736
14-bit	16,384	4,398,046,511,104
16-bit	65,536	281,474,976,710,656

enough color data present in the image to blend the extremes between light and dark areas of the image. Because post-processing in forensic imaging is typically used to obtain visual information in the photograph that resides in the under/ overexposed areas of the photograph, the tonal range of the photograph is, in essence, pushed to its usable limits. In these cases, the bit-depth of the image being

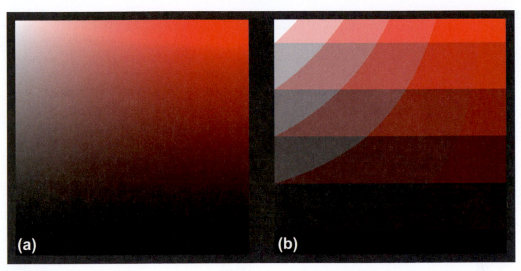

FIGURE 12.25
Posterization occurs when the photograph or image file used does not contain a sufficient tonal range of color data to create a smooth transition between highlight and shadows in an image. When sufficient data exists in the image file, the transition between colors and areas of contrast is gradual, as depicted in panel (a). If the image lacks dynamic range, the transition between colors and areas of contrast is abrupt as depicted in panel (b), which can potentially create artifacts in the image.

used becomes important to avoid posterization artifacts in the digitally developed images. For this reason, photographing in RAW is recommended. Depending on the camera used, RAW files can be recorded as either 12-bit or 14-bit images. Using the highest bit-depth of RAW is recommended for maximum flexibility in post-processing. Some cameras are capable of photographing in TIFF format; however, the manufacturer's specification for TIFF recording should be determined as some TIFF files can have a bit-depth as low as eight-bits per channel. If the post-processing software being used necessitates conversion of the RAW file to another workable format for post-processing, a 16-bit TIFF file should be used, as this will preserve the bit depth of the original image. In general, when post-processing in Photoshop, the user should always be mindful of methods and techniques that could degrade usable detail in the image (Figure 12.25).

CALIBRATING IMAGES IN PHOTOSHOP

The resolution of a camera is directly related to its pixel dimension, or the number of pixels that span the surface of the sensor in the vertical and horizontal directions. For example, if a Nikon D3x camera is used at its full resolution setting, the sensor has a specified pixel dimension of 6048p × 4032p, which is equal to about 24.5 mega pixels (6048p × 4032p = 24,385,536 pixels). The resolution of the image or the number of ppi establishes the size of the image document in Photoshop.

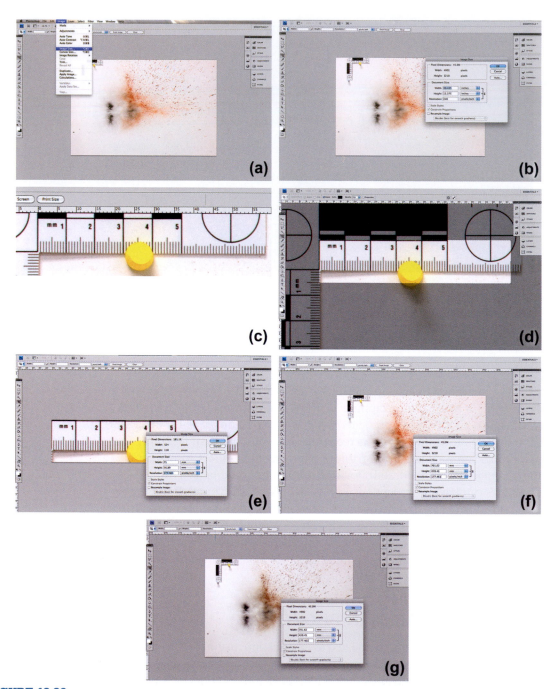

FIGURE 12.26

The above example illustrates the steps taken to generate an actual sized image of gunshot related spatters that can be used in an analysis of the bloodstain patterns. The image document size and resolution was viewed by accessing the image size menu in Photoshop (a, b). The size of the metric scale within the photograph was also compared to the metric ruler in Photoshop (c), which disclosed that

The printable size of an image document can be determined by dividing the pixel dimension by the resolution. For example, if an image is displayed at a resolution of 300 ppi, the above image from a D3x camera can be used to make a print that is 20″L × 13.5″H. Unfortunately, the camera cannot determine the true scale of the subject being photographed. For example, if a tool mark is photographed at a 1:1 reproduction using the same D3x camera, the scale of the image should be roughly 36 × 24 mm, which is the approximate size of the sensor for the D3x camera. However, printing the image can result in a 20″ × 13.5″ photograph of the tool mark, which obviously will not be an actual size representation of the evidence. Images that are actual size (also referred to as 1:1, life size, or natural size images) are often needed in forensic disciplines that involve detailed analysis and comparisons, such as tool mark examinations, fingerprint analysis, footwear impression comparisons, and bloodstain pattern analysis. For example, in the case of footwear impression comparisons, test impressions made from known footwear can be prepared on transparencies in order to directly compare them with impressions photographed at the crime scene. Because the transparency prepared from the actual shoe will be "life-size," examination quality photographs of the crime scene impression will also need to be "life-size" to conduct a proper comparison.

As previously mentioned, examination quality photographs are taken of physical evidence that may be used for the purpose of comparison to a known object or to document the fine detail of evidence. These images are usually taken with the intent that they will be calibrated for actual size prints and are therefore photographed in a particular manner, one that aims at minimizing distortion in the photograph: the camera is set to full resolution, imaged with an uncompressed file format; the photograph is taken with a properly framed right angle scale in view while the subject fills the entire frame of the photograph, the camera is positioned with the sensor parallel to the plane on which the evidence resides to minimize distortion. With a scale in view, these images can be imported into Photoshop and calibrated to generate 1:1 prints of the image.

Once the image is opened in Photoshop, the pixel dimension and resolution of the image can be observed via the following path (Figure 12.26(a)):

Image > Image Size…

the image was not at the proper scale. The bars of the millimeter scale in the photograph do not correspond with the millimeter scale in Photoshop; the photograph is slightly smaller. To correct this, a known distance in the scale is cropped from the photograph (d). In this case, a section corresponding to 75 mm was cropped. The image size dialogue box for the cropped scale was then accessed and the width of the photograph was corrected to 75 mm (e). This change also changed the resolution or distribution of pixels per inch (ppi) of the image. The new resolution was recorded and the original image was restored by reverting the crop. The image size dialogue box for the original image was then opened and the resolution was changed to the resolution value of the cropped scale (f). Selecting "OK" executes the calibration of the image, which can be verified by comparing the scale in the calibrated image to the scale in Photoshop (g). Correspondence between the millimeter increments in both scales indicates a successful calibration of the image.

This will open the image size dialogue box (Figure 12.26(b)). In the dialogue box, there will be a section indicating the pixel dimension of the image and the document size, which is based on the resolution of the image. Using the example in Figure 12.26, the pixel dimension is 4902p × 3210p, which works out to about 16 megapixels. The document size is based on a resolution of 240 ppi, which is approximately 20″ × 13″. If we zoom into the right angle millimeter scale in the corner of the photograph and compare it to the millimeter ruler in Photoshop, it can be seen that the image is not to scale (Figure 12.26(c)) as the millimeter bars in the photograph lose correspondence with the Photoshop scale. In order to calibrate the image and correct the scale, the crop tool is selected and used to crop out a carefully selected known distance in the millimeter scale. The ends of the crop tool should be well aligned with the measurement bars in the scale. The crop box should also be well assigned with the edge of the scale. If the crop box does not align with the edges of the scale, it should be rotated to adjust the alignment. In the above example, a distance of 75 mm was cropped from the scale (Figure 12.26(d)). Once the scale has been cropped, the image size dialogue box should be opened (Figure 12.26(e)). The scale of the document size should be selected to match the scale in the photograph. The box at the bottom marked "resample image" should also be deselected. In the above example, because the scale is an ABFO no. 2 mm scale, the units of the document size are changed to millimeters. The distance captured in the crop of the scale is equal to 75 mm, therefore, a value of 75 mm is entered into the width in the document size dialogue box. Once the width is entered and tabbed through, the resolution/ppi of the image will change. The new resolution should be noted for the next step of the calibration process. Once the new resolution value is recorded, undo the crop of the scale by either selecting "undo" from the edit menu or by accessing the history pallet. This should revert the cropped scale to the original uncropped image. Once the uncropped image has been restored, the image size dialogue box should be reopened (Figure 12.26(f)). The resolution value of the uncropped image should be replaced with the resolution value determined from the cropped scale. In the above example, the value of the resolution field was replaced with 177.461, which was the resolution of the cropped scale with the width of the image adjusted to 75 mm. Once this number is entered in the resolution field, ensure that the document size parameters are linked (a "chain" icon should be present to the right of the values) and resample image should be deselected. Clicking "OK" in the dialogue box will subsequently calibrate the image by resizing the pixels to the designated scale. The actual size of the image can be viewed in the document size section of the dialogue box. The calibration results can be verified by zooming into the scale in the photograph and comparing it to the Photoshop ruler. Using the above example, the millimeter scale in the photograph now corresponds with the millimeter scale in Photoshop in both the horizontal and vertical directions, indicating a successful calibration of the image (Figure 12.26(g)). This image can then be used to print an actual size image directly from Photoshop with an adequate high-quality printer.

It should be noted that in the above steps, image resampling was deselected from the process. Image resampling will resize the photograph by either adding pixels (when enlarging an image) or deleting pixels (in reductions) from the image through interpolation. Because interpolation can reduce the resolvable detail in an image, image resampling should not be used when calibrating an image.

OTHER SOFTWARE PROGRAMS

There are many additional software programs available to the police photographer that will aid in enhancing photographic images. The freeware version of Photoshop is Gimp (available at www.gimpshop.com) and is nearly identical to Photoshop in terms of functions. HDR programs are also available for use with bracketed exposures. Photomatix (available from www.photomatix-pro.en.softonic.com) is a program that can merge two or more photographs for HDR images. Although not freeware, Photomatix performs the merge function very quickly and easily and is very useful in combining two or more images where light and dark need to be controlled, such as taking photographs of luminol developed bloodstains. The police photographer should explore the many photographic software products available that may assist in performing one of the most important and challenging tasks in law enforcement–police photography.

Bibliography

References

Blitzer, H. L., & Jacobia, J. (2002). Forensic digital imaging and photography. San Diego, CA: Academic Press.

Blitzer, H. L., Stein-Ferguson, K., & Huang, J. (2008). Understanding forensic digital imaging. Burlington, MA: Academic Press/Elsevier.

Eastman Kodak Co. (1995). Photography through the microscope. Rochester, NY: Eastman Kodak.

Eastman Kodak Co. (1990). Ultra violet and fluorescence photography. Rochester, NY: Eastman Kodak.

Fish, J. T., Miller, L. S., Braswell, M. C., & Wallace, E. W. (2014). Crime scene investigation (3rd ed.). Burlington, MA: Anderson/Elsevier.

Gibson, H. L. (1980). Photography by infrared—Its principles and applications (3rd ed.). New York: John Wiley & Sons.

Kasai, A. (1997). Essentials of digital photography. Indianapolis, IN: New Riders Publishers.

Krejcarek, P. (1996). Digital photography: a hands on introduction. Albany, NY: Delmar Publishers.

International Center of Photography. (1984). Encyclopedia of photography. New York: Crown.

Marin, N., & Buszka, J. M. (2013). Alternate light source imaging: forensic photography techniques. Burlington, MA: Anderson/Elsevier.

Robinson, E. M. (2010). Crime scene photography (2nd ed.). Burlington, MA: Academic Press/Elsevier.

Saferstein, R. (2010). Criminalistics: an introduction to forensic science (10th ed.). Englewood Cliffs, NJ: Prentice-Hall.

Siljander, R., & Fredrickson, D. (1997). Applied police and fire photography (2nd ed). Springfield, IL: Charles C. Thomas Publishers.

Staggs, S. (1997). Crime scene and evidence photographer's guide. Temecula, CA: Staggs Publishers.

London, B., Upton, B., & Upton, J. (2001). Photography (7th ed.). Englewood Cliffs, NJ: Prentice-Hall.

Additional Reading

Eastman Kodak Company published a number of books and pamphlets of interest to police photographers. Kodak's Index to Photographic Information (L-1) lists more than 300 books, guides, and pamphlets that provide information about selecting and using Kodak products. Kodak's

Professional Photographic Catalog (L-9) lists all Kodak products, cameras, accessories and finishing equipment, and supplies. To obtain downloadable copies, visit: www.kodak.com.

Additional companies and their products have been mentioned throughout the text. Below is a list of how these companies may be contacted.

Corning Glass Works – One Riverfront Plaza, Corning, NY 14831 (607-974-9000). www.corning.com.

Edmund Scientific – 101 E. Gloucester Pike, Barrington, NJ 08007–1380 (800-363-1992). www.edmundoptical.com.

Electrophysics Corporation – 373 W. Route 46, Bdg. E, Fairfield, NJ 07004 (973-882-0211). www.electrophysics.com.

FJW Optical Systems – 322 Woodwork Ln., Palantine, IL 60067 (847-358-2500). www.findrscope.com.

Porter's Camera Store, Inc. – Box 628, Cedar Falls, IA 50613 (319-268-0104). www.porters.com.

West American Rubber Co. – 750 N. Main St., Orange, CA 92868 (714-532-3355). www.warco.com.

There are a number of web sites on the internet that may be accessed for additional information. Students should use one of the many search engines to search for related web sites. All of the major camera manufacturers have web sites with technical information regarding their products. Below is a list of a few sites that also provide links to other sources.

Company sells photoshop software for digital imaging. www.adobe.com.

Information on digital imaging and fingerprint comparisons software. www.mediacy.com.

Information on crime scene photography. www.crimelibrary.com.

Company sells infrared cameras, filters and equipment. www.x-raycameras.com.

Information on crime scene photography. www.crime-scene-investigator.net.

Information about digital cameras and accessories. www.dcviews.com.

Information about digital photography. www.dpfwiw.com.

Information about general photography. www.photo.net.

Company sells infrared filters. www.serialporteng.com.

Information about cameras and general photography. www.cameragear.com.

Company sells infrared, ultraviolet filters and microscope attachments. www.maxmax.com.

Online popular photography magazine. www.popphoto.com.

Information about forensic photography. www.rescuehouse.com.

Information about forensic science and photography. www.forensicpage.com.

Company provides software for photographic imaging. www.heliconsoft.com.

Information about digital cameras. www.steve's-digicams.com.

Company sells software for forensic photography. www.reindeergraphics.com.

Glossary of Terms

Aberrations Optical defects in a lens that cause imperfect images.

Achromatic lens A lens that is at least partially corrected for chromatic aberration.

Adapter ring A device designed to permit the use of filters, supplementary lenses, etc., of a single diameter in connection with several lens mounts whose diameters differ.

Aerial perspective An impression of depth or distance in a photograph by means of progressively diminishing detail due to aerial haze.

Aero Applied to a lens, camera, or film intended for use in photography from aircraft.

Afocal Applied to a lens system that has both foci at infinity; afocal systems include certain wide-angle and telephoto attachments for lenses that do not change the lens extension.

Alligatoring Cracks that form on the surface of paint layers, resembling alligator skin

Alternate light sources (ALS) Single portable lighting units that are capable of providing light, from ultraviolet to infrared

Alternative light source A light emitting device capable of producing light waves ranging from the ultraviolet through infrared wavelengths.

Ambient light Light already existing in an indoor or outdoor scene, independent of any light supplied by the photographer.

Anamorphic A lens or optical system in which the magnification is different in two planes at right angles; used in wide-screen movie processes to "squeeze" a wide image into standard format and to "unsqueeze" it in projection onto a wide screen.

Anastigmat   A lens that has been corrected for astigmatism, and therefore focuses vertical and horizontal lines with equal brightness and definition. Anastigmat lenses are also free of common aberrations.

Angle finder   A viewfinder containing a mirror or prism so that pictures may be taken while aiming the camera sideways.

Angle of view   The angle subtended at the center of the lens by the ends of the diagonal of the film or plate.

Angstrom unit (AU)   A unit of length equal to one ten-thousandth of a micron. Commonly used as a method of expressing length of light rays.

Aperture priority automatic camera   An automatic exposure camera that automatically adjusts the shutter speed to correctly expose the picture, once the photographer has set the lens opening.

Aperture   A small opening, usually circular. In cameras, the aperture is usually variable, in the form of an iris diaphragm, and regulates the intensity of light that passes through a lens.

Aplanat   A lens of the rapid-rectilinear type, sometimes better corrected for spherical aberration, but not for astigmatism.

Apochromatic   Refers to lenses that are most completely corrected for chromatic aberration. These lenses focus rays of all colors to very nearly the same plane.

ARGUS   Autonomous Real-Time Ground Ubiquitous Surveillance Imaging System; camera system that is capable of infrared photography, facial recognition, is equipped with a microphone, and can capture digital images of a 25 square mile area from 20,000 feet altitude and record high resolution images of objects as small as six inches on the ground.

Arson   Crime involving setting a building or other location on fire intentionally.

ASA   American Standards Association rating of film emulsion. For example, Kodak Tri-X Film has an ASA rating of 400. The higher the ASA number, the more sensitive the film is to light. Also referred to as "speed" of the film. See also ISO, Exposure index, and DIN.

Astigmatism   A lens aberration in which both the horizontal and vertical lines in the edge of the field cannot be accurately focused at the same time.

Asymmetrical (nonsymmetrical)   Applied to a lens having differently shaped elements on either side of the diaphragm, or both.

Autofocus   Use of an infrared sensing module to determine distance of the subject in concordance with high-speed, motor-driven focusing.

Automatic diaphragm   A lens aperture that stays at its widest opening until the moment of exposure, when it closes down to the aperture at which it is set. After the exposure, it returns to the widest opening.

Automatic exposure camera   A camera with a built-in metering system that automatically adjusts the lens opening, shutter speed, or both, for proper exposure.

Automatic flash   An electronic flash with a photocell that measures the amount of flash illumination reflected back by the subject. When enough light for a properly exposed picture is reflected by the photocell, it prevents the flash from emitting any more light.

Automatic focus   A camera or lens that automatically adjusts the focus by electronic means.

Autopsy   Examination of a body after death.

Auxiliary lens   A lens element that is added to the regular camera lens to shorten or increase its focal length.

Axial-Lighting   Technique used for illuminating small items for photographic details by using a beam splitter to project light onto an object so that it reflects back directly toward the camera lens and the object appears as if it is the light source.

Axis of lens   An imaginary line that passes through the center of a lens and contains the centers of curvature of the lens surfaces.

Background   Generally, the part of a scene beyond the main subject of the picture.

Backlight illumination   A lighting technique used often for small, opaque objects, whereby the object is placed on a transparent surface, which is raised several inches from the background, and the background is illuminated with two or four light sources.

Barndoor   Folding wings used in front of studio spotlights to aid in directing light, and to shade portions of the subject from direct illumination.

Barrel distortion   A term applied to the barrel-shaped image of a square object; this occurs when the diaphragm is placed in front of a simple convex lens.

Barrier filter   Filter used in fluorescence photography that is placed in front of the camera lens to remove exciting radiation and transmit the fluorescence.

Bayonet lock   A means of quickly attaching or removing a lens from a camera by turning through only part of a revolution.

Beam splitter   An optically flat glass (usually 5″ × 7″) mounted at a 45-degree angle to a light source, splitting the beam of light so that one beam is directed onto the object to be photographed. Used in axial-lighting.

Bellows attachment   Extension tubes used for large images at medium to close working distance, which alter the lens-to-sensor distance by extending the lens.

Bertillon system   Developed by Alphonse Bertillon, a system of identification utilizing measurements of physical body parts, particularly around the head and face.

Between-the-lens shutter   A shutter located between the front and back elements of a double lens.

Big Bertha   A custom-made camera, usually consisting of a 4 × 5 or 5 × 7 Graflex body combined with a powerful telephoto lens. Its most important feature is its lens. It is a very bulky camera.

Bit Depth   The number of data points used to define the color of an individual pixel, calculated by the expression 2^x, where x = bit depth of the file format being used. For example, an 8-bit JPEG image produces 2^8 or 256 colors per color channel.

Black light tubes   A tube that is opaque to most visible light but freely transmits the long-wave ultraviolet radiation and appears visually black.

Blackout (adj.)   Applied to photoflash lamps, a lamp having a visually opaque coating transmitting only infrared radiation, and used for photography in total visual darkness.

Blow-up   Photographic slang for enlargement.

Boom   A stand, usually on wheels, that has an extension arm on which a microphone or lamp may be attached.

Bounce flash   Camera flash that is directed at a surface other than the object being photographed so that the light bounces off the surface and provides the subject with a soft, even illumination.

Bounce light   Flash or tungsten light bounced off ceilings or walls to give the effect of natural or available light.

Bracketing   Taking additional photos of a subject over a range of varying exposures, when unsure of the correct exposure.

Breathing brightness range   Variation of light intensities from maximum to minimum. Generally refers to a subject to be photographed. For example, a particular subject may have a range of one to four, that is, four times the amount of light is reflected from the brightest highlight as from the least bright portion of the subject.

Brilliance   A term denoting the degree of intensity of a color or colors.

Bulb   Shutter setting in which the leaves remain open as long as the button is depressed, and close as soon as the button is released; marked "B" on cameras.

Burned out   Applied to an overexposed negative or print lacking in highlight detail.

Burning in   A method of darkening parts of a print in which certain parts of the image are given extra exposure while the rest of the image is protected from the light.

Cable release   A flexible shaft for operating the camera shutter.

Camcorder   A device used for recording video that includes a built-in recorder/playback unit.

Camera angle   The point of view from which a subject is photographed.

Candid photography   A term applied to pictures taken without posing the subject. The object is to catch natural expression.

Candle-meter-second   A unit of exposure consisting of the light from a standard candle burning for 1 s at a distance of 1 m from the plate.

Candle   A unit of luminous intensity; approximately equal to the intensity of a 7/8-inch sperm candle burning at 120 grains per hour.

Candlepower   Luminous intensity expressed in terms of the standard candle.

Capacitor   An electrical circuit element consisting of one or more pairs of plates separated by some insulating material; sometimes called a condenser, but the term capacitor is preferred because it is more specific.

Cardinal points   In a thick lens or lens system, the two principal points, two nodal points, and two focal points.

Catch lights   The small reflections of a light source, found in the eyes of a portrait subject.

CD   Compact Disk, a storage medium for computers; used to store digital photographs.

Centimeter   A measure of length; 1/100th of a meter; abbreviation: cm.

Characteristic curve   A curve plotted to show the relation of density to exposure. Sometimes referred to as the H and D curve.

Charge-coupled device (CCD)   Semi-conductor chip onto which an image is focused in a digital camera

Chromatic aberration   A defect in a lens that prevents it from focusing different colored light rays in the same plane.

Circle of confusion   An optical term describing the size of an image point formed by a lens.

Circle of illumination   The total image area of a lens, only part of which is actually used in taking a picture.

Clandestine photography   See Covert photography

Clinical camera   A camera designed especially for use in hospitals and clinics.

Close-up lens   A lens attachment that permits a lens to focus more closely than normal. Usually sold in sets, with each close-up lens a different strength for focusing at varying distances.

Coating lens   A thin, transparent coating applied to a lens to reduce surface reflection and internal reflection; also cuts down transmission of ultraviolet rays, acting somewhat like a haze filter.

Collage   A composite photograph made by pasting up a number of individual prints.

Collimate   To produce parallel rays of light by means of a lens or a concave mirror.

Collimating lens   A lens adjusted so as to produce a parallel beam of light.

Collinear   The line-to-line relation existing between the corresponding parts of the object and its image formed by a lens.

Color contrast   A property by which the form of an object can be recognized by its variation in color, whether or not the brightness of all parts of the object is equal.

Color Depth   The total number of colors displayed by an image. For example, if an 8-bit JPEG image is used, this file format can store 256 colors/red/green/blue channel. The total number of colors would be 256^3 or 16,777, 216.

Color sensitivity   The response of a photographic emulsion to light of various wavelengths.

Color temperature   A comparison of the color of a light source expressed in degrees Kelvin.

Color   The sensation produced in the eye by a particular wavelength or group of wavelengths of visible light.

Coma   A lens aberration in which a coma or pear-shaped image is formed by oblique rays from an object point removed from the principal axis of the lens.

Comparison microscope   Microscope used to view and analyze multiple objects side-by-side. In investigations, it is primarily used for examining a questioned bullet or casing and comparing rifling markings and ejector markings with a test bullet or casing fired from the suspect weapon.

Complementary colors   One color is complementary to another when a combination of the two produces white light.

Complementary metal oxide semiconductor   Semi-conductor chip onto which an image is focused in a digital camera

Composition   The balancing of shapes and tones to produce a pleasing effect.

Compound shutter   A trade name for an American (or German) shutter similar to the Compur, except that its slow speeds are controlled by means of a pneumatic piston retard instead of a gear escapement.

Compression   The manner in which the storage size of an image file is reduced.

Compur Shutter   A trade name for a between-the-lens shutter containing independent mechanisms for time (and bulb) exposures and for instantaneous exposures varying from 1 s to as high as 1/500th of a second.

Concave lens   A lens that has one or two concave surfaces.

Concave-convex lens   A lens having one concave and one convex surface.

Concave   Hollowed out; curved inward; applied to negative lenses that are thinnest in the center.

Condenser   An optical system in projection printers used to collect the divergent rays of a light source and concentrate them upon the objective lens.

Contrast filter   A color filter used to make a colored subject stand out very sharply from surrounding objects.

Contrast   Subject contrast is the difference between the reflective abilities of various areas of a subject. Lighting contrast is the difference in intensities of light falling on various parts of a subject. Inherent emulsion contrast is the possible difference between the maximum and minimum densities of the silver deposits with a minimum variation of exposure. It is determined by the manufacturer. Development contrast is the gamma to which an emulsion is developed. It is controlled by the developer, time, temperature, and agitation.

Convertible lens   A lens containing two or more elements that can be used individually or in combination to give a variety of focal lengths.

Convex   The opposite of concave; curved outward; applied to a lens that is thicker in the center than at the edges.

Copy board   A board or easel to which photographs or other originals are fastened while being copied.

Copy camera   A camera intended for photographing text or documents.

Copy stand   A device used in photographing documents or copy that holds the camera and the document stable.

Corex   A trademark of the Corning Glass Works for a type of glass that is highly transparent to ultraviolet light.

Covering power   The capacity of a lens to give a sharply defined image to the edges of the sensitized material it is designed to cover, at the largest possible aperture.

Covert photography   Tactic for photographing an area in which the camera is hidden in an attempt to gather intelligence and evidence on criminal activity.

Crop   To trim or cut away the unnecessary portions of a print in order to improve composition.

Curtain aperture   The slit in a focal plane shutter that permits light to reach the film. The slit size may be fixed or variable.

Curvature of field   The saucer-shaped image of a flat object formed by an uncorrected lens.

Cyan   A blue-green (minus red) color.

Cyanoacrylate Fuming   Processing fingerprints using cyanoacrylate (super glue), which leaves white crystalline prints.

Darkfield illumination   A photographing technique whereby transparent objects may be photographed showing detail and contrast. A light source is placed behind or underneath the object and directed through it at a 45-degree angle, making the object appear bright against a dark background.

Data sheet   Documentation that should be included with every evidence photograph and includes the date, time, case number, location, and officer's name.

Debris   Fragments of a destroyed object scattered around a scene.

Decimeter   A measure of length; 1/10th of a meter, abbreviation: dm.

Dedicated flash   An electronic flash that is designed for specific camera makes and models. When the flash is attached to the camera and turned on, the camera's shutter speed will be automatically adjusted to the correct setting. Other settings may be made automatically as well.

Definition   The clarity, sharpness, resolution, and brilliance of an image formed by a lens.

Dense   Very dark; applied to a negative or positive transparency that is over-exposed, overdeveloped, or both.

Density   A term used to express the light-stopping power of a blackened silver deposit in relation to the light incident upon it.

Depth of field   The distance measured between the nearest and farthest planes in the subject area that gives satisfactory definition.

Depth of focus   The distance that a camera back can be racked back and forth while preserving satisfactory image detail in focal plane for a given object point.

Detective camera   An early name for what is now called a candid camera.

Diaphragm   A device for controlling the amount of light that passes through a lens. It is usually an iris diaphragm, but may be in the form of slotted discs of fixed sizes.

Diapositive   A positive image or a transparent medium such as glass or film; a transparency.

Diffraction   An optical term used to denote the spreading of a light ray after it passes the edge of an obstacle.

Diffusion   The scattering of light rays from a rough surface, or the transmission of light through a translucent medium.

Digital Camera   A camera without film, using a computer chip to record a visual image for computer downloading.

Digital imaging   The creation of photographs using digital technology, allowing photographers to take images and manipulate or enhance them on a computer rather than in a darkroom.

Digital-Single-Lens-Reflex (DSLR)   The combination of digital imaging (as opposed to film) and the mechanisms of a single lens reflex camera.

DIN   A European system of measuring film speed; little used in this country.

Diopter   A measure of lens power; the reciprocal of the focal length of the lens in meters.

Direct finder   A viewfinder through which the subject is seen directly, such as the wire finder on various cameras.

Dispersion   The separation of light into its component colors, created by passing white light through a prism.

Distance meter   An instrument used for estimating the distance to a particular object. Also known as a range finder.

Distortion   Defects caused by uncorrected lenses, resulting in images that are not the proper shape.

Dodge   To shade a portion of the negative during printing.

Dodging   The process of holding back light from certain areas of sensitized material to avoid overexposure of these areas.

Dots per inch   DPI, a unit of measurement for resolution of computer printers.

Double exposure   The intentional or unintentional recording of two separate images on a single piece of sensitized material.

Double image   A blurred picture, caused by movement of the camera or of the subject during exposure.

Duplicator   A split lens cap used to photograph a person twice on a single film without a dividing line between the two exposures.

Dynamic Range   The span highlights and shadows, or light intensity, recorded in an image.

Eastman Kodak   One of the first companies to produce automatic cameras at a price that was affordable to most people.

Effective aperture   The diameter of the lens diaphragm as measured through the front lens element; the unobstructed useful area of a lens; it may actually be larger than the opening in the lens diaphragm, due to the converging action of the front lens element.

Efficiency of a lens   The ratio of the light actually transmitted by a lens to that incident to it.

Efficiency   As applied to shutters, the perceptual relationship between the total time a shutter remains open (counting from half-open to half-closed position) and the time required for the shutter to reach the half-open and the fully closed positions.

Equivalent focus   The focal length of a group of lenses that is considered as one lens.

Excitation   The addition of energy to an object.

Exciter filter   Filter used in fluorescence photography that is placed between the radiation source and the subject and transmits radiation.

Exposure index   A speed rating for film and paper; can be used interchangeably with ASA and ISO.

Exposure indicator   A device attached to a camera to indicate the number of exposures; also to a plate holder to show whether the plate has been exposed.

Exposure meter   An instrument for measuring light intensity and determining correct exposure.

Exposure values for digital cameras   Compensation that allows the photographer to make adjustments to the automatic exposure feature of the camera. Values are measured in steps, typically between [+] 2.0 EV through [−] 2.0 EV in half or third increment steps.

Exposure   The product of time and intensity of illumination acting upon the photographic material. Intensity × Time = Exposure.

Extension tubes   Hollow metal tubes that go between camera and lens to permit closer-than-normal focusing. The longer the extension, the closer the lens will focus.

Extension   The distance between the lens and the sensitive material in a camera.

Extinction meter   An exposure meter that measures the light by the minimum visibility of the image or target.

Eyepiece   The lens element of a microscope, viewfinder, or telescope, to which the eye is applied in order to view the image.

f number   A system denoting lens apertures. Examples f/5.6; f/11; f/16; f/32.

f-Stop   The degree to which the aperture diaphragm is open or closed

f-System   Relationship between the diameter of the lens opening, or aperture, and the focal length of the lens, in which the "f" indicates the speed of the lens or, in other words, the amount of light the lens lets through in proportion to its focal length.

Far point   The farthest object from the camera that is still acceptably sharp when the camera is focused at a given distance.

Fast lens   A lens that has a large relative aperture. Examples f/1.2; f/1.5; f/1.9.

Faurot foto focuser   An attachment placed in the lens of 4 × 5 camera to take photographs of fingerprints.

Field   The area covered by a lens or a viewfinder.

Filament   That part of an incandescent lamp, composed of resistance wire, that becomes luminous when heated by the passage of an electric current.

File Format   The type of data file used to record an image, such as the JPEG, TIFF, and RAW formats.

Fill-in   Secondary illumination directed so as to keep shadow areas from photographing too dark; also known as fill light.

Film-less photography   see Digital Imaging

Filter factor   The number by which the correct exposure without the filter must be multiplied in order to obtain the same effective exposure with the filter.

Filter size   The diameter of the filter retaining threads on the front of a lens in millimeters. Common filter sizes include 49, 52, 55, 58, 62, and 67 mm.

Filter, light or color   A piece of colored glass or gelatin that is usually placed in front of the camera lens to compensate for the difference in color sensitivity between the film and the eye. Also used to modify or exaggerate contrast to provide primary color separation in color photography.

Finder   A viewer through which the picture to be taken may be seen and centered.

Fingerprint camera   A fixed-focus camera with built-in lights, used to photograph fingerprints, stamps, and other small objects.

Fingerprint camera   Camera, traditionally used by fingerprint technicians, that is specially built for photographing fingerprints without needing to be focused.

Fisheye lens   An extreme wide-angle lens. Most fisheye lenses cover over 180° angle of view and produce circle-shaped pictures on film.

Fixed focus   A term applied to a camera in which the lens is set permanently in such a position as to give good average focus for both near and distant objects.

Flash gun   The battery case, lamp socket, and reflector used with photoflash lamps.

Flash meter   An instrument for measuring the amount of light produced by a flash unit.

Flash synchronization   The adjustment and timing of camera and flash so that the flash fires when the camera shutter is open. Most 35 mm single-lens-reflex cameras synchronize with electronic flash at shutter speeds of 1/125th of a second or slower.

Flashtube   A glass or quartz tube, usually wound in helical shape, containing two electrodes and filled with xenon or other inert gases at a very low pressure; used as the light source in flash units and photographic stroboscopes.

Flatness of field   The quality of a lens that produces sharpness of image both at the edges and at the center of the negative.

Floodlamp   In general, any lamp or lighting unit that produces a broad beam or flood of light; colloquially used as a contraction for photoflood lamp.

Florida v. Victor Reyes   2002 murder trial in which the defendant was acquitted after police used computer software to enhance a smudged palmprint photograph and the defense demonstrated the ease with which photographs can be manipulated on Photoshop.

Fluorescence   Emission of light by a substance as a result of radiation being absorbed.

Focal length   The distance between the center of the lens and the point at which the image of a distant object comes into critical view. The focal length of a thick lens is measured from the emergent nodal point to the focal plane.

Focal plane shutter   A shutter that operates immediately in front of the focal plane. A shutter of this type usually contains a fixed- or variable-sized slit in a curtain of cloth or metal that travels across the film to make the exposure.

Focal plane   The plane at which the image is brought to a critical focus. In other words, the position in the camera occupied by the film emulsion.

Focus   The plane toward which the rays of light converge to form an image after passing through a lens. (The most important function for the police or fire photographer to perform before snapping the shutter.)

Foot-candle   The intensity of light falling on a surface placed one foot distant from a point light source of one candlepower.

Foreground   Generally, the part of a scene that is closer to the camera than the main subject.

Fresnel lens   A lens consisting of a small central plano-convex lens surrounded by a series of prismatic rings; also known as an echelon lens.

Full aperture   The maximum opening of a lens or lens diaphragm.

Full spectrum   Covers the infrared, visible, and ultraviolet spectrums. In photography, a full spectrum camera is one in which the internal filter is removed from in front of the sensor and replaced with quartz glass so that the camera is sensitive to the full spectrum of light.

Ghost images   The reflection of the light from a bright subject, by the elements of the lens or its mounting, to form a spurious image.

Ghost   The reflection of an image on one or more lens surfaces caught by the negative.

Gray scale   A monochrome strip of tones ranging from pure white to black with intermediate tones of gray. The scale is placed in a setup for a color photograph and serves as a means of balancing the separation negatives and positive dye images, and is cropped from the finished print.

Green v. City and County of Denver   The first appellate court case (1943) passing upon the admissibility of color photographs, upholding their use as evidence.

Guide number   A rating of a flash unit's power. It can be defined as the proper exposure setting for a photo taken with the flash 10 feet from the subject, multiplied by 10. For example, a flash with a guide number of 56 will produce enough light for an exposure of f/5.6 at 10 feet.

Gun   Any device for igniting flashlamps or flash powder; also, the gunstock for supporting small cameras and heavy lenses with greater firmness.

High dynamic range (HDR)   Measured in stop differences exposure values between brightest and darkest points of an image to show detail.

High-key   Applied to a print having the majority of its tones as light grays and white.

Highlights   The brightest parts of the subject, represented by the denser parts of the negative and the light gray and white tones of the print.

Hold back   To shade portions of an image while printing, in order to avoid excessive density; similar to dodge.

Homicide   The act of killing another person.

Hot shoe   A standardized method of mounting an electronic flash on a camera. The hot shoe fittings on both the camera and flash have an electrical contact in the center that fires the flash when the shutter is released.

Hue   The name by which we distinguish one color from another: blue, red.

Hyperfocal distance   The distance from the camera, such that if an object at that point is in sharp focus, then all objects from one-half this distance to infinity give satisfactory definition on the ground glass screen.

Identification   A photograph showing the head and shoulders, both front and side views, of a person.

Illumination   The illumination at a point on the surface of a body is the intensity of light received, and is expressed as the number of lumens per square foot of the number of foot-candles.

Image   The representation of an object formed by optical or chemical means.

Incandescent   Glowing with heat (such as a tungsten filament in an incandescent lamp).

Incident light   A meter reading designed to be held at the subject position, facing the camera, to measure light strength at the subject plane.

Index of refraction   The mathematical expression of the deviation of a light ray entering a given medium at an angle to its surface.

Infinity   A distance so far removed from an observer that the rays of light reflected to a lens from a point at that distance may be regarded as parallel. Also, a distance setting on a camera focusing scale, beyond which all objects are in focus.

Infrared   Invisible rays of light beyond the red end of the visible spectrum.

Interpolation   A method by which pixels are added to an image file during the decompression of a "lossy" file format. Interpolation is also used by software to add pixels to an image when it is enlarged beyond its native resolution.

Inverse square law   A physical law that states that illumination intensity varies inversely with the square of the distance from a point of light.

Invisible rays   The rays, such as X-rays, ultraviolet, and infrared, that are not visible to the eye.

Iris diaphragm   A lens control composed of a series of overlapping leaves operated by a revolving ring to vary the aperture of the lens.

ISO   International Standards Organization rating of film speed. Used interchangeably with ASA.

JPEG (Joint Photographer Expert Group)   A "lossy" compressed image file format used in modern digital cameras.

JPEG or JPG   Joint Photographic Experts Group—a lossy compression technique for color images. While it can reduce file size to about 5% of the normal size, some detail is lost in the compression.

Kelvin   A thermometer scale starting at absolute zero (−273 °C. approximately) and having degrees of the same magnitude as those of the Celsius thermometer. Thus 0 = 273 °K; 100 °C = 373 °K, etc.; also called the absolute scale.

Key   The prevailing tone of a photograph, such as high-key, low-key, medium-key.

Land camera   Camera developed by the Polaroid Corporation in about 1950 that makes finished photographs in about 10 s by the diffusion-transfer process; also known as a "Polaroid" camera.

Latent prints   Surface fingerprints that are not immediately perceivable by the naked eye, or are incomplete.

Lateral chromatic magnification   Refers to the formation of colored images of different sizes in the same plane, of an object removed from the principal axis of the lens.

Lens cap   A cover used to protect a lens from dust and damage when not in use.

Lens hood   A shade used to keep extraneous light from the surface of a lens.

Lens paper   A fine, soft tissue paper used for cleaning lenses.

Lens shade   A detachable camera accessory used to shield the lens from extraneous light rays.

Lens speed   The largest lens opening at which a lens can be set. A "fast" lens has a larger maximum opening than a "slow" lens. For example, an f/2.8 lens is faster than an f/4 lens.

Lens   An optical term applied to a piece of glass that is bounded by two spherical surfaces, or a plane and a spherical surface. The term is also applied to a combination of several glass elements, such as a photographic objective lens.

Light copy   Original material to be copied, containing only black and white areas or lines, without halftones.

Light meter   A device that measures the intensity of light. Can be either built into a camera or a separate hand-held device.

Line pairs per millimeter   lp/m, a traditional measure of resolution for video and digital images; 10 lp/m is equivalent to 20 pixels per millimeter.

Long-wave ultraviolet   Ultraviolet rays with wavelengths between 320 and 400 nm.

Lossless Compression   A compressed image file format that does not delete pixel data to reduce the file size.

Lossy Compression   A compression algorithm that deletes pixel from an image in order to reduce the size of it.

Low-key   The balance of light or dark tones of a photograph. If light tones prevail with few or no dark tones, the photograph is said to be "high-key"; if the opposite, "low key."

Luco v. United States   One of the first known U.S. court cases to use a photograph as evidence (1859).

Lumen   A measurement of light equivalent to that falling on a foot-square surface, which is one foot away from a point light source of one candlepower.

Lumenized   A trademark of the Eastman Kodak Company for an anti-reflection coating applied to lenses and other glass surfaces.

Luminescence　The phenomenon of induced light emission when a material is subjected to short-wave electromagnetic radiation.

Luminol　Chemical used for detecting blood.

Luminosity　The intensity of light in a color as measured by a photometer.

Luminous light　Light sources that emit radiations within the visible spectrum.

Lux　Lumens per square meter.

Macro lens　A primary lens that can be focused from a very short distance out to infinity. May be a fixed focal length lens or a zoom lens.

Macrophotography　Close-up photography, the taking of a picture larger than the size of the subject.

Magenta　A reddish-blue (minus green) color.

Medium-key　Applied to a print having the majority of its tones as medium grays, with only a small proportion of solid black or pure white.

Megacycle　1,000,000 cycles, abbreviation: mc.

Megapixel　One million pixels. Digital cameras are commonly rated by their number of sensor pixels, which can be calculated by multiplying the horizontal number of pixels by the vertical resolution. For example, a sensor with 4928 horizontal pixels and 3280 vertical pixels would denote a 16.2 Megapixel sensor.

Meniscus lens　A positive or negative, crescent-shaped lens consisting of one concave and one convex spherical surface.

Metadata　Data stored within an image file that provide information about the photograph and camera settings used, when the exposure was captured. Metadata may also store and post processing information.

Microphotography　Taking a photograph through a microscope. Not necessarily using the lens of the microscope, but the lens of the camera.

Miniature camera　A term more or less generally applied to a camera using film 2 × 3 inches or less in size.

Mirror lens　A type of long telephoto lens that uses several mirror optic surfaces to "fold" the light path, reducing the size and weight of the lens.

Modeling　Applied to the representation of the third dimension in a photograph by the controlled placement of highlights and shadows.

Monochromatic A single color.

Mug shot A photograph showing head and shoulders, both side and front views, usually made of an arrested person during booking.

Multi-coating The application of several coats of materials to the surface of lens elements to improve light transmission and reduce flares.

Multiple camera A camera that makes a number of small photographs on a single, large film or plate.

Multiple flash Provides more than one source for the flash when taking a photograph, creating fewer harsh shadows.

Neutral Without color—gray; chemically, a solution that is neither acid nor alkaline.

Nicol prism A type of prism used to produce polarized light.

Night vision photography The employment of a light amplification device in adverse lighting conditions or darkness.

Night vision A mode included on most cameras that allows for photographs to be taken in the dark.

Nodal points The points on the axis of a thick lens, such that a ray traversing the first medium, passing through one nodal point, emerges from the second medium in a parallel direction, and appears to originate at a second point.

Normal lens A lens with a focal length of approximately the diagonal measurement of the film image area. A 50 mm lens is considered the normal lens for 35 mm photography. Normal lenses view the subject as do unaided human eyes, neither reducing nor enlarging the subject size.

Objective lens A lens that is used to form a real image of an object.

Oblique lighting Lighting that is used when photographing impressions; should be low and to the side of the impression.

Opacity The resistance of a material to the transmission of light.

Opal glass A white, milky, translucent glass used as a diffusion medium in enlargers.

Opaque Refers to an object that is incapable of transmitting visible light. A commercial preparation used to black out certain negative areas.

Optical axis An imaginary line passing through the centers of all the lens elements in a compound lens.

Original   In copying, that which is to be reproduced.

Overexposure   The result of too much light being permitted to act on a negative, with either too great a lens aperture or too slow a shutter speed or both.

Overt photography   Tactic for photographing an area in which a camera is readily visible under the assumption that its presence will deter someone from engaging in criminal activity.

Packard shutter   A trade name of a type of shutter, operated by a rubber bulb and tube, much used on studio cameras.

Painting with light   A film camera technique that simulates multiple flash, but requires only one flash unit. It can be used only with subjects that are absolutely stationary.

Pan   An abbreviation for panchromatic.

Panchromatic film   A film that is sensitive to all colors of the visible spectrum.

Panoramic head   A revolving tripod head, graduated so that successive photographs may be taken that can be joined into one long panoramic print.

Parallax   The apparent displacement of an object seen from different points. Commonly encountered in photography in the difference between the image seen in the viewfinder and that actually taken by the lens.

PC cord   Shutter cord.

Pentaprism   A five-sided prism used in single-lens-reflex viewing hoods to turn the image right-side up and laterally correct.

People v. Jennings   1911 U.S. court case that ruled in favor of the use of fingerprint photographs for identification purposes.

Perspective grid   A square or rectangle of known size included in a photograph of a flat surface, providing perspective that allows measurements to be made to scale.

Perspective   The illusion of three dimensions created on a flat surface.

Phosphorescence   The ability of a substance to continue to luminescence for a long time after removal of the exciting stimulus.

Phot   A unit of luminance; one lumen per square millimeter.

Photo CD   A Compact Disk used to store digitized photographs taken either with film cameras or with digital cameras.

Photoflash lamp   A light bulb filled with aluminum wire or shreds in an atmosphere of oxygen; the heating of the filament ignites the primer, which in turn fires the aluminum, giving a short, brilliant flash of light.

Photoflood lamp   An electric lamp designed to be worked at higher-than-normal voltage, giving brilliant illumination at the expense of lamp life. Also called a floodlamp.

Photogrammetry   The science of mapping by the use of aerial photographs.

Photographing viewpoints   The direction from which a photograph is approached; usually a crime scene should be photographed from multiple locations representing various viewpoints.

Photomacrography   Enlarged photography of small objects by the use of a long bellows camera and a lens of short focal length.

Photomicrography   Photography through a microscope.

Photomontage   A picture composed of several smaller pictures.

Phototopography   The mapping or surveying of terrain by means of photography.

Pincushion distortion   A term applied to the pincushion-shaped image of a square object, obtained when the diaphragm is placed behind the lens.

Pixel   A unit of measurement for resolution of digital images; one pixel contains at least three dots (dots per inch, DPI).

Pixelated   When an enlargement of a digitized photograph shows the individual pixels to the point that the image is not readily recognizable.

Point of impact   In a vehicle accident, the point on the vehicle(s) that came into contact with another vehicle or object.

Pola screen   A screen that transmits polarized light when properly oriented with respect to the vibration plane of the incident light. When rotated to a 90-degree angle it will not transmit the polarized light.

Polarized light   Light that vibrates in one manner only, in straight lines, circles, or ellipses. Light is commonly polarized by passing a light beam through a Nicol prism or a polarizing screen.

Polarizing filter   A filter that removes reflections from water, glass, and other surfaces; it also increases color saturation.

Polaroid   The first company to introduce film that could produce finished pictures in black and white or color in less than 1 min.

Posterization   Occurs when a photo image does not contain sufficient tonal range of color data to create a smooth transition between highlights and shadows in an image.

Prefocused   Applied to a lamp having a special type of base and socket, which automatically centers the filament with respect to an optical system.

Press camera   See View camera.

Primary colors   Any one of the three components of white light—blue, green, and red.

Process lens   A highly corrected lens used for precise color separation work.

Programed automatic exposure camera   An automatic exposure camera that automatically sets both the shutter speed and lens opening to properly expose the picture.

Props   Accessories used to add interest or provide variety in an illustration or a portrait.

Quartz lens   A special lens used for ultraviolet photography.

Racking   Moving either the lens board or the camera back to and fro while focusing.

Radiant energy   A form of energy of electromagnetic character. All light that causes a photochemical reduction is radiant energy.

Radiation   Transfer of energy via electromagnetic waves.

Rangefinder camera   A camera equipped with a range finder focusing system, which provides a double image of the subject in a small central area of the viewfinder. When the camera is in focus, the double image appears as a single image.

Raster Graphics   images of a dot matrix data structure representing a rectangular grid of pixels or points of color.

Ratio   The degree of enlargement or reduction of a photographic copy with respect to the original.

RAW   An image file format in digital cameras with minimally processed data. It retains more image information than JPEG and can produce better results in image applications such as Photoshop.

Reciprocity failure   Underexposure that may occur as a result of a long exposure time after the proper f-number has been determined and the lens is set at a small aperture.

Reciprocity law   A law that states that the blackening of photosensitive materials is determined by the product of light intensity and time of exposure. Thus, intensity is the reciprocal of time and, if one is halved, then the other must be doubled in order to obtain the same blackening.

Rectilinear lens   A lens corrected so that it does not curve the straight lines of the image.

Reddin v. Gates   One of the first U.S. court cases to hold that a relevant photograph of an injured person was admissible evidence (1879).

Reflection   The diversion of light from any surface.

Reflector   Any device used to increase the efficiency of a light source. Examples are flashlight reflectors and tinfoil reflectors for outdoor pictures.

Refraction   The bending of a light ray when it passes obliquely from a medium of one density to a medium of a different density.

Reproduction ratio   The ratio of the actual size of an object to its reproduced size on film. A 1:1 ratio means life-size, a 2:1 ratio means 2 times the actual size and 1:4 ratio means 1/4 life-size.

Resolution   The level of detail that can be seen in an image—generally calculated by multiplying the DPI of an image by its width.

Resolving power   The ability of a lens to record fine detail, or of an emulsion to reproduce fine detail.

Retouching   A method for improving the quality of a negative or print by use of a pencil or brush.

Reverse adapter   An adapter ring that permits a normal lens to be mounted backwards onto a camera for improved results when taking extreme close-up photos.

Ringlight flash   Circular attachment that connects directly to the front of the camera lens for close-up flash photography

RUP   Reflective Ultraviolet Photography

Safety film   Film with a cellulose acetate base; so called because it burns very slowly.

Scale   Scale is the ratio of a linear dimension in the photograph to the corresponding dimension in the subject.

Scanners   Stationary digital camera that uses a singular row of light-sensitive sensors mounted on a bar, which passes over a document and records the image one line at a time.

Secondary colors   Colors formed by the combination of two primary colors. Yellow, magenta, and cyan are the secondary colors.

Sectoring   A method of photographing a scene that is achieved by dividing a large area into zones (or sectors) so that both the overall pattern and the fine detail can be captured.

Selective absorption   The capacity of a body to absorb certain colors while transmitting or reflecting the remainder.

Sepia toning   A process that converts the black-silver image to a brownish image. The image can vary considerably in hue, depending on the process, the tone of the original, and other factors.

Set   An interior or exterior scene or part of a scene, together with furniture or natural objects, built in a studio for photography, or on a motion picture lot.

Sex offenses   An unlawful act of a sexual nature against another person or persons.

Shadow area   The darker portions of a picture or the lighter portions of a negative.

Shadows   A term applied to the thinner portions of a negative and the darker parts of a positive slide or print.

Shoot   To make an exposure.

Short-wave ultraviolet   Ultraviolet rays with wavelengths between 200 and 280 nm.

Shutter priority automatic camera   An automatic exposure camera that automatically adjusts the lens opening to correctly expose the picture once the photographer has set the lens opening.

Shutter   On a camera, a mechanical device that controls the length of time light is allowed to strike the sensitized material.

Silhouette   A photograph that shows only the mass of a subject in black, against a white or colored background.

Skid marks   In a car accident, marks made by the tires of the car (usually the front tires) that deviate from the general line of travel.

Skylight filter   A very pale pink filter used with color film to reduce excess blue found in outdoor scenes. Commonly left on the lens at all times to serve as a lens protector.

Skylight   A large window, usually inclined and facing north, used as a principal light source in certain photographic studios.

Slave sensor   A device with a photocell that fires a flash unit when it senses the light from another flash unit. The light from both flash units will be in synchronization with the camera.

Slide   A positive print on glass, or a film transparency bound between glasses for projection; also the removable cover of a sheet-film plate, or film-pack holder.

SLR   Single-lens-reflex camera, a type of camera design that permits the photographer to view through the image-taking lens instead of a separate viewfinder window.

Soft-focus (adj.)   Applied to a lens that has been deliberately undercorrected to produce a diffused image; also applied to pictures made with such a lens.

Soft-focus lens   A special type of lens, used to produce a picture with soft outlines. Such lenses are well adapted to portrait work.

Soft   A term used in describing prints and negatives that have low contrast.

Spectrogram   A photograph of a spectrum, made by using a spectrograph.

Spectrophotometer   An instrument used for comparing the intensities at the corresponding wavelengths of two spectra.

Spectrum   A colored band that is formed when white light is passed through a prism or a diffraction grating; it contains all the colors of which white light is composed; plural: spectra.

Speedgun   A device used to ignite flashlamps in synchronism with the opening of the camera shutter.

Spherical aberration   A lens defect that causes rays parallel to the axis and passing near the edge of a positive lens to come to a focus nearer the lens than the rays passing through the center portion.

Split field lens   A semicircular close-up lens in a rotating mount. Attaches to the front of a lens and enables it to render near and distant objects in focus at the same time.

Spot lamp   A type of mushroom-shaped electric lamp that has an integral reflector and produces a narrow, concentrated beam of light.

State v. Thorp   1934 U.S. court case approving the use of ultraviolet photography as evidence.

Step-down ring   A filter-size adapter ring that permits a lens to use filters smaller than the lens filter size.

Step-up ring   A filter size adapter ring that permits a lens to use filters larger than the lens filter size.

Stereo camera   A camera that has two lenses or the equivalent through which the pair of pictures that make up a stereogram may be taken simultaneously.

Stereoscope   A device that contains lenses, prisms, or mirrors, through which a stereogram is seen as a single, three-dimensional picture.

Stills   Photographs, as distinguished from motion pictures.

Stop down   To use a smaller aperture.

Stop   A lens aperture or a diaphragm opening such as f/4, f/5.6, etc.

Strobe unit   An electronic unit that can be used many times for flash photography.

Subtractive process   A process in color photography that uses the colors magenta, cyan, and yellow. Contrast with additive color process.

Suicide   The act of intentionally bringing about one's own death.

Sunshade   A hood placed over a lens to keep stray light from its surface; similar to lens hood.

Superproportional reducer   A reducing solution that lowers the highlight density faster than it affects the shadow density.

Supplementary lens   An attachable lens, by which the focal length of a camera objective is increased or decreased.

Synchro-flash   A term applied to flash photography, in which a flash bulb is ignited at the same instant that the shutter is opened, the flash bulb being the primary source of illumination.

Synchro-sun   A term used in flash photography, in which flashlight and sunlight are used in combination.

Synchronizer   A device for synchronizing the shutter of a camera with a flashlamp, so that the shutter is fully opened at the instant the lamp reaches its peak intensity.

T-Mount An interchangeable lens mounting system for slide duplicators, microscope and telescope attachments, lenses without automatic diaphragms, and other optical accessories. A T-mount is a metal ring with female 42 mm threads on one side to screw onto the lens attachment and a male camera mount on the other side.

T-number, T-stop A system of marking lens apertures in accordance with their actual light transmission, rather than by their geometrical dimensions, as in the f-stop system.

Tangent of an angle The ratio of the length of the opposite leg to the adjacent leg of a right triangle.

Tele-converter A lens accessory that mounts between a camera body and normal, telephoto, or telephoto zoom lenses to double (or triple) the effective focal length. A 2X converter will make an 80–200 mm zoom lens seem like a 160–400 mm zoom lens.

Telephoto lens A lens of long focal length that has a separate negative rear element; it is used to form larger images of distant objects; it is similar in result to a telescope.

Tessar A trade name for a type of anastigmat lens composed of two pairs of lens elements; one pair is cemented together, the other pair is separated by an air space.

Three-quarter A term describing a portrait pose, standing or seated, including the figure approximately to the knees.

Thyristor A type of circuitry used in automatic electronic flash units that returns unused energy to the capacitor after each shot. This design substantially reduces recycling time and power consumption.

TIFF Tagged Image File Format—a computer file format for storing raster graphics images.

Tilt-top A device attached to a tripod head that permits the camera to be set at various angles in elevation.

Time exposure An exposure in which the shutter is opened and closed manually with a relatively long interval between.

Time-gamma-temperature curve A curve of developing time plotted against developed contrast, or gamma. The contrast for any given time may be read directly from the curve, or vice versa. The curve applies only for one particular developer and emulsion.

Tire impressions Imprints made on the ground or road from the tires of a vehicle.

Tone   In photography this usually applies to the color of a photographic image or, incorrectly, to any distinguishable shade of gray. To change the color of a photographic image from its natural black to various colors, either by means of metallic salts, or by mordanting certain dyes to the image; such dyes do not stain the gelatin; note the difference from tinting.

Translucent   A medium that passes light but diffuses it so that objects cannot be clearly distinguished.

Transmission   The rate of the light passed through an object to the light falling upon it.

Transmitting filter   Filter, usually made of quartz glass, in which coloring agents are contained to control the transmittance of ultraviolet rays.

Tripod socket   A threaded opening in the base of a camera, used to fasten the camera to the tripod head.

Tripod   A three-legged stand used to support a camera.

Tungsten   A metallic element of an extremely high melting point, used in the manufacture of incandescent electric lamps. In photography, tungsten is used to refer to artificial illumination as contrasted with daylight. For example, film emulsion speeds are given both in tungsten and daylight.

Ultraviolet filter   A filter that transmits ultraviolet light, as used for photography, by the reflected ultraviolet light method. Known as a Kodak Wratten No. 18A filter.

Ultraviolet rays   Rays that comprise the invisible portion of the electromagnetic spectrum just beyond the visible violet. Ultraviolet wavelengths are comparatively short and therefore disperse more easily than visible wavelengths. This is a factor to be taken into account in high altitude photography because these rays are photographically actinic.

Underexposure   The result of insufficient light being allowed to pass through the lens to produce all the tones of an image; or of sufficient light being allowed to pass for too short a period.

Uniform System   A system of marking diaphragm aperture used until recently, in which an f/4 lens was marked U.S. 1; f/5.6 was equal to U.S. 2; f/8 equal to U.S. 4; f/11 equal to U.S. 8, etc.

Unipod   Similar to tripod but with only one telescoping leg; it is compact and easily portable.

Variable focal length lens   A type of zoom lens that requires refocusing as it is zoomed.

Vehicle damage   The destruction that occurs with relation to a vehicle involved in a crash.

Vernier scale   A device used on a camera to indicate distance.

Vertical illumination   See axial-lighting

Video camera   Portable machine used to record video and is attached to a separate recorder/playback unit.

View camera   A style of camera that consists of a bellows connecting a lens support and film holder, mounted on a rail or pair of rails. View cameras offer the lens and film planes a great deal of unrestricted physical movement for controlling depth of field and perspective. Also known as Press cameras.

Viewfinder   A viewing instrument attached to a camera, used to obtain proper composition.

Vignetting   Underexposure of the extreme edges of a photographic image; occasionally caused by improper design of lenses or too small a sunshade; sometimes intentionally done in portraiture.

Visible light   The small portion of electromagnetic radiation that is visible to the human eye. Approximately, the wavelengths from 400 to 700 millimicrons.

White balance   The setting used to adjust the color of an exposure for a given type of illumination.

Wide-angle lens   A lens of short focal length and great covering power that is used to cover a larger angle of view than a normal lens will include from a given viewpoint.

Will West–William West Case 1903   Leavenworth Prison case in which a man (Will West) was incorrectly identified (as William West) using several identification methods, until a fingerprint comparison proved he was not. Subsequently, most police departments began using photographs, Bertillon measurements and fingerprints on their "mug shot" files.

Zone focusing   A type of focusing system that has two or more focus settings for varying subject distance ranges, rather than a continuous adjustable focusing ring.

Zoom lens   A lens that can be varied in apparent focal length while maintaining focus on a given object; it gives the effect of moving to or from the subject when used on a motion-picture camera.

Index

Note: Page numbers followed by "*f*" indicate figures; "*t*" tables; "*b*" boxes.